BARRON'S

E-Z AMERICAN SIGN LANGUAGE

THIRD EDITION

David A. Stewart, Ed.D.
Formerly of Michigan State University

Elizabeth Stewart, B.Sc.
Signing Online

Jessalyn Little, M.Ed.
Vancouver School Board
Vancouver, BC

Lisa Dimling, Ph.D.
Bowling Green State University
Bowling Green, Ohio

Illustrated by
Beth Roberge Friedrichs

BARRON'S

Dedicated to the memory of my brilliant husband—author of this book—
inspiring his family, friends, and students to continue his work. —Liz

Dedicated to Joe, Emmett, Elliott and Elise  —Beth

Acknowledgments

Many thanks to my colleagues and the many ASL students who provided feedback on the content and flow of the text. A special thanks to the following people who helped review the manuscript and put it together: Brenda Cartwright, Lynn Duckwall, Judy Foren, Tanna Girod, Kelly Grondin, Michael Kellett, and Liz.

The excerpt on page 7 is reprinted by permission of the publisher, *The Study of Language*, George Yule, Press Syndicate of the University of Cambridge University Press, 1985.

The excerpt on page 13 is reprinted by permission of the publisher, *The Mask of Benevolence*, Harlan Lane, DawnSignPress, 1992.

The excerpt on page 31 is reprinted by permission of the publisher, from C.A. Padden, "The Relation Between Space and Grammar in ASL Verb Morphology" in *Sign Language Research: Theoretical Issues*, Ceil Lucas, ed. (1990): 18, Washington, D.C.: Gaullaudet University Press. Copyright © 1990 by Gallaudet University.

The excerpt on page 99 is reproduced with permission of DawnSignPress.

The excerpt on page 105 is from *Deaf in America: Voices from a Culture*, by Carol Padden and Tom Humphries. Copyright © 1988 by the President and Fellows of Harvard College. Reprinted by permission of Harvard University Press.

The excerpt on page 249 is reprinted with permission of the publisher, for Dennis Cokely and Charlotte Baker, eds., *American Sign Language: A Teacher's Resource Text on Grammar and Culture* (1980), Washington, D.C.: Galluadet University Press. Copyright © 1980 by Dennis Cokely and Charlotte Baker.

The excerpt on page 285 is reprinted from *Meeting Halfway in American Sign Language* (1993). Copyright © 1993 Deaf Life Press. Used with permission.

"How We Are" (pages 209 and 432) is reprinted with permission of the publisher, from J. D. Schein, *At Home Among Strangers* (1989): 40, 68. Washington, D.C.: Gallaudet University Press. Copyright © 1989 by Gallaudet University.

"Language for the Eye" by Dorothy Miles (page 433): *Viewpoint on Deafness, A Deaf American Monograph*. Copyright © 1992. Donald Eastwood Read, Executor, granted permission.

"On His Deafness" (page 433): from *Communication Issues Among Deaf People: Deaf American Monograph*, by Robert F. Panara. Copyright © 1990.

"Words From a Deaf Child" (page 434): *Communication Issues Among Deaf People, A Deaf American Monograph*. Copyright © 1990.

"My Clipped Wings" (page 435) is reprinted with permission by Ken Glickman from National Association of the Deaf's *Communication Issues Among Deaf People*. Author's other work can be found at his website at http://deafology.com.

Every effort has been made to contact the copyright holders. Barron's Educational Series and the author apologize for any unintentional omissions. We would be pleased to insert the appropriate acknowledgment in future editions of this book.

ISBN: 978-0-7641-4458-5

Library of Congress Catalog Card No. 2010041277

Library of Congress Cataloging-in-Publication Data
E-Z American Sign Language / David A. Stewart [et al.] ;
  illustrated by Beth Roberge Friedrichs. — 3rd ed.
    p. cm. — (E-Z)
  Rev. ed. of: American Sign Language the easy way / David A. Stewart, Elizabeth Stewart, Jessalyn Little. 2nd ed. c2007.
  Includes index.
  ISBN-13: 978-0-7641-4458-5
  ISBN-10: 0-7641-4458-8
  1. American Sign Language. I. Stewart, David Alan, 1954–
II. Stewart, David Alan, 1954– American Sign Language the easy way.
  HV2474.S67 2011
  419'.7--dc22   2010041277

Printed in the United States of America
9 8 7 6 5 4 3 2 1

CONTENTS

Note to the Student

E-Z American Sign Language is designed to make you a better signer. Here are some suggestions for using this book:

- *Think visually.* American Sign Language (ASL) is understood by seeing it because all information in ASL is visual. How you make a sign is important, but just as important are the facial expressions and body movements you use when signing. Read about the facial grammar of ASL in Chapter 1 to help you make the transfer from a communication based on sounds to one that's entirely based on "seeing."
- *Learn the ten basic ASL grammar rules.* Examples of how these rules are used in a dialogue are given in the 36 lessons that follow. Most of the rules are frequently repeated to help you gain greater familiarity with them.
- *Study the chapters that focus on a particular aspect of ASL* such as directional verbs (Chapter 6), classifiers (Chapter 11), and body- and gaze-shifting (Chapter 9). These chapters will give you a better understanding of the spatial qualities of ASL.
- *Master signing the dialogues.* Each lesson has a dialogue, and they become progressively more difficult throughout the book. Practice signing each dialogue until you are comfortable with the signing. You can do this best with a partner or a fluent ASL signer, but if you are alone, practice signing in front of a mirror or videotape yourself. This practice will help you develop fluency in your signing. The dialogues are broken up in the sections called "Practice Activities." Practicing the shorter pieces of the dialogues will help you gain greater fluency when practicing the entire dialogue.
- *Learn to analyze ASL language structures and signs.* Each dialogue is analyzed in a section called "What's in the Signs (Notes about the Grammar)." Read this section carefully so that you get a feel for how ASL is structured. Some signs are discussed separately in a section called "What's in a Sign (Notes about Vocabulary)." Read this section to learn about the reasons some signs are produced in a certain way.
- *Follow all suggestions for further practice* that require you to develop your own dialogues and practice signing them.

- *Create ASL sentences and write the English translations of these sentences.* Translation is important for learning the differences between ASL and English grammar because in ASL you do not sign each word you say in English and the ASL grammar is different from English grammar.
- *Learn the different meanings of some ASL signs.* A listing of these signs and their alternative meanings is presented in most chapters.
- *Learn about Deaf culture.* Five chapters introduce you to different aspects of Deaf culture.

Mastering ASL will require more than just mastering the dialogues and ASL rules presented in this book. Communicating with Deaf people will help you learn more about ASL and help you expand your vocabulary of signs.

Introduction: American Sign Language

American Sign Language has had a durable history. Its origin can be traced to the emergence of a large community of deaf people centered around the first public school for deaf children in France, founded about 1761; the language that arose in this community is still being used in France today. In 1817, a Deaf teacher from this school helped establish the first public school for deaf children in the United States. Although his language was incorporated into the early curriculum, the children's own gestural systems mingled with the official signed language, resulting in a new form that was no longer identifiable as French Sign Language. Some signs and structures in ASL today still reflect their French Sign Language origins, although the two languages are distinct.

—CAROL PADDEN AND TOM HUMPHRIES
Deaf in America: Voices from a Culture

HOLD THAT SIGN . . .

The founding of the first school for the Deaf in America in 1817 is a landmark in the history of American Sign Language, or ASL as it is most often called. Located in Hartford, Connecticut, and now known as the American School for the Deaf, the school brought together two main sources in the development of ASL signs and grammar. The first was the school's first two teachers. One was Laurent Clerc, the Deaf man from France described by Padden and Humphries. He and the French Sign Language he knew were brought to the United States by an American, Thomas Gallaudet, who learned to sign from Clerc.

The other source of ASL was the Deaf pupils in attendance at the school. They came at a time when schooling was not mandatory and most of the population lived in farming communities. So how did they sign or did they sign prior to attending the school? For

1

some of these children, the school marked the first time they were in the company of other Deaf people, so what signs they had were mainly homemade. But other Deaf children, and especially those with Deaf parents, introduced to the school signs indigenous to America—signs that were used in the Deaf community. For about the next forty years, this pattern was repeated in other states where schools for the Deaf were springing up, many of them employing Deaf teachers who had graduated from other schools for the Deaf. The work of these early pioneers of education had a lasting influence on the shape of ASL as we know it today. In this chapter, you are introduced to various aspects of ASL.

WHAT IS AMERICAN SIGN LANGUAGE?

American Sign Language is the language of the American Deaf community. This is a simple yet practical definition. If someone asked you what Italian is, you would likely respond that it is the way most people in Italy speak. This approach might appear unusual given the trend in most ASL textbooks to define ASL by clarifying misconceptions about it. But why learn about misconceptions? Learn ASL with a clean conscience and a clear goal: ASL is how most Deaf Americans sign, and it is how you will sign as you venture through this book.

SIGNING AS A CHOICE OF COMMUNICATION

I have taught ASL to over two thousand students, and my strongest impression of this language can be summed up in a simple observation: once a student has tasted the excitement of communicating with her hands she never loses her appetite for learning more about signing. I have not met a sign language teacher who has observed otherwise. Not all students learn to sign well nor do they all continue in their study of signing. But once their curiosity is piqued, they continue to have an interest in signing. I was asked by a student if I signed in my dreams. Whether a Deaf person signs in his dreams is a moot question, so I flipped it around and told her to tell me how she dreams after she becomes a fluent signer. Such is the nature of learning about sign language.

For many of you, ASL is a new language that forces you to confront your prejudices about communicating with your hands. You might wonder about what you can talk about in signs. Would you wonder about this if you were learning to speak Spanish? Probably not. But ASL is not just a different language, it is a different medium for talking, and this fact may make you hesitant and perhaps even suspicious about what you can and cannot say in ASL. You are in good company because Deaf people wonder how it is possible to talk in speech about such things as the destructive force of twisters and the tender moments of a child playing alone. To Deaf people the picture of communication painted by vowels and consonants, pitch and loudness pales in comparison to the vibrant images that jump off the fingers and hands, face, and body of a person signing.

Being able to communicate with your hands should not be a surprise because you have been doing it for years albeit to a far lesser extent than Deaf people. From the earliest days of human communications, people have relied on symbols created by the hands to communicate with the other groups of people they encountered as they followed a herd of animals or moved across the continent in search of food and shelter. Native Americans used signs for intertribal communications because mastering many spoken dialects is difficult. Hunters in the African savannah still use signs to help them hunt better. It is hard to imagine a hunter yelling, "Sneak up on the wildebeest on your left!" A neon sign could hardly be more invasive. Yet, it is easy to imagine hunters and others using natural gestures and created signs to communicate.

For Deaf people, signing *is* necessary for communication. How did Deaf people living 3,000 years ago in Athens communicate with one another? In sign language, the same way they communicate today. Then why, until recently, did so many nondeaf people know so little about signing? There are at least three reasons for this. First, Deaf people make up just a small fraction of the population in any area. Therefore many nondeaf people never encounter a Deaf person in their walk through life. Second, speech is the dominant form of communication in society and gets the most attention. Third, Deaf people tend to socialize with one another and with those nondeaf people who know how to sign.

Given these reasons for why nondeaf people know so little about signing, it is reasonable to assume that if you know someone who communicates with the hands, you know someone who is Deaf. Or is it? Consider how much gestural and nonverbal communication you encounter in your everyday conversations. A stare ("Don't do it"), an affectionate smile ("I am comfortable around you"), pushing the hand quickly to the side ("Get rid of it"), brushing the index finger back and forth across the chin ("I'm thinking about it"), and placing the hand on the forehead ("I don't believe this happened") convey information. They are not random acts unrelated to a conversation taking place. In fact, we use nonverbal communication so naturally that we don't talk about these gestures other than to say, "Don't talk with your hands." But we do talk with our hands, and for Deaf people it is the most natural way of talking.

Awareness of ASL has been growing since William C. Stokoe published his research on the linguistics of ASL forty years ago. ASL courses in high schools and colleges are booming. The television and movie industry has discovered the value of including Deaf actors and actresses in films. Even if the part is small as in *River Wild* and *Mr. Holland's Opus*, the effect is that ASL is steadily working its way into households across the nation. Sign language interpreters are also indirectly promoting exposure to ASL whether they are interpreting in schools, in a doctor's office, or for the President on the campaign trail. Their visibility translates to ASL visibility. Just how effective is this movement toward greater awareness of ASL? Answer this question yourself by thinking about your first encounter with signing and the reason why you are reading this book.

THE BEGINNING OF SIGNS

At some point you will wonder where in the world signs came from. Compared with the study of other languages, the study of sign language is relatively new, with ASL being the most widely studied sign language in the world. But even ASL has had only forty years under the microscope of psycholinguists and sociolinguists who are seeking to determine its roots, map out its grammar and vocabulary, and survey its linguistic versatility in all phases of communication. Although we have learned much, we still have much more to learn.

It was mentioned earlier that even though ASL did not begin with the schooling of Deaf children, schools for the Deaf have helped spread its use. Moreover, because Deaf communities tend to form around schools for the Deaf, there is a close association among ASL, schools for the Deaf, and the Deaf community.

As with any language, we like to know about its roots. We also want to know why we use a particular word and where this word comes from. Sign language is no exception, and like gazing at the stars, we are curious about whether any of the signs used almost 200 years ago are still used today. Some of them are. The signs HELP, OTHER, and SEARCH-FOR are similar to signs in French Sign Language. The ASL noun-adjective grammar structure creates phrases such as SHIRT BLUE and BIRD YELLOW, the same sort of structure used in French Sign Language. Sign language used in other countries may also have influenced the development of ASL, but we are just learning about the nature of this influence.

We can say that ASL is a versatile language, which is something we say about English. Many words were introduced to English by speakers from other languages: the word *skunk* comes from the Native Americans, *patio* comes from Spaniards, *corral* comes from people in southern Africa, and *okay* comes from slaves brought from West Africa. Okay? Surprisingly, ASL is flexible enough to borrow from English. The sign OK is made by fingerspelling O-K. Signs for many countries are typically taken from the native sign language used in that country.

Deaf people create new signs as necessary to accommodate changing lifestyles and the influence of technology. Signs of recent origin are CREDIT-CARD, COMPUTER, DISK, and NETWORK. Creating new signs is a part of ASL's evolution. It is also a part of Deaf culture. It is unthinkable that you will wake up one day speaking words that you have invented. Likewise you should not think that learning ASL is an invitation to make up signs. The signs you need for communicating are there already. Your task is to learn them.

It should also be clear that if you wish to communicate with Deaf people from other countries, then you must learn their sign language because ASL is common only in the United States and in all provinces of Canada other than Quebec where Language des Signes Québécoise is the dominant sign language. Thus, British Sign Language is as Greek to Deaf Americans as Mexican Sign Language is to Deaf Brazilians. Although there is no international sign language, the World Federation of the Deaf created a standardized system of signs to meet the needs of Deaf people throughout the world to promote understanding. The sign system Gestuno was created by the World Federation of the Deaf in 1975 utilizing signs commonly used by Deaf people across the world, and those which occur in a naturally spontaneous manner (World Federation of the Deaf, 1975). Gestuno is often used at international conferences such as the Annual World Federation of the Deaf and International Congress on the Education of the Deaf to facilitate communication.

THE PHYSICAL DIMENSIONS OF ASL

ASL is a visual-gestural language. It is visual because we see it and gestural because the signs are formed by the hands. Signing alone, however, is not an accurate picture of ASL. How signs are formed in space is important to understanding what they mean. The critical space is called the signing space and extends from the waist to just above the head and to just beyond the sides of the body. This is also the space in which the hands can move comfortably. As you will learn in this book, the signing space has a role in ASL grammar. One further dimension of ASL is the movement of the head and facial expressions, which help shape the meaning of ASL sentences. In fact, facial grammar is examined in its own chapter. All the foregoing dimensions have given ASL its unique grammar.

How are signs formed? Handshape, orientation, location, and movement describe a sign. The *handshape* is the shape of the hands when the sign is formed. The handshape may remain the same throughout the sign, or it can change. If two hands are used to make a sign, both hands can have the same handshape or be different. The *orientation* is the position of the hand(s) relative to the body. For example, the palms can be facing the body or away from the body, facing the ground or facing upward. The *location* is the place in the signing space where a sign is formed. Signs can be stationary such as THINK and LOVE, or they can move from one location in the signing space to another, like the signs LONG and EXCITE. The *movement* of a sign is the direction in which the hand moves relative to the body. There is a variety of movements that range from a simple sliding movement (e.g., NICE) to a complex circular movement (e.g., TRAVEL-AROUND).

Some signs are iconic in that their meanings can be guessed from the sign alone. A majority of signs are not iconic, and their meaning must be learned. There is usually a reason, however, for why a sign has taken the shape it has. In the sign LEARN, the movement of the hand represents taking knowledge from a book and inserting it in the brain.

Thus, signs are used to create in space images that convey our thoughts to other people; this is the makeup of ASL. The dynamics of moving the hands in space determines how signs are formed and the shape of ASL grammar. Two or more concepts can be simultaneously expressed in ASL. This feat cannot be accomplished in a spoken language because speech is temporal in that one word rolls off the tongue at a time. Because of the spatial and gestural qualities of ASL, there can be no convenient written form of ASL. What we can do is write English glosses of ASL signs. An English gloss is the best approximation of the meaning of a sign. It gives us a way of laying out ASL so that it can be studied and discussed, but it is not a written form of ASL. In this book, English glosses are written in uppercase lettering. For example, the English sentence "What are you doing tonight?" would be written in English gloss using ASL signs and would read, "TONIGHT, YOU DO-what?" When signed in ASL, the sign TONIGHT is signed first, to indicate time, then the subject YOU is signed, the verb DO, and finally the question WHAT, which is commonly placed at the end of the sentence. This method of ordering sentences with the subject first, object next, and verb at the end is not found in English.

THE CULTURAL DIMENSION OF ASL

Learning ASL is not simply about learning another language. It is also about access. Even though we can learn something about any culture from reading about it, we acquire a deeper understanding when we can experience the culture or hear firsthand accounts from the people who are a part of the culture. ASL gives us access to Deaf culture.

ASL is one of the defining characteristics of the Deaf community. People in the Deaf community are seldom defined by their ethnicity as they are in other communities such as the Hispanic community and the Irish community. Although some ethnic groups such as Deaf African-Americans do form their own communities, the Deaf community as it is normally described crosses all ethnic populations. They are bounded instead by their language, ASL. To learn more about Deaf culture and to tap into the resources of the Deaf community, you need a solid grasp of ASL. The cultural dimension of ASL is discussed in depth in Chapter 3 called "The Deaf Community."

REVIEW EXERCISES

1. Write down the reasons why you are learning ASL. Compare your reasons with others who are learning ASL. Compile a list of the most common reasons.

2. Schools for the Deaf are closely associated with ASL because they bring together large numbers of Deaf pupils who use ASL as their major language of communication. When these pupils leave the school, they spread their knowledge of ASL to other Deaf people as well as to nondeaf people. Look up the names of the schools for the Deaf in your state, province, or region. E-mail or use the Internet to find out when one of the schools was first established and how many pupils are now enrolled in the school.

3. Name the three main sources of influence on the early development of ASL.

4. Describe the four characteristics used to describe a sign.

5. Why is it difficult to have a written form of ASL and what is an English gloss?

ANSWER EXPLANATIONS

1. Individual answer.

2. Find them from the Internet. For example, Michigan School for the Deaf and Blind.

3. Sources: Laurent Clerc (Deaf teacher from France), Thomas Gallaudet, and the Deaf Community.

4. Handshape, orientation, location, and movement. See page 5.

5. It is difficult to have a written form of ASL because ASL has spatial and gestural qualities that are difficult to label. English gloss is the best approximation of the meaning of a sign.

The Basics

Facial Grammar

In one study, it was noted that a signer, in the middle of telling a story, produced a signed message such as MAN FISH CONTINUOUS, which we would translate as *the man was fishing*. However, other ASL users, watching the signer, would translate the message as *the man was fishing with relaxation and enjoyment*. The source of this extra information was a particular facial expression in which the lips were together and pushed out a little, with the head slightly tilted. This nonmanual signal was clearly capable of functioning as the equivalent of an adverb in English and was an integral part of the message.

—GEORGE YULE
The Study of Language

HOLD THAT SIGN . . .

What's in a sign may not be what's in the mind. To capture the sense of what a signer is signing, you must read the signer's face and body. When you listen to someone speak, you listen not only to the words but also to how the words are spoken. The tone of the voice, the rise and fall of the pitch, the length of the pause, and the steadiness of voice are all features that you latch onto with little effort in your spoken communication. These traits are nonexistent in signing, but they do have parallel traits that are crucial to ASL's grammar. The raised eyebrow, the tilted head, the open mouth, and a sign held slightly longer than others shape the meaning of the signs that are made by the hands. We call these nonmanual signals *facial grammar*, which allow you to use facial expressions, your body, and gestures to add meaning and additional information to your signing. Mastering ASL cannot occur without a mastery of facial grammar. Read this chapter and you should be ready to use your face to say what your hands cannot.

THE FIRST RULE OF SIGNING: MAINTAIN EYE CONTACT

ASL is a visual language, and eye contact is the starting profile of any two people who are about to sign to each other. You cannot understand signing if you are not watching someone sign. That's the easy part. What is harder to learn is how to maintain eye contact even when you are signing. That is, even when you have someone's attention, you must continue to look at this person while you are signing.

You achieve eye contact with someone by drawing their attention to you. Deaf people will lightly tap a person on the shoulder to indicate that eye contact is desired so that a conversation can begin. Looking away from someone can mean several things. Perhaps you are finished with a conversation. Or it may be that you are distracted by something. Or, just as likely, your eyes are being called upon for a role in structuring an ASL sentence.

BREAKING THE FIRST RULE OF SIGNING

Eye contact is not always maintained throughout a conversation. The eyes will gaze elsewhere but only if such movement is relevant to what is being signed. Eye contact and eye gazing send several signals to the other person. These signals are influenced by the signs that are made as well as by the facial expressions that accompany the signing. Some grammatical signals are associated with the eyes and an example of each follows:

1. *Ask a particular type of question*. The sentence "Are you ready?" is translated as YOU READY? in ASL. In the absence of any nonmanual signals from the face, signing YOU and READY would give us the sentence "You are ready." To indicate that a question is being asked, the signer looks directly at the person, raises the eyebrows, and tilts the head slightly forward. Nonmanual signals for other types of questions require a different set of facial expressions and body movement.

2. *Draw attention to a particular place in the signing space in which a person or thing has been established*. ASL signing relies heavily upon establishing reference places in the signing space. After establishing a reference place, the signer can point to it or look at it to draw attention to the referent that is in that place. In this way, the eyes can incorporate referents that are in the signing space into a sentence.

3. *Highlight key information in a sentence*. Eye contact accompanied by a raised eyebrow, the head tilting forward, and a sign held slightly longer than other signs can indicate the topic of a sentence.

4. *Reinforce the direction in which certain signs might be moving*. A signer can make the sentence "I watched him walk past me" by simply gazing from the right to the left side of the signing space.

5. *Reveal emotions about a topic*. Adjectives such as *surprised* and *suspicious* can be expressed by opening the eyes wide or narrowing them.

Each of these examples as well as others will be expanded upon in this book. They are mentioned here to emphasize the importance of the eyes in enhancing the meaning when signing.

COMMON TYPES OF NONMANUAL SIGNALS

1. Questions

   a. Did you see the game last night? (LAST NIGHT, GAME SEE FINISH YOU?)
   b. What time did you arrive home yesterday? (YESTERDAY, YOU HOME ARRIVE, TIME?)

Both of these sentences ask questions. Asking a question calls for a particular kind of non-manual signal. To know what type of nonmanual signal to use, you must first know what type of question you will ask. Sentence a asks for a yes or no response and is called a yes/no question. Sentence b is a wh-question and asks for information about something.

For all types of questions, the signer *maintains eye contact with the person to whom she or he is signing*.

Yes/No Questions

For yes/no questions, the signer (1) *raises the eyebrows* and (2) *tilts the head forward*. If the question is short, then the signer can raise the eyebrows and tilt the head throughout signing the question. This is the case with the following questions:

FINISH YOU? (Are you finished?)
SEE FINISH YOU? (Have you seen it?)
TIRED YOU? (Are you tired?)
YOU HUNGRY? (Are you hungry?)

If the question is long, then the signer usually adds the nonmanual signal at the end of the sentence while signing those signs that are directly associated with asking questions. In the following sentences, the nonmanual signals should be added while signing the underlined phrases:

LAST-WEEK, MOVIE <u>SEE FINISH YOU</u>? (Did you see the movie last week?)
TOMORROW, SCHOOL GO-to <u>WANT YOU</u>? (Do you want to go to school tomorrow?)
YOUR SCIENCE BOOK, <u>HAVE YOU</u>? (Do you have your science book?)
ME LEAVE NOW, <u>DON'T-MIND YOU</u>? (Do you mind if I leave?)

Questions Seeking Information

For questions that ask for information such as wh-questions, the signer (1) *squeezes the eyebrows* and (2) *tilts the head forward*. If the questions are short, then the signer can make the nonmanual signals throughout the question as in the following questions:

TIME? (What time is it?)
DO-what YOU? (What are you going to do about it?)
YOU LIVE WHERE? (Where do you live?)
WHAT YOU EAT? (What did you eat?)

If the question is long, then the signer should add the nonmanual signals at the end of the sentence and especially on the sign that is asking the question. Nonmanual signals are typically added while signing the underlined phrases in the following sentences:

LAST MONDAY, YOU SWIM <u>WHERE</u>? (Where did you swim last Monday?)
BEFORE, YOU ENGINE FIX <u>HOW</u>? (How did you fix the engine before?)
YOUR ASL CLASS, STUDENT <u>HOW-MANY</u>? (How many students are in your ASL class?)
YOU WORK FINISH, <u>TIME</u>? (What time does your work finish?)

2. Rhetorical Questions

  a. me-MEET-you WHEN? NEXT-WEEK THURSDAY. (I will meet you next week on Thursday.)
  b. ME ARRIVE LATE WHY? MY CAR FLAT-TIRE. (I arrived late because I had a flat tire.)

Both of these sentences are examples of rhetorical questions. The signer asks a question and then answers it. No question is being asked to someone else. ASL rhetorical questions are not translated as questions in English. When signing a rhetorical question, the signer must use the appropriate nonmanual signals to indicate that a question was asked and that she or he will answer it. For rhetorical questions, the signer (1) *maintains eye contact*, (2) *raises the eyebrows*, (3) *tilts the head forward*, and (4) *holds the last sign of the rhetorical question slightly longer than the other signs*. Even though this last feature is not a facial expression, the time during which the sign is held is still a part of the nonmanual signals that the signer is sending. The signer typically relays the nonmanual signals while signing the entire rhetorical question, which tells the *addressee* (the person to whom the signer is signing) that what is being signed is a rhetorical question. Examples of rhetorical questions are underlined in the following:

<u>ME GO-to WORK TIME</u>? TIME 12. (I go to work at twelve o'clock.)
<u>YOU LINE-UP FOR-FOR</u>? MOVIE FINISH NOT-YET.
(You are lining up because the movie isn't over yet.)
<u>ME GO-to NEW-ORLEANS HOW</u>? FLY. (I am flying to New Orleans.)
<u>ME HOMEWORK FINISH WHAT</u>? GEOGRAPHY.
(I have finished my geography homework.)

Notice that the nonmanual signals for rhetorical questions are the same whether a yes/no question or a question seeking information is asked.

3. Topicalization: Topic/Comment Sentences

a. BOY THERE BROWN HAIR, MY SON. (That boy with the brown hair is my son.)

b. YOU TAKE-UP MATH, ME SHOCKED. (I am shocked that you are taking math.)

Both of these sentences are examples of a common ASL sentence structure known as topic/comment. The signer describes a topic and then makes a comment about it. The nonmanual signals consist of the following: (1) *maintain eye contact with the person being addressed* provided the eyes are not needed for relaying other grammatical information, (2) *raise the eyebrows and tilt the head slightly forward* when signing the topic, (3) *hold the last sign of the topic a little longer than the other signs*, and (4) *pause slightly between signing the topic and the comment*. When the comment is signed, the signer reverts to a neutral signing posture and facial expression, or uses eye gazing, facial expressions, and body posture suitable to the intended meaning of the comment.

The four parts of the nonmanual signals are conveyed during the signing of the topic, which is underlined in each of the following sentences:

<u>you-HELP-me STUDY ASL</u>, ME HAPPY.
(I'm happy when you help me study ASL.)
<u>STORY ABOUT THREE RABBIT</u>, EXCITING.
(The story about the three rabbits is exciting.)
<u>CAR RED THERE</u>, ME WANT. (I want that red car.)

4. Conditional Sentences

a. SUPPOSE ME SIGN FORGET, you-HELP-me PLEASE. (Please help me if I forget a sign.)

b. YOUR CAR BREAK-DOWN, YOU LATE WILL YOU. (If your car breaks down, you will be late.)

Conditional sentences require nonmanual signals to alert the addressee to the stated condition. The signal is (1) *the eyebrows raised*, (2) *the head tilted slightly to one side*, (3) *the last sign of the conditional clause held slightly longer than the other signs*, and (4) in some cases, *the body inclined forward*. The head is usually tilted forward, but it may be tilted slightly backward depending upon the style of the signer and the context of the sentence. If the intent of the sentence "If you go to the store, I am taking your credit cards away" is humor, then it might be signed with the head tilted slightly backward. The sign SUPPOSE in the first sentence is an obvious indication of a conditional sentence. In the second sentence, the signer must rely on nonmanual signals to inform the addressee of the condition, "If your car breaks down." The conditional clauses requiring a nonmanual signal are under-lined in the following sentences:

YOU LOSE, ME HAPPY STILL. (If you lose, I will still be happy.)
SUPPOSE MY AUNT SHOW-UP, ME GO HOME.
(If my aunt shows up, I'm going home.)
TOMORROW RAIN, TOURNAMENT CANCEL.
(If it rains tomorrow, the tournament will be canceled.)
SUPPOSE HE HUNGRY, you-GIVE-him APPLE.
(If he's hungry, give him an apple.)

As with all signed sentences, if there is no grammatical reason for looking away, the signer should maintain eye contact with the addressee.

REVIEW AND PRACTICE

1. Describe four types of grammatical signals associated with the eyes.

2. Describe the nonmanual signals that accompany (a) a yes/no question, (b) a question seeking information, (c) a rhetorical question, (d) a topic/comment sentence struc-ture, and (e) a conditional sentence.

3. In ASL, it is important to say with your face what you are signing with your hands. Many people do this most of the time when speaking. Many beginning signers, on the other hand, find themselves concentrating so hard on the formation of a sign that they often just have a neutral expression on their faces. With a partner or while stand-ing before a mirror, practice making facial expressions to suit each of the following actions. Beside each action make notes about what happens to your eyebrows, head, shoulders, and hands.
   (a) You are looking for someone in an auditorium.
   (b) The ice cream you were given is not the one you ordered.
   (c) Your car has two flat tires.
   (d) You are thanking someone for finding your wallet.
   (e) You find out that the money in your returned wallet is missing.
   (f) You are telling the stranger at your door to go away.
   (g) You just spilled a can of soda pop on your computer keyboard.
   (h) You have just tasted something that is very sour.
   (i) You are telling a friend that you have just won a new car in a raffle.

ANSWER EXPLANATIONS

1. Yes/No questions, questions seeking information, rhetorical questions, topic sentences, and conditional sentences.

2.
   (a) Yes/No question: raised eyebrows and forward tilting head.
   (b) Question seeking information: squeezed eyebrows and forward tilting head.
   (c) Rhetorical question: raised eyebrows, forward tilting head, and holding last sign longer.
   (d) Topic/comment sentence structure: raised eyebrows, forward tilting head, pause between sentences, and holding last sign longer.
   (e) Conditional sentence: raised eyebrows, forward tilting head, and holding last sign longer.

3. Use the following facial expressions to suit each of the respective actions:
   (a) question seeking information.
   (b) topic/comment.
   (c) rhetorical.
   (d) conditional.
   (e) topic/comment.
   (f) conditional.
   (g) topic/comment.
   (h) topic/comment.
   (i) topic/comment.

The First Ten Rules of ASL Grammar

Signed languages exist in space and naturally take advantage of spatial reasoning to convey messages. In ASL, for example, I-SHOW-YOU is one sign moving outward from the signer; YOU-SHOW-ME moves inward toward the signer. Where English would require three words in each case, there is only one sign with its incorporated movement. If I sign MY BROTHER and point to the left and MY SISTER and point to the right, "My brother met my sister" can be rendered by a single sign moving from left to right. I can then attribute qualities unambiguously to my brother or my sister by making the signed attributions either to the left or to the right. Many ASL verbs, such as GIVE, NAME, PREACH, SAY-NO, ASK, HATE, MOCK, are executed with movements that incorporate who is doing the action to whom. Since that information is in the modified sign itself, ASL, like many spoken languages, such as Russian, does not have to restrict word order, as English does. For example, the three signs HORSE, COW, and KICK . . . might be arranged in any order in ASL . . . and there would still be no doubt about which animal was kicking which. Word order is available, therefore, to serve other purposes; thus, it is common for an ASL sentence to put the topic first and then the comment, as in the sentence with two signs: GIVE-HIM-THE-BOOK, I-DON'T-WANT-TO.

—HARLAN LANE
The Mask of Benevolence

HOLD THAT SIGN . . . .

Harlan Lane is fascinated with ASL's grammatical freedom and its grammatical structures. How a language can have both of these seemingly contradictory features will become plain as you get accustomed to the three dimensions of ASL. First, ASL is visual; you must see it to understand it. Second, ASL is spatial; signers create meaning in the space in front of them. Lastly, ASL is gestural; the hands form signs that articulate thoughts. Even though ASL grammar shares some similarities with spoken languages, its visual, spatial, and gestural features combine to create some grammatical structures that are unparalleled in the world of spoken languages. Thus, as you learn about ASL, look for similarities with English and other spoken languages, but also get ready for a journey through new linguistic territory. In particular, the spatial qualities of ASL grammar allow a signer to express more than one thought simultaneously—a characteristic that cannot be duplicated in English. To help you get started in mastering a new grammar, this chapter introduces and provides you with an overview of the ten basic ASL rules. Each of these rules is further explained in the following lessons that teach you how to sign.

TOPIC/COMMENT

In a simple topic/comment sentence, the topic is described first followed by the comment.

HE WON 3 MILLION DOLLARS, HE HAPPY.

Many sentences are built around the simple concept of a topic and a comment. We can add to this concept the observation that ASL tends to structure sentences in the order that events occur. There must be a topic before there can be a comment about the topic. Hence, we have the rule for the common topic/comment structure in ASL.

From the preceding sentence, the topic and comment follow:

topic:	HE WON 3 MILLION DOLLARS,
comment:	HE HAPPY.

The English translation of this sentence is "He won $3,000,000 and he is happy," or "He's happy that he won $3,000,000."

Here are more examples of topic/comment sentences with the topic underlined:

<u>**ASL TEST**</u>**, EASY. (The ASL test is easy.)**
<u>**DOG GOOD**</u>**, you-GIVE-it COOKIE. (The dog is good, give it a cookie.)**
<u>**HER MONEY LOST**</u>**, SHE UPSET. (She's upset that she lost her money.)**
<u>**BOY STAND BESIDE CHAIR**</u>**, HE MY BROTHER.**
(The boy standing beside the chair is my brother.)

The topic can vary according to what it is that the signer wants to emphasize. Let's look at the following sentence:

Two years ago I had a wonderful vacation.

With just this sentence to consider, we might suppose that *vacation* is the topic and *wonderful* is the comment. This could be represented in signs as follows:

topic:	2-YEARS-AGO <u>ME VACATION</u>
comment:	WONDERFUL

What if the point of the discussion was the last time a signer had a great vacation? Then the topic changes as the following ordering of the ASL sentence demonstrates:

topic:	<u>ME WONDERFUL VACATION</u>
comment:	2-YEARS-AGO

In English the same sentence structure can be used to represent either of these two topics because a speaker would highlight the topic using the tone of voice.

NONMANUAL SIGNALS

The following nonmanual signals play a role in identifying the topic in a topic/comment sentence structure. The signer (1) *maintains eye contact with the person being addressed*, (2) *raises the eyebrows and tilts the head slightly forward when signing the topic*, (3) *holds the last sign of the comment a little longer than the other signs*, and (4) *pauses slightly between signing the topic and the comment*.

   When signing the comment, the signer uses facial expressions that convey the emotion of what is signed. If the comment is SHE UPSET, then the signer should project a face associated with being upset. But the face does not always correspond with the emotions projected by the signs. For example, if the signer is being sarcastic, humorous, silly, or serious, then she or he might wish to convey these feelings rather than the feelings associated with the comment itself. If a signer is in fact being funny, then she or he might have a hint of smile on the face while signing SHE UPSET. Similarly, the lips might be pursed and the eyebrows squeezed together while signing a comment, if a signer is serious about something.

TENSE WITH TIME ADVERBS

The time adverb is placed at the beginning or near the beginning of a sentence.

   a. LAST NIGHT, SUNSET BEAUTIFUL. (The sunset was beautiful last night.)
   b. IN-2-DAYS, YOU GO-to WORK. (You go to work in two days.)
   c. ME YESTERDAY, STAY HOME. (I stayed home yesterday.)

Sentences a and b start off with a time adverb, whereas sentence c has the time adverb near the beginning of the sentence. Placing a time adverb at or near the beginning of a sentence marks the tense of the sentence. Using time adverbs is the most common means of indicating tense. Unlike English, verb signs never undergo changes to indicate tense. Because there are no changes to a verb sign, the time that an action occurred must come before the verb sign.

   After a time adverb has indicated tense in a sentence, all sentences after this sentence will have the *same* tense. There is no need to repeat the time adverb with each sentence.

Tense can be changed only by signing a different time adverb, changing the topic of discussion, or using a sign that is not a time adverb but tells about time.

The signs FINISH, WILL, and NOT-YET are signs that tell about time. Each of these will be discussed in more detail later in the book. They are briefly mentioned at this point because of their effect on tense. The placement of each of these signs in a sentence varies. The sign FINISH is often used to indicate that an action has been completed. It is either placed before or after the verb as in the following sentences:

> Before the verb: HE MOVIE FINISH SEE. (He saw the movie.)
>
> After the verb: ME WORK FINISH. (I have finished working.)

The sign WILL is often used in its emphatic sense to stress that an action is indeed going to take place in the future. It can be placed before or after a verb or at the end of a sentence. Three examples of how the sign WILL is used follow:

> Before the verb: ME WILL SEND-you LETTER. (I will send you a letter.)
>
> After the verb: me-MEET-you WILL, TOMORROW ME PROMISE.
> (I promise I will meet you tomorrow.)
>
> End of a sentence: PHONE HOME TWICE WEEK, ME WILL. (I will phone home twice a week.)

The sign NOT-YET is used to show that an action has not yet occurred. It is often placed at the end of a sentence as in sentence a, which follows, or it can be used by itself in response to a question as demonstrated in sentence b.

a. ME HOMEWORK FINISH, NOT-YET. (I haven't done my homework yet.)
b. Signer A: YOU EAT FINISH YOU? (Have you finished eating?)
    Signer B: NOT-YET. (Not yet.)

SIMPLE YES/NO QUESTIONS

In short sentences that ask a yes/no question, the order of the signs is variable.

a. YOU EXERCISE WANT?
b. YOU WANT EXERCISE?
c. WANT EXERCISE YOU?
d. EXERCISE YOU WANT?

In short questions such as those in sentences a–d, the signer is asking a simple yes/no question, and the correct English translation for all of them is "Do you want to exercise?"

However, the signs alone do not ask the question. The signer must use the correct non-manual signals, which for yes/no questions are: (1) *eye contact with the addressee*, (2) *raised eyebrows*, and (3) *the head tilted forward*. Recall that with short questions the nonmanual signals can be made throughout the question.

LONG YES/NO QUESTIONS

Long yes/no questions use a topic/question format.

In longer yes/no questions, you first describe the topic and then place the sign that is asking the question at or near the end of the sentence.

   a. CAT BLACK TREE CLIMB, YOUR? (Is that black cat climbing the tree yours?)
   b. CLEAN DISHES WASH CLOTHES, HE? (Will he clean the dishes and wash the clothes?)
   c. GO-to STORE BUY FOOD MILK, READY YOU? (Are you ready to go to the store and buy food and milk?)

You may recognize that questions a–c follow a variation of the topic/comment sentence structure. For convenience, we will refer to this structure as a topic/question structure to help you recall it more easily. The nonmanual signals in long questions usually fall on the last sign or phrase. In the preceding long questions, the nonmanual signals will accompany the signs YOUR?, HE?, and READY YOU?

INFORMATION-SEEKING QUESTIONS

Simple questions that ask for information have variable sentence structures and rely on nonmanual signals to distinguish them from declarative sentences.

   a. AGE YOU? (How old are you?)
   b. TIME? (What time is it?)
   c. BOOK TITLE? (What is the title of the book?)

Questions a–c are simple and are distinguished from simple declarative statements by the nonmanual signals that would accompany them. Both questions ask for information; therefore, the signer (1) *maintains eye contact*, (2) *squeezes the eyebrows together*, and (3) *tilts the head forward*.

Wh-questions also seek information. Although the wh-question sign can come at the beginning of a sentence, most wh-questions follow a topic/question format and place the wh-question sign at or near the end of the question.

d. SHE WORK HERE, HOW LONG? (How long has she worked here?)
e. CITY DESTROY BUILDING, WHY? (Why did the city destroy the building?)

In sentences d and e, the wh-question sign or phrase comes at the end of the question. It follows a topic/question format because a topic is described followed by a question about it. It would still be correct to turn the questions around.

f. HOW LONG SHE WORK HERE?
g. WHY CITY DESTROY BUILDING?

Questions f and g are similar in structure to English. Many beginning signers find it difficult to ask a wh-question using the topic/question format as shown in sentences d and e. Yet, this format is very common in ASL, and for this reason it will be emphasized throughout this book.

It is also common practice to include the pronoun at the end or near the end of a wh-question. This is shown in the following examples:

PICNIC FOOD BRING, WHAT YOU? (What food are you bringing to the picnic?)
HE BORN, WHEN HE? (When was he born?)
YESTERDAY FIX FENCE, HOW YOU? (How did you fix the fence yesterday?)
you-PICK-ON-me, WHY YOU? (Why are you picking on me?)

PRONOMINALIZATION

Pronouns are indicated by pointing to either (a) a person or thing that is present or (b) a place in the signing space that is used as a referent point for a person or thing. Pointing is mostly done with the index finger, but eye gazing and other handshapes are sometimes used.

To understand how pointing is used to indicate pronouns, you must first understand the dimensions and techniques for using the signing space. The *signing space* is the space in which a signer signs. The following diagram shows the typical dimensions of the signing space for a signer.

The signing space is roughly defined as the space from the waist to just above the head and to the left and right side of the body. This space is also the comfort zone of signing—the signer can move the hands about without stretching them to the point of discomfort.

PRONOUNS IN THE PRESENCE OF A PERSON OR OBJECT

If a person or object is present, then the signer merely points to them and the pointing becomes the pronoun. This is illustrated in the following diagram. Pointing to the person yields the pronoun SHE/HER or HE/HIM. Pointing to an animal or object is translated as IT.

Similarly, whomever or whatever the signer points to will be understood as the pronoun of the person or object indicated. For example, if several people are present, the signer sweeps the index finger past all of them to show the pronoun THEY or THEM. The pronoun ME is made by pointing to oneself and the pronoun YOU is made by pointing to the addressee. Notice that the pronouns WE/US cannot be established in the signing space because they include the signer who is always present. To sign WE/US, the signer moves the index finger in an arc from one shoulder to the other shoulder.

PRONOUNS IN THE ABSENCE OF A PERSON OR OBJECT

The principle of identifying pronouns in the absence of a real person or object is similar to the principle of identifying pronouns when the referent is present. The signer uses the signing space to insert reference points that will represent a specific person or object. For example, the following diagrams illustrate the common referent points in the signing space for pronouns.

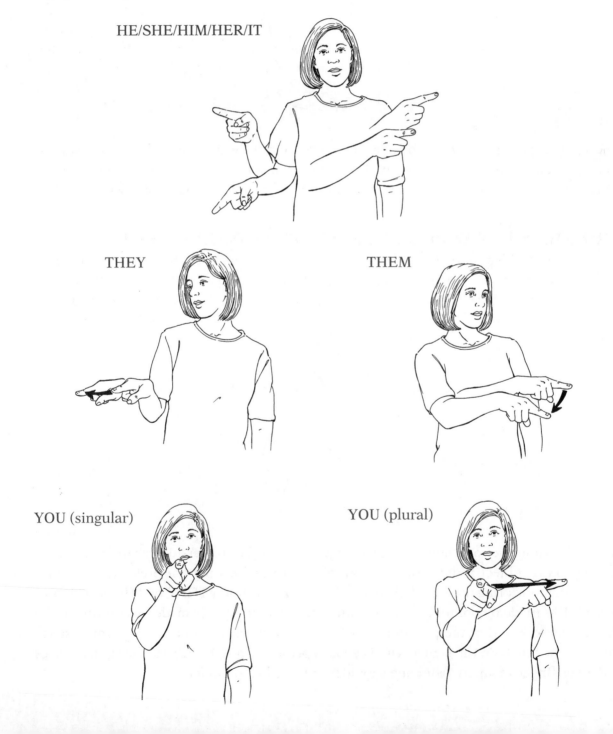

HE/SHE/HIM/HER/IT

THEY

THEM

YOU (singular)

YOU (plural)

The phrases "point-right" or "point-left" are used in ASL sentences to show which side of the signing space the signer is placing the reference point for HE/HIM, SHE/HER, or IT. The phrases "sweep-right" and "sweep-left" are used when showing which side of the signing space the signer is placing THEY or THEM. You will note in the signing lessons that these phrases are used to help you learn about placing people and places in the signing space. In other instances, determining the location is left for you to decide.

Before the signing space can be used to sign pronouns, the signer must first establish a referent in the space. The procedure for doing this is to name the person or object and then point to a spot in the signing space. This spot becomes the location for the pronoun associated with the referent. How this works can be shown with the following sentence:

My brother is deaf, and he is visiting me.

To establish the pronoun *he*, the signer must place the person called *brother* in the signing space. From an earlier diagram we saw that the pronoun HE is typically set up either to the right or left side of the signer. If the signer chooses the right side, we would then get the following ASL sentence:

MY BROTHER point-right, HE VISIT ME.

MY

BROTHER

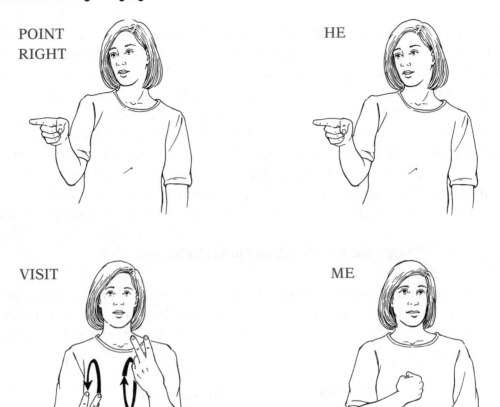

POINT RIGHT

HE

VISIT

ME

After the signer has signed MY BROTHER point-right, a place has been identified in the signing space that is the reference point for "brother." Pointing to this place will always mean the sign HE until the signer either no longer talks about the brother or changes the location of brother in the signing space.

Another example of how pronouns are established in the signing space is seen in the following sentence:

The teachers showed up for class yesterday, but the students did not.

The tense of the sentence is first established. Then, the signer sets up the location for teachers and students in the signing space. Following this, the signer can point to these locations and tell what the teachers and students did yesterday. This is done in the following ASL sentence:

YESTERDAY, TEACHERS (sweep-left) STUDENTS (sweep-right)
THEY-sweep-left SHOW-UP, THEY-sweep-right DIDN'T (not).

This sentence can be broken down to show its various components.

YESTERDAY	establishes the tense of the sentence
TEACHERS sweep-left	establishes the location of "teachers" in the signing space
STUDENTS sweep-right	establishes the location of "students" in the signing space
THEY sweep-left	sweep-left to refer to the teachers
SHOW-UP	
THEY sweep-right	sweep-right to refer to the students
DIDN'T.	

YESTERDAY

TEACHERS

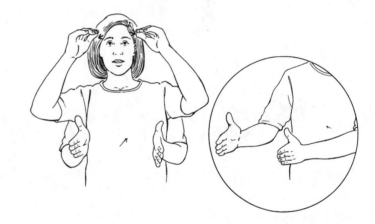

sweep left

STUDENTS

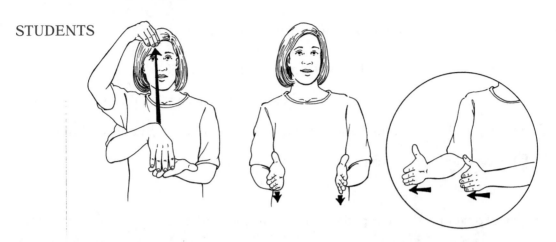

sweep-right   THEY-sweep-left

SHOW UP   THEY

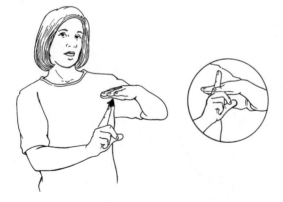 

DIDN'T

Note that in the above illustrations, the hands move to the side for TEACHERS and STUDENTS. This movement indicates the plural form of TEACHER.

Multiple reference points can be established in the signing space as long as the signer and the addressee can recall what each place in the signing space represents. Because of the need to memorize the meaning of each location, you should not attempt to have more than three or four reference points in the signing space at any one time.

As you progress through this book, you will come across repeated examples of pronominalization as well as be introduced to pronouns such as two-of-us, that make special use of the signing space.

SUBJECTIVE VERSUS OBJECTIVE PRONOUN FORMS

The subjective forms of the pronoun are SHE, HER, HE, HIM, YOU, ME, THEY, THEM, WE, US, and IT. The handshape for signing them is the index finger pointing out.

The objective forms of the pronoun are HER, HERS, HIS, YOUR, YOURS, MINE, THEIR, OUR, OURS, and ITS. The handshape for signing them is an open hand with the palm facing outward.

Both the subjective and objective forms of the pronoun make the same movement.

RHETORICAL QUESTIONS

In a rhetorical question, the signer asks a question and then answers it.

a. ME KNOW ASL? YES. (I know ASL.)
b. ME LOST WHY? NOT PAY-ATTENTION STREET NAME. (I didn't pay attention to the name of the street and got lost.)

The rhetorical question is a common grammatical structure in ASL. As shown in sentences a and b, the signer asks a question and then answers it. There is no expectation that someone else will answer the question.

Rhetorical questions often make use of signs for wh-questions such as WHY and HOW. However, a proper translation to English will seldom include a direct reference to these signs. For example, when WHY is used, the proper translation will often include the conjunction "because."

Notice the liberty taken in omitting the word *yes* in the translation of sentence a. A good translation is *not* a matter of finding a word for each of the signs made. An English translation attempts to capture the signer's intended meaning including the nonmanual signals and the manner of signing. Nevertheless, sentence a could also be correctly translated as "Yes, I know ASL."

Recall that the correct nonmanual signal for rhetorical wh-questions is signed during the question and is *not* the same as that for other wh-questions. Also, it is important to hold the last sign of the rhetorical question before answering the question.

ORDERING OF SIMPLE SENTENCES

In simple sentences the verb can be placed before or after the object of the sentence.

a. ME PLAY GAME.
b. ME GAME PLAY.

Sentences a and b translate to "I play a game." The difference between them is that sentence a has a subject-verb-object (SVO) word ordering. SVO is a basic sentence structure in English. Sentence b has a subject-object-verb (SOV) word order. SOV is not a sentence structure in English, but it is basic in ASL. For this reason, beginning signers will tend to use SVO word ordering more frequently than SOV word ordering.

Not all simple sentences can have an SOV word order. The phrase

BOB KATE KISS.

yields the translation "Bob and Kate kiss." Whereas, the phrase

BOB KISS KATE.

means "Bob kisses Kate." It is possible to sign a variation of BOB KATE KISS so that *it appears* that the verb comes after the object. You can do this by using the pronominalization rule. For example, you first fingerspell BOB (or use a name sign for Bob) and then point to the right. You do the same for KATE but point to the left. At this stage, you have established reference points in the signing space for Bob and Kate. You then make the sign KISS moving from the right side to the reference point for Kate, which is on the left side.

The movement of the verb shows who kisses whom. But is this an example of SOV word ordering? Let's look at this sentence:

BOB point-right KATE point-left he-KISS-her.

In this sentence, the verb sign KISS has the subject and the object incorporated into its movement.

CONDITIONAL SENTENCES

In a conditional sentence, first the condition is described then the outcome of this condition is described.

In all types of conditional sentences, nonmanual signals are critical. Review the appropriate nonmanual signals for conditional sentences in "Facial Grammar" (pages 11–12).

SUPPOSE

The condition can be clearly marked with the use of the sign SUPPOSE as shown in the following sentences:

a. SUPPOSE HE SHOW-UP, DO-what YOU? (If he shows up, what are you going to do about it?)
b. SUPPOSE SHE SEE ME, ME HAVE-TO LEAVE. (I will have to leave if she sees me.)
c. SUPPOSE TONIGHT SNOW, TOMORROW YOU CANCEL SCHOOL. (If it snows tonight then you will cancel school tomorrow.)

The conditional clause is always at the beginning of the sentence, and it must clearly describe the condition.

The outcome of the condition is described in the second part of the sentence. The preceding sentences show three different types of outcomes. In sentence a the outcome is a question; in sentence b it is a statement; and in sentence c it is a command.

Notice that the three English translations do not all have the condition stated at the beginning of the sentence. In sentence b the condition is at the end of the sentence. Another suitable translation for sentence b is "If she sees me, I will have to leave." Even though there is flexibility in the ordering of conditional clauses in English, ASL always states the condition first followed by the outcome.

IF

The fingerspelling of I-F is also used to construct a conditional clause. Although I-F can be used interchangeably with the sign SUPPOSE, it is often used to give greater emphasis to a condition. I-F is fingerspelled with the upright fingers of the "f" handshape often wiggling depending on the type of emphasis a signer is trying to give. It is also common for a signer to hold the letter F for a short time to increase the emphasis given to the condition. Some uses of I-F as a condition follow:

a. I-F SHE CAN'T COME, YOU LOSE CONTRACT. (If she can't come, you lose the contract.)
b. I-F YOU WIN GAME, YOUR TEAM CHAMPION. (If you win the game, your team will be the champions.)

In sentences a and b the signer uses I-F to emphasize the consequences of the condition. In sentence a the signer might be warning someone and in essence is saying "She must come or you are going to lose the contract." In sentence b the signer might be pleading "You had better win this game so your team can be champions."

NONMANUAL SIGNALS

All conditional sentences must be accompanied by nonmanual signals. There are some conditional sentences where the nonmanual signal is the only indicator that a condition is being stated. If we take out the sign I-F in sentence a, we have

SHE CAN'T COME, YOU LOSE CONTRACT.

In the absence of nonmanual signals, this sentence translates to "She can't come so you lose the contract." If the nonmanual signals for conditional sentences are added to the phrase SHE CAN'T COME, then the translation will be the same as if the signs I-F or SUPPOSE were used.

NEGATION

You can negate a thought by placing a negative sign before the verb or by first describing a topic and then signing the appropriate negative sign or giving a negative head shake.

a. ME NOT WATCH FOOTBALL GAME. (I'm not watching the football game.)
b. ME CHEAT, NEVER. (I never cheat.)
c. ME GO HOME NOW? NEG-headshake. (No, I am not going home now.)

Sentence a is an example of negating a thought by placing a negative sign before the verb. The sign NOT negates the action sign WATCH.

Sentence b is an example of a topic/comment sentence. The topic is about cheating. The signer uses a negative sign NEVER to make a comment about cheating, which is that it never happens.

Sentence c does not have a negative sign. To respond negatively to the rhetorical question ME GO HOME NOW?, the signer uses the nonmanual signal of shaking the head to say "no."

Shaking the head to say "no" can accompany any negative sign. It can also accompany the topic that is being negated. Although it is good practice to use this nonmanual signal when expressing a negative thought, it is not always necessary to do so. Some negative signs call up different nonmanual signals. An example of this occurs in the following rhetorical statement:

ME MONEY HAVE? NONE!

In this sentence, if the signer is adamantly denying having any money, then the nonmanual signals might be tightly closed lips and raised eyebrows with the head tilted forward. The eyebrows raised and the head tilted together would be proper if the signer is surprised at the question and is denying having any money. The eyebrows might be squeezed together, the head tilted forward, and tightly closed lips if the signer is angry at an accusation that she or he has money.

Most negative signs can be used as adjectives or adverbs such as NO, NOT, NONE, NOTHING, NEVER, NOT-YET, DON'T-WANT, NOT-POSSIBLE, NO-GOOD, ILLEGAL, NOT-FAIR, and NOT-WORTHWHILE. A few negative signs are verbs including DENY, DECLINE, CAN'T, WON'T, REFUSE, DON'T, DON'T-BELIEVE, DON'T-KNOW, DON'T-LIKE, and FORBID.

REVIEW EXERCISES

State the number and the name of the rule associated with each of the following explanations.

1. In a wh-question, the sign for the wh-word is usually placed at or near the end of the question.

2. First the topic is described and then the sign that is asking a yes/no question about the topic is placed at or near the end of the sentence.

3. The sign NOT can be placed before the verb or at the end of the sentence.

4. The topic of a sentence is first described, followed by a comment about the topic.

5. A signer points to a place in the signing space to establish a referent point for a person or thing.

6. A sign such as LAST-YEAR can be used to establish the tense of a sentence.

7. Nonmanual signals can be used in place of the signs IF and SUPPOSE.

8. In some sentences, the verb can follow the object.

9. A question is asked and then the signer answers it.

10. The order of signs in this type of question is variable.

ANSWERS

1. Rule #5. Information-seeking questions

2. Rule #4. Long yes/no questions

3. Rule #10. Negation

4. Rule #1. Topic/comment

5. Rule #6. Pronominalization

6. Rule #2. Tense with time adverbs

7. Rule #9. Conditional sentences

8. Rule #8. Ordering of simple sentences

9. Rule #7. Rhetorical questions

10. Rule #3. Simple yes/no questions

Introduction to the Dialogues

Perhaps the most compelling feature of signed languages, certainly one that has attracted much discussion, is their ability to exploit the visuo-spatial dimension. Unlike oral languages where space is referred to, in sign languages, space is physically available for representation. The space around and on the signer's body is exploited at all levels: formationally similar signs may contrast only in location; verb agreement is marked using spatial position; and discourse topics are distinguished from one another by where the signs are articulated.

—CAROL A. PADDEN
The Relation Between Space and Grammar in ASL Verb Phonology

HOLD THAT SIGN . . . .

Your quest to become a fluent ASL signer will come into clearer focus when you cease to think entirely of language as being organized temporally. Oral languages are temporal; only one thought or word can be expressed at a time. Sign languages are spatial; not only can more than one thought be expressed simultaneously, but thoughts and events are also shaped in space or on the signer's body. Carol Padden draws attention to the need to "exploit" the spatial and visual dimensions that play an important role in shaping ASL grammar. This book introduces you to ten basic rules about ASL grammar, and learning them is an important step toward understanding how ASL grammar is entwined in space. In the ASL lessons that follow, dialogues are used to show you how these rules are applied to the formation of ASL sentences. Studying and practicing the dialogues will teach you how the hands, face, body, and space are manipulated to form sentences.

The dialogues presented in this book are intended to be simple in that they mirror the type of conversation that you might have in your daily encounters with people—*mirror* is used in the sense that each signer in the dialogue speaks in short, authentic sentences.

The sentences in each of the dialogues are analyzed in a section called "What's in the Signs (Notes about the Grammar)" to show you which rule best fits the sentence. The term *best fits* is used because in some instances more than one rule applies—but the rule that is the focus of the sentence is the only one that is analyzed.

This section is then followed by one called "What's in a Sign (Notes about Vocabulary)," which explains the particular ways in which some of the signs are used. In addition, this section is where synonyms for a sign are described. That is, some signs are also used to mean different things. For example, the sign START can also be used to mean BEGIN, ORIGINATE, ORIGINAL, and INITIATE. Facial expressions can also be used to indicate a particular meaning of some signs.

The next section of each lesson is called "Practice Activities." The purpose of this section is to break down the dialogue into units that you can practice until you have mastered them. Following this, you are to practice signing the entire dialogue. It is recommended that you practice the dialogue with a partner so that you can get used to using facial grammar and the signing space when signing. You should also practice signing the dialogues by yourself in your own "space" so that you can slow down the signing without feeling any pressure to complete a sentence. After all, fluency doesn't mean signing as fast as you can. Indeed, fast signing is *not* the object of this book. Rather, you are encouraged to become articulate signers. Your ASL instructor and Deaf people judge the clarity and pacing of your signing.

The final section of each lesson contains activities for additional practice. Many of these activities guide you in creating your own ASL sentences and dialogues, which is a good reflection of how well you have learned the material presented in the lessons.

Interspersed throughout the lessons are several chapters that introduce key grammatical information about signing with respect to the use of directional verbs (Chapter 6), body- and gaze-shifting (Chapter 9), classifiers (Chapter 11), and numbers (Chapter 4). With the exception of the chapter on body- and gaze-shifting, they include a list of new signs for you to learn, although there are no dialogues in which to practice them.

FINGERSPELLING

When a signer does not know the sign for a word or if there is no sign for the word, such as a name, the signer will often spell out the word letter by letter. This is called fingerspelling. To begin fingerspelling, you must first learn the handshapes of the manual alphabet. See Appendix, page 487.

- Right-handed signers fingerspell with the right hand. Left-handed signers fingerspell with the left hand.
- Fast fingerspelling does not mean that person is a better fingerspeller.
- The hand is raised in a comfortable position by bending the elbow.
- The palm is facing at a 45-degree angle across the body.
- The arm does not move when fingerspelling. Each handshape is clearly formed.
- Pause slightly between words.
- In words containing double letters, the hand is moved slightly to the outside for the repeated letter or the fingers will tap the letter twice.

Getting Started

LESSON 1   GETTING STARTED

LANGUAGE GOALS

The student will
1. **use Rules**   **#1.** topic/comment,
      #3. simple yes/no questions, and
      #5. information-seeking questions.
2. be introduced to a directional verb sign.
3. use correct nonmanual signals in sentences that correspond to Rules #1, #3, and #5.
4. respond affirmatively to a yes/no question.
5. use ten new signs in a master dialogue.

THE MASTER DIALOGUE

1.   Tina: EXCUSE-me, ME NAME T-I-N-A. NAME YOU?
         Excuse me, I'm Tina, what's your name?

    Judy: ME J-U-D-Y. NICE me-MEET-you.
         I'm Judy. It is nice to meet you.

2.   Tina: NICE me-MEET-you. YOU TAKE-UP ASL?
         It's nice to meet you. Are you taking ASL?

    Judy: YES, ME TAKE-UP ASL. YOU?
         Yes, I am taking ASL. How about you?

3.   Tina: SAME-HERE (me-SAME-you). ME TAKE-UP ASL.
         Same as you, I'm taking ASL, too.

THE MASTER SIGNS

ASL

EXCUSE-me	ME
	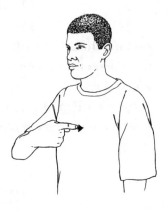
me-MEET-you	NAME

THE MASTER SIGNS

NICE

SAME-HERE (me-SAME-you)

TAKE-UP

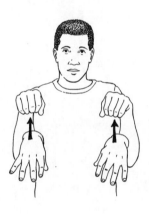

YES

YOU

WHAT'S IN THE SIGNS (NOTES ABOUT THE GRAMMAR)

1. RULES #1. TOPIC/COMMENT AND #5. INFORMATION-SEEKING QUESTIONS

EXCUSE-me, ME NAME T-I-N-A. NAME YOU?

There are three parts to this sentence. The first part is a form of common courtesy, used when attempting to get someone's attention:

EXCUSE-me

The signer does not sign the object of the sentence which is *me*. The object is implied from the context of the sentence. The English translation of the phrase is simply "Excuse me." If the signer wishes to refer to an object other than herself or himself, then the object must be signed.

The second part of the sentence

ME NAME T-I-N-A

is an example of a simple topic/comment sentence structure.

topic:	ME NAME
comment:	T-I-N-A.
translation:	My name is Tina.

The use of the sign ME when introducing oneself may be confusing to English speakers who are accustomed to using *my*, the possessive form of *me*, when referring to things that belong to them. It is still correct ASL to sign MY NAME. You are introduced to the phrase ME NAME in the dialogue because it is a common occurrence in the Deaf community. Learn and practice this phrase to help you begin to think in ASL.

The third part of the sentence is a demonstration of a question that seeks information:

NAME YOU?

This translates as "What is your name?" The pronoun can also be placed at the beginning of the phrase, YOU NAME? What is most important about this sentence is the nonmanual signals or the facial grammar that accompanies the sentence.

2. RULE #3. SIMPLE YES/NO QUESTIONS

An example of a simple yes/no question is shown in the following sentence:

YOU TAKE-UP ASL?

When this sentence is signed with the appropriate nonmanual signal, its English translation is "Are you taking ASL?"

The sign YOU is used in the dialogue to ask a simple yes/no question in the following sentence:

YES, ME TAKE-UP ASL. YOU?

The signer is saying that she or he is taking ASL. The topic of the sentence then becomes "taking ASL." The sign YOU asks a question about the topic. The sign YOU? can be translated into "How about you?" or, more specifically, "Are you taking ASL?"

3. INTRODUCTIONS

In the dialogue, Judy signs

ME J-U-D-Y. NICE me-MEET-you.

The first part of this sentence

ME J-U-D-Y

is a response to the question NAME YOU? The signer simply fingerspells her first name. If the last name is also fingerspelled, then the signer should pause slightly after fingerspelling the first name.

The second part of this sentence

NICE me-MEET-you

is a common form of courtesy that a person uses when introduced to someone. Using the lowercase for the pronouns *me* and *you* in the sign me-MEET-you means that they are not signed directly. Rather they are implied in the direction in which the sign is moved. The sign MEET is called a directional verb sign and Chapter 6 explains more about the grammatical qualities of this type of verb sign.

4. RESPONDING AFFIRMATIVELY TO A YES/NO QUESTION

To respond affirmatively to a yes/no question, the signer can sign YES directly as in the sentence

YES, ME TAKE-UP ASL.

In this sentence the signer also repeats the topic of the question—ME TAKE-UP ASL. The signer could also nod when signing YES or simply nod and not sign YES.

5. FACIAL GRAMMAR/NONMANUAL SIGNALS

See "Facial Grammar" in Chapter 1 to review the appropriate nonmanual signals to use with the following sentence structures:

a. topic/comment
b. yes/no questions
c. information-seeking questions

WHAT'S IN A SIGN (NOTES ABOUT VOCABULARY)

1. EXCUSE-ME

A common error made by beginning signers is to sign ME when making the sign EXCUSE-me. The sign ME should *not* be signed. The illustration for the sign EXCUSE-me shows one hand brushing across the other hand twice. This is the general manner in which this sign is made. However, it is common practice to brush the hand several times and in some cases to continue making the sign until a desired result is achieved. The repeated brushing of the hand is used, for example, when a person must pass between two or more people carrying on a conversation in signs.

2. ASL

ASL is the abbreviated form for American Sign Language. The arm should not move when forming the handshapes A, S, and L.

3. ME-MEET-YOU

The general sign for MEET has the two hands moving from the side of the signing space to the center where they meet. For the sign me-MEET-you, one hand is held away and to the front of your body while the other hand is held in front of your body. The hand by the body then moves out to meet the other hand, which is held stationary. The following illustrations show the difference between MEET and MEET-you:

MEET   ME-MEET-YOU

What would the meaning of the sign be if the hand that is held away from the body moved to meet the hand that is held stationary by the body? The answer is you-MEET-me. The direction in which the sign moves indicates the subject and the object of the sentence. We can show this relationship by writing:

subject-VERB-object
me-MEET-you
you-MEET-me

4. SAME-HERE

When making the sign SAME-HERE, your thumb should be pointed toward your chest and your little finger should be pointed toward the person with whom you are indicating agreement.

5. ASL SYNONYMS

Some signs can be used to mean other things.

Sign	Also used for
ASL	AMERICAN-SIGN-LANGUAGE
EXCUSE-me	FORGIVE
NICE	CLEAN
SAME-HERE	ME-TOO, SAME-as-you, me-SAME-as-you
TAKE-UP	ADOPT

PRACTICE ACTIVITIES

1. MODEL FOR RULES #1. TOPIC/COMMENT AND #5. INFORMATION-SEEKING QUESTIONS

Signer A:	1. Introduce self; 2. ask for the other person's name.	
	Introduction:	ME NAME T-I-N-A.
	Request for name:	NAME YOU?
Signer B:	1. Introduce self.	
	Introduction:	ME J-U-D-Y.
Signer A:	1. Make a greeting.	
	Greeting:	NICE me-MEET-you.
Signer B:	1. Make a greeting.	
	Greeting:	NICE me-MEET-you.

Practice

Signer A: ME NAME (fingerspells name). NAME YOU?
Signer B: ME (fingerspells name).
Signer A: NICE me-MEET-you.
Signer B: NICE me-MEET-you.

2. MODEL FOR RULE #3. SIMPLE YES/NO QUESTION

Signer A: 1. Ask a question.

           Question: YOU TAKE-UP ASL?

Signer B: 1. Answer affirmatively;
           2. repeat the question using the sign YOU.

           Answer: YES, ME TAKE-UP ASL.
           Repeat the question: YOU?

Signer A: 1. Answer the question;
           2. repeat the topic.

           Answer: SAME-HERE.
           Repeat the topic: ME TAKE-UP ASL.

Practice

Signer A: YOU TAKE-UP ASL?
Signer B: YES, ME TAKE-UP ASL. YOU?
Signer A: SAME-HERE. ME TAKE-UP ASL.

3. MASTERY LEARNING

When you feel comfortable signing these phrases, practice signing the entire master dialogue shown at the beginning of the lesson. Practice the dialogue until you can sign the part of each character smoothly while using the appropriate facial grammar.

4. FURTHER PRACTICE WITH INTRODUCTIONS

Practice asking people their names using the following sentence.

EXCUSE-ME, ME NAME (spell your name), NAME YOU?

After each person has spelled his or her name to you, respond by saying

(spell the other person's name), NICE me-MEET-you.

LESSON 2   LEARNING ASL

LANGUAGE GOALS

The student will

1.   use Rules   #1. topic/comment,
                    #4. long yes/no questions,
                    #5. information-seeking questions, and
                    #7. rhetorical questions.
2.   use the correct nonmanual signals in sentences that correspond to Rules #1, #4, #5, and #7.
3.   use ten new signs in a master dialogue about learning ASL.

THE MASTER DIALOGUE

1.   Judy: YOU TAKE-UP ASL WHY?
              Why are you taking ASL?

      Tina: ME TAKE-UP ASL WHY? ME ENJOY.
              I am taking ASL because I enjoy it.

2.   Judy: SAME-HERE. ME SIGN, ME FEEL GOOD.
              The same with me, I feel good when I sign.

      Tina: YOU MORE ASL LEARN, READY YOU?
              Are you ready to learn more ASL?

3.   Judy: YES, ME READY. YOU?
              Yes, I'm ready. How about you?

      Tina: LEARN MORE ASL, ME READY ALWAYS.
              I am always ready to learn more ASL.

4.   Judy: ME AGREE.
              I agree with that.

THE MASTER SIGNS

AGREE

ALWAYS

ENJOY

FEEL

GOOD

LEARN

THE MASTER SIGNS

MORE

READY

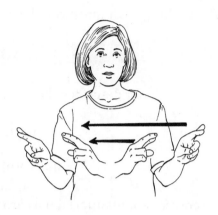

SIGN

WHY

WHAT'S IN THE SIGNS (NOTES ABOUT THE GRAMMAR)

1. RULE #5. INFORMATION-SEEKING QUESTIONS

When asking a wh-question, the wh-sign is commonly placed at the end of the sentence.

YOU TAKE-UP ASL WHY?

First, the signer describes the topic and then adds the wh-sign.

topic	YOU TAKE UP ASL
question	WHY?

The correct nonmanual signals are (1) *the squeezed eyebrows* and (2) *the head tilted forward slightly*.

2. RULE #7. RHETORICAL QUESTIONS

In the dialogue, Tina responds to the question "YOU TAKE-UP ASL WHY?" with the following rhetorical question and answer:

ME TAKE-UP ASL WHY? ME ENJOY.

Recall that the correct nonmanual signals for a wh-question that is part of a rhetorical question are the same as that for yes/no questions: the signer (1) *tilts the head forward* and (2) *raises the eyebrows*.

3. RULE #4. LONG YES/NO QUESTIONS

The sign READY can be used to ask a simple question that was demonstrated in the dialogue:

YOU MORE ASL LEARN, READY YOU?

The question has two parts. In the first part, YOU MORE ASL LEARN, the signer describes the topic. In the second part, the signer asks a question about the topic, READY YOU? Because this is a yes/no question the signer (1) *tilts the head forward* and (2) *raises the eyebrows*.

4. RULE #1. TOPIC/COMMENT

The topic/comment sentence structure was used twice in the dialogue:

ME SIGN, ME FEEL GOOD.
LEARN MORE ASL, ME READY ALWAYS.

Breaking them down we get

topic:	comment:	translation:
ME SIGN,	ME FEEL GOOD.	I feel good when I sign.
LEARN MORE ASL,	ME READY ALWAYS.	I am always ready to learn more ASL.

The facial grammar accompanying the sentence helps the addressee clearly identify the topic of the sentence.

WHAT'S IN A SIGN (NOTES ABOUT VOCABULARY)

1. ALWAYS

The sign ALWAYS is often placed at the end of a sentence because it is usually making a comment about a topic. By placing it at the end of the sentence, its importance to the meaning of the sentence is emphasized.

2. GOOD

Signs that indicate feelings or emotions such as GOOD and ENJOY, are often accompanied by nonmanual signals that reinforce the feelings being expressed. For example, if you are feeling good, then this should easily be detected from your facial expression.

3. FEEL

The sign FEEL is made either with a single movement up the chest or a double movement. Some signers will use a single movement when stating how they feel ("I feel dizzy") and a double movement when inquiring how someone else feels ("How do you feel?").

4. ASL SYNONYMS

Some signs can be used to mean other things.

Sign	Also used for
ENJOY	PLEASURE, PLEASANT
GOOD	WELL
LEARN	ACQUIRE

PRACTICE ACTIVITIES

1. MODEL FOR RULES #5. INFORMATION-SEEKING QUESTIONS AND #7. RHETORICAL QUESTIONS

Signer A: 1. Describe the topic;

2. use a wh-sign to ask a question about the topic.

Topic:	YOU TAKE-UP ASL
Question:	WHY?

Signer B: 1. Repeat the wh-question to form a rhetorical wh-question;

2. answer the question.

Rhetorical question:	ME TAKE-UP ASL WHY?
Answer:	ME ENJOY.

Signer A: 1. Acknowledge the answer with a remark.

Remark:	SAME-HERE.

Practice

Signer A: YOU TAKE-UP ASL WHY?
Signer B: ME TAKE-UP ASL WHY? ME ENJOY.
Signer A: SAME-HERE.

2. MODEL FOR RULE #3. SIMPLE YES/NO QUESTIONS

Signer A:	1. Describe the topic;	
	2. ask a yes/no question about the topic using READY.	
	Topic:	YOU MORE ASL LEARN,
	Question:	READY YOU?
Signer B:	1. Answer the question affirmatively.	
	Answer:	YES, ME READY.

Practice

Signer A: YOU MORE ASL LEARN, READY YOU?
Signer B: YES, ME READY.

3. MODEL FOR RULE #1. TOPIC/COMMENT

a.	Signer:	1. Describe the topic while using nonmanual signals to highlight the topic;	
		2. sign the comment related to the topic.	
		Topic:	ME SIGN,
		Comment:	ME FEEL GOOD.

Practice

Signer: ME SIGN, ME FEEL GOOD.

b.	Signer A:	1. Describe the topic using nonmanual signals to highlight the topic;	
		2. sign the comment related to the topic.	
		Topic:	LEARN MORE ASL,
		Comment:	ME READY ALWAYS.
.	Signer B:	1. Make a remark about the comment	
		Remark:	ME AGREE.

Practice

Signer A: LEARN MORE ASL, ME READY ALWAYS.
Signer B: ME AGREE.

4. MASTERY LEARNING

When you feel comfortable signing these phrases, practice signing the entire dialogue shown at the beginning of the lesson. Be sure to include the appropriate nonmanual signals. Practice the dialogue until you can sign each character smoothly.

5. FURTHER PRACTICE

Create your own dialogue using the signs you have learned in Lessons 1 and 2. Keep the sentences and dialogue short and then practice signing them. Write the approximate English translation for your dialogue. For example:

Signer A:	ME FEEL GOOD. YOU?
	I feel good. How about you?
Signer B:	SAME-HERE. NAME YOU?
	The same with me. What's your name?
Signer A:	ME NAME S-T-Y-L-E-S. YOU?
	My name is Styles. What's your name?
Signer B:	B-R-E-N-N-A-N. NICE me-MEET-you.
	Brennan. It is nice to meet you.

LESSON 3   COURTESY PHRASES

LANGUAGE GOALS

The student will
1. use Rules   #3. simple yes/no questions,
                 #5. information-seeking questions, and
                 #7. rhetorical questions.
2. use ten new signs and the numbers 1–5 in a master dialogue about learning ASL.

THE MASTER DIALOGUE

1.   Tina: HOW YOU?
               How are you?

      Judy: FINE. YOU?
               I am fine. How about you?

2.   Tina: FINE. ASL CLASS WHERE?
               I am fine. Where is the ASL class?

      Judy: ASL CLASS WHERE? ROOM NUMBER 4.
               The ASL class is in room number 4.

3.   Tina: ROOM 5?
               Room 5?

      Judy: NO. ROOM 4.
               No. Room 4.

4.   Tina: THANK-YOU.
               Thank you.

      Judy: WELCOME (or THANK-YOU). SEE-YOU-LATER.
               You're welcome. See you later.

THE MASTER SIGNS

CLASS

FINE

HOW

NO

THANK-YOU

THE MASTER SIGNS

NUMBER

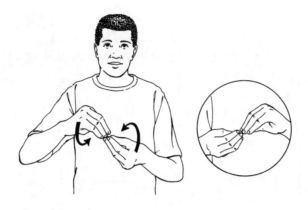

ROOM

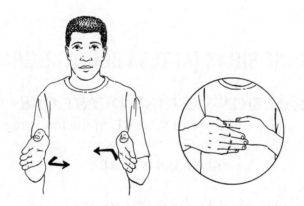

SEE-YOU-LATER

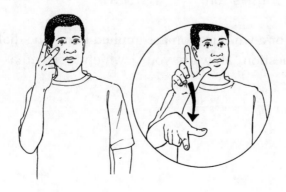

THE MASTER SIGNS

WELCOME

WHERE

Numbers 1–5 (see Chapter 4, "One Million New Signs" for illustrations of numbers)

WHAT'S IN THE SIGNS (NOTES ABOUT THE GRAMMAR)

1. RULE #5. INFORMATION-SEEKING QUESTIONS

The dialogue introduces the use of the sign WHERE in the following wh-question:

ASL CLASS WHERE?

The signer describes the topic and asks a question about it.

topic:	ASL CLASS
question:	WHERE?

The nonmanual signals for a wh-question are applied here. The dialogue also introduces the common courtesy question "How are you?," which is signed as HOW YOU?, and the common response, FINE.

2. RULE #7. RHETORICAL QUESTIONS

In a rhetorical question, the signer asks a question and then answers it as in the following:

ASL CLASS WHERE? ROOM NUMBER 4.

Although the sign WHERE is in the ASL sentence, it does not appear in the English translation. To translate to English, a person must first observe the entire expression and then translate the sense of the ASL meaning into English. In this sentence the sense relates to the room in which the ASL class is. Therefore, a proper English translation directly points this out, "The ASL class is in room number 4." Recall that the correct nonmanual signals for rhetorical questions with wh-signs are different than the nonmanual signals used for wh-questions and other information-seeking questions.

3. RULE #3. SIMPLE YES/NO QUESTIONS

A simple question is asked simply by (1) *raising the eyebrows* and (2) *tilting the head forward* when signing.

ROOM 5?

WHAT'S IN A SIGN (NOTES ABOUT VOCABULARY)

1. THANK-YOU

A common error when signing THANK-YOU is to add the sign YOU. This is not only unnecessary but can be confusing. The meaning is vague in the following sentence:

THANK-YOU, YOU.

It reads like an incomplete sentence. Another signer would look at this and wonder what was supposed to come after the sign YOU.

2. WELCOME

The English translation of WELCOME is either "welcome" or "you're welcome" depending upon the context of the sentence. It is not necessary to add the sign YOU or YOU'RE before WELCOME because the pronoun *you* is already a part of the sign WELCOME.

3. SEE-YOU-LATER

This sign is a modification of three signs—SEE, YOU, and LATER. The sign YOU is dropped as you develop fluency in signing this phrase.

4. NUMBERS 1–5

For counting, the numbers 1–5 are typically formed with the palm of the hand facing toward the signer's body. However, when signing a phone number, the numbers are all signed with the palm facing out.

5. ASL SYNONYMS

Some signs can be used to mean other things.

Sign	Also used for
CLASS	CATEGORY
ROOM	BOX
THANK-YOU	THANK, THANKS
WELCOME	YOU'RE-WELCOME

PRACTICE ACTIVITIES

1. MODEL FOR USING COURTESY PHRASES

Signer A: 1. Use a courtesy question to ask how a person is.

Courtesy question: HOW YOU?

Signer B: 1. Respond to the question with a common courtesy sign;
2. repeat the courtesy question by just signing YOU?

Response: FINE.
Courtesy question: YOU?

Signer A: 1. Respond to the question with a common courtesy sign.

Response: FINE.

Practice

Signer A: HOW YOU?
Signer B: FINE. YOU?
Signer A: FINE.

2. MODEL FOR RULES #5. INFORMATION-SEEKING QUESTIONS AND #7. RHETORICAL QUESTIONS

Signer A: 1. Describe the topic you want to ask a question about;
              2. sign the wh-sign WHERE.

Topic:	ASL CLASS
Question:	WHERE?

Signer B: 1. Repeat the wh-question to form a rhetorical wh-question;
              2. answer the question.

Rhetorical question: ASL CLASS WHERE?

Answer: ROOM NUMBER 4.

Practice

Signer A: ASL CLASS WHERE?
Signer B: ASL CLASS WHERE? ROOM NUMBER 4.

3. MODEL FOR RULE #3. SIMPLE YES/NO QUESTIONS

Signer A: 1. Ask a yes/no question about the room number.

Question: ROOM 5?

Signer B: 1. Respond negatively to the question;
              2. state the room number.

Negative:	NO.
Statement:	ROOM 4.

Signer A: 1. Acknowledge the answer with a courtesy remark.

Remark: THANK-YOU.

Signer B: 1. Acknowledge the courtesy remark with another one;
              2. sign a remark commonly used when departing company.

Remark:	THANK-YOU.
Remark:	SEE-YOU-LATER.

Practice

Signer A: ROOM 5?
Signer B: NO. ROOM 4.
Signer A: THANK-YOU.
Signer B: SEE-YOU-LATER.

Repeat practice: Repeat this exercise replacing the number 4 with the numbers 1, 2, 3, and 5.

4. MASTERY LEARNING

When you feel comfortable signing these phrases, practice signing the entire dialogue shown at the beginning of the lesson. Practice the dialogue until you can sign the part of each character smoothly. Pay particular attention to the nonmanual signals you use to accompany each phrase you sign. It is better to exaggerate your facial expressions slightly than to project none at all or to project one that is inappropriate for the sentence being signed.

5. FURTHER PRACTICE

Create your own dialogue using the signs you have learned in Lessons 1–3. Keep the sentences short and write an English translation for your dialogue. Practice signing your dialogue with a partner.

LESSON 4 VOCABULARY BUILDING: DESCRIPTIVE SIGNS

LANGUAGE GOALS

The student will
1. use Rules   **#5.** information-seeking questions and
                    #8. ordering of simple sentences.
2. use FEEL with a repeated motion to ask a question.
3. use FEEL with a single motion to express a feeling.
4. use forty new signs to describe feelings.

THE MASTER DIALOGUE

1. Michael: FEEL+ YOU?
                  How are you feeling?

2. Rachel: ME FEEL SATISFIED. FEEL+ YOU?
                  I'm feeling satisfied. How do you feel?

3. Michael: HUNGRY.
                  I'm hungry.

THE MASTER SIGNS

FEEL+

ALSO USED FOR

EMOTION
SENTIMENT

THE MASTER SIGNS

ALSO USED FOR

HUNGRY

FAMISHED, PASSION, STARVED

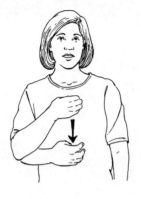

SATISFIED

APPEASE, CONTENT, SATISFACTION

plus the following thirty adjectives or signs for feelings:

ANGRY

ANGER, FURY, RAGE, WRATH

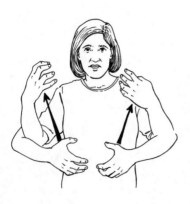

THE MASTER SIGNS

ALSO USED FOR

ASHAMED

SHAME

BAD

NAUGHTY

BORED/BORING

THE MASTER SIGNS

ALSO USED FOR

COLD

WINTER, CHILLY

COMFORTABLE

CONVENIENT

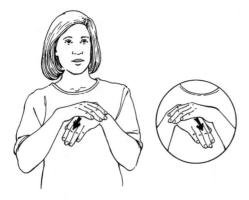

CRAZY

DAFT, LUNATIC

THE MASTER SIGNS

ALSO USED FOR

DEPRESSED

DESPONDENT, DOWNCAST

DISCOURAGED

DEVASTATED

DUMB

DOLT, IDIOT, MORON, OAF, STUPID

THE MASTER SIGNS

ALSO USED FOR

EMBARRASSED

FLUSTERED, HUMILIATED

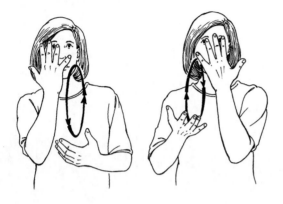

ENTHUSIASTIC

EAGER, ZEAL, MOTIVATED

EXCITED

AGITATED, ECSTATIC,
EXCITING, THRILLED

THE MASTER SIGNS

FRUSTRATED

ALSO USED FOR

FRUSTRATE, FRUSTRATION

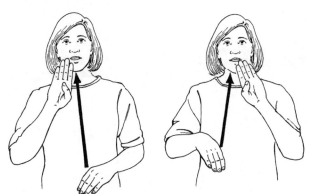

(repeating small
movement, up to
the mouth)

FUNNY

HUMOR

(slightly brush fingers
down tip of nose)

HAPPY

GLAD, JOY

(repeating movement,
upward and outward
on the chest)

THE MASTER SIGNS

ALSO USED FOR

HOT

HUMBLE

MEEK, MODEST,
UNASSUMING

JEALOUS

ENVIOUS

THE MASTER SIGNS

ALSO USED FOR

LAZY

LONELY

LONESOME

LOUSY

THE MASTER SIGNS

ALSO USED FOR

LUCKY

FORTUITOUS, FORTUNATE

MAD

ANGRY, CROSS, GROUCHY

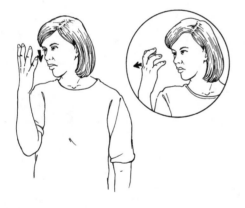

SAD

DISMAL, DREARY, GLOOMY,
MOROSE, SORROWFUL,
UNFORTUNATE

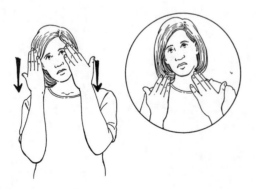

THE MASTER SIGNS

ALSO USED FOR

SCARED

AFRAID, FRIGHTENED

SHOCKED

ASTOUNDED, HORRIFIED, STARTLED

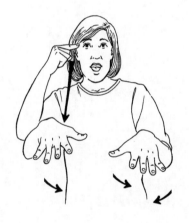

THE MASTER SIGNS

ALSO USED FOR

SHY

BASHFUL, RETICENT, TIMID

SLEEPY

SO-SO

FAIR

THE MASTER SIGNS

ALSO USED FOR

STRANGE

BIZARRE, ODD, PECULIAR,
UNUSUAL

TERRIBLE

APPALLING, AWFUL,
DREADFUL, FRIGHTFUL,
HORRIBLE

TERRIFIC

EXCELLENT, FABULOUS,
FANTASTIC, GREAT,
MARVELOUS, SUPER,
WONDERFUL

THE MASTER SIGNS

ALSO USED FOR

THIRSTY

THIRST

TIRED

EXHAUSTED, FATIGUED

WARM

TEPID

WHAT'S IN THE SIGNS (NOTES ABOUT THE GRAMMAR)

1. RULE #5. INFORMATION-SEEKING QUESTIONS

A simple question asking about how a person is feeling can be formed using the sign FEEL as shown in the following:

FEEL+ YOU?

The plus sign (+) after the sign FEEL means to repeat the sign. To express the appropriate nonmanual signals (1) *the head tilts forward* and (2) *the eyebrows squeeze together*.

2. RULE #8. ORDERING OF SIMPLE SENTENCES

In response to the question FEEL+ YOU? a simple sentence following a subject-verb-adverb structure can be used to get the following:

ME FEEL SATISFIED.

It is not necessary to sign the subject and the verb in response to a question about how you feel. Because the question is directed at you, you can simply respond by stating how you feel as Michael did in the dialogue:

HUNGRY.

WHAT'S IN A SIGN (NOTES ABOUT VOCABULARY)

1. FEEL

The sign for FEEL is made with one movement of the middle finger moving up the middle of the chest.

2. FUNNY

The sign for FUNNY can also use a repeated motion. When the sign is made with a slow, single motion, it means STRANGE as in "I feel strange" or "That's strange."

PRACTICE ACTIVITIES

In the master dialogue substitute adjectives from the list of master signs introduced in this lesson. You should match your facial expression with the feelings that the adjective indicates. Practice signing each adjective in a dialogue until you feel comfortable that you can match the sign with the appropriate facial expression.

Signer A:	FEEL+ YOU?
Signer B:	ME FEEL **SATISFIED**. FEEL+ YOU?
Signer A:	**HUNGRY**.

LESSON 5   TAKING UP CLASSES

LANGUAGE GOALS

The student will
1. use Rules   #1. topic/comment,
                  #2. tense with time adverbs,
                  #5. information-seeking questions,
                  #7. rhetorical questions, and
                  #8. ordering of simple sentences.
2. use twelve new signs in a conversation about taking a class together
    with someone.

THE MASTER DIALOGUE

1. Judy: HELLO. WHAT'S-UP?
            Hello, what's up?

    Pat: HI. NOW ME CLASS GO-to.
            Hi. I am going to my class now.

2. Judy: REALLY? YOU MORNING CLASS NAME?
            Is that so? What is the name of your morning class?

    Pat: MY MORNING CLASS NAME? SCIENCE.
            The name of my morning class is Science.

3. Judy: YOU TAKE-UP SCIENCE, ME SURPRISED.
            I am surprised that you are taking science.

    Pat: YOU SURPRISED, WHY?
            Why are you surprised?

4. Judy: ME TAKE-UP SCIENCE, me-SAME-as-you.
            I am taking science, too.

    Pat: REALLY? TWO-of-us TAKE-UP SCIENCE, WONDERFUL.
            Is that so? That's wonderful that the two of us are taking science.

THE MASTER SIGNS

GO-to

HELLO/HI

MORNING

MY

NOW

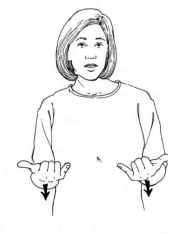

REALLY, IS THAT SO.

THE MASTER SIGNS

SURPRISED

SCIENCE

TWO-of-us

WHAT

(alternate sign
is to shrug
shoulders
upward)

WHAT'S-UP, WHAT'S HAPPENING

THE MASTER SIGNS

WONDERFUL

WHAT'S IN THE SIGNS (NOTES ABOUT THE GRAMMAR)

1. INITIATING A CONVERSATION

The sign WHAT'S-UP is commonly used to initiate a conversation or to inquire about what's happening. It is typically signed all by itself

WHAT'S-UP?

and is translated as "What's up?" or "What's happening?"

2. RULE #8. ORDERING OF SIMPLE SENTENCES

Some simple sentences can have a subject-object-verb (SOV) or a subject-verb-object (SVO) word order as in the following sentence:

a. ME CLASS GO-to.
b. ME GO-to CLASS.

The meaning of both phrases is "I am going to class." The meaning usually does not change with the placement of the GO-to sign. A signer might place a key sign at the end of the sentence if she or he wishes to emphasize that concept. If a signer wishes to emphasize the action verb "GO-to" then sentence a should be used. Likewise, if CLASS is being emphasized, then sentence b would be appropriate.

3. RULE #5. INFORMATION-SEEKING QUESTIONS

A signer creates a wh-question by setting up the topic and then using a wh-sign to ask a question about the topic. This is seen in the questions YOU MORNING CLASS NAME? and YOU SURPRISED, WHY?

topic:	YOU MORNING CLASS
question:	NAME?

The nonmanual signals are the same as for information-seeking questions—(1) *the eyebrows are squeezed* and (2) *the head is tilted forward.*

4. RULE #2. TENSE WITH TIME ADVERBS

In the sentence

NOW ME CLASS GO-to.

the time frame is established by placing the time adverb NOW at the beginning of the sentence. A proper translation of this sentence is "I am going to class now."

5. RULE #7. RHETORICAL QUESTIONS

In the dialogue, Pat asks a question and then responds to it:

MY MORNING CLASS NAME? SCIENCE.

6. RULE #1. TOPIC/COMMENT

With the following sentence structure:

YOU TAKE-UP SCIENCE, ME SURPRISED.

the signer describes the topic and then makes a comment about it as shown in the following sentence:

topic:	YOU TAKE-UP SCIENCE,
comment:	ME SURPRISED.
translation:	I am surprised that you are taking science.

In ASL, events are typically laid out in the order that they occur. In the preceding sentence, Pat was surprised only after he had found out that someone was taking science. Therefore, the comment ME SURPRISED comes at the end of the sentence. Two more examples of the topic/comment structure are in the following dialogue:

topic:	comment:	translation:
ME TAKE-UP SCIENCE,	me-SAME-as-you.	I am taking science, too.
TWO-of-us TAKE-UP SCIENCE,	WONDERFUL.	That's wonderful that the two of us are taking science.

WHAT'S IN A SIGN (NOTES ABOUT VOCABULARY)

1. GO-to

Which direction should the hands move when signing GO-to? The sign GO-to is typically moved forward to the right or left side of the body. Where it is moved will establish the location of the object of the sentence. In the sentence

ME CLASS GO-to.

you might sign GO-to to the left side of the body. This action places the object of the sentence, CLASS, to the left of the body. Future references to CLASS will always be to the left of the body until you change the location of CLASS. ASL grammar is dependent upon where signs are made in the signing space. Thus, how the hands are moved for the sign GO-to can be important in telling the meaning of a sentence.

2. REALLY

The translation of the sign REALLY depends upon the dialogue. The same sign is used for the signs REAL, TRUE, SURE, and CERTAIN, among others. In the dialogue, the sign REALLY could have been translated as "Is that a fact?", which has the same meaning in English as "Is that so?"

3. TWO-of-us

The sign for TWO-of-us is an example of Rule #6. pronominalization. To make this sign, the 2 handshape is moved between the signer and one other person. This other person might be present physically as she is in the dialogue, or the person might just exist in the signing space. The movement of the 2 handshape is not random. The hand is usually twisted so that the middle finger points toward the signer and the index finger points toward the other person. Depending on the context, this sign can be translated to mean "both of us," "you and I," and "we."

4. me-TOO

This sign is made in the same way as the sign SAME-HERE.

5. ASL SYNONYMS

Some signs can be used to mean other things.

Sign	Also used for
MY	MINE
NOW	PRESENTLY, TODAY
REALLY	CERTAIN, CERTAINLY, REAL, SURE, SURELY, TRUE, TRULY
SURPRISED	AMAZED
WHAT'S-UP?	WHAT'S-HAPPENING?
WONDERFUL	EXCELLENT, FABULOUS, FANTASTIC, GREAT, MARVELOUS, SUPER, TERRIFIC

PRACTICE ACTIVITIES

1. MODEL FOR INITIATING A CONVERSATION AND RULE #2. TENSE WITH TIME ADVERBS

Signer A: 1. Sign a greeting;
2. use the sign WHAT'S-UP to ask a question.

Greeting:	HELLO.
Question:	WHAT'S-UP?

Signer B: 1. Sign a greeting;
2. establish the tense of the sentence with a time adverb;
3. describe an action.

Greeting:	HI.
Tense:	NOW
Action:	ME CLASS GO-to.

Practice

Signer A: HELLO. WHAT'S-UP?
Signer B: HI. NOW ME CLASS GO-to.

2. MODEL FOR RULES #2. TENSE WITH TIME ADVERBS, #5. INFORMATION-SEEKING QUESTIONS, AND #7. RHETORICAL QUESTIONS

Signer A: 1. Describe the topic you want to ask a question about;
2. make the sign asking the question.

Topic:	YOU MORNING CLASS
Question:	NAME?

Signer B: 1. Ask a rhetorical question by repeating the question;
2. answer the question.

Rhetorical question:	MY MORNING CLASS NAME?
Answer:	SCIENCE.

Practice

Signer A: YOU MORNING CLASS NAME?
Signer B: MY MORNING CLASS NAME? SCIENCE.

3. MODEL FOR RULES #1. TOPIC/COMMENT AND #5. INFORMATION-SEEKING QUESTIONS

Signer A:	1. Describe the topic;
	2. make a comment about it.

Topic:	YOU TAKE-UP SCIENCE,
Comment:	ME SURPRISED.

Signer B:	1. Respond to the comment with a wh-question using WHY.

Response:	YOU SURPRISED, WHY?

Signer A:	1. Describe the topic;
	2. make a comment about it.

Topic:	ME TAKE-UP SCIENCE,
Comment:	me-SAME-as-you.

Signer B:	1. Describe the topic;
	2. make a comment about it.

Topic:	TWO-of-us TAKE-UP SCIENCE,
Comment:	WONDERFUL.

Practice

Signer A: YOU TAKE-UP SCIENCE, ME SURPRISED.
Signer B: YOU SURPRISED, WHY?
Signer A: ME TAKE-UP SCIENCE, me-SAME-as-you.
Signer B: TWO-of-us TAKE-UP SCIENCE, WONDERFUL.

4. MASTERY LEARNING

Review the notes on facial grammar and nonmanual signals prior to practicing the sentences. When you feel comfortable signing these phrases, practice signing the entire dialogue shown at the beginning of the lesson. Practice the master dialogue until you can sign the part of each character smoothly.

5. FURTHER PRACTICE

Create your own dialogue using the signs you have learned in Lessons 1–5. Keep the sentences short and write an English translation for them. Practice signing the dialogue with a partner.

LANGUAGE GOALS

The student will
1.   use Rules   #1. topic/comment,
                       #5. information-seeking questions, and
                       #8. ordering of simple sentences.
2.   use correct procedures for indicating the time.
3.   use nine new signs and the numbers 6–12 in the master dialogue.

THE MASTER DIALOGUE

1.   Mike: YOUR ASL CLASS START WHEN?
               When does your ASL class start?

      Pat: MY ASL CLASS START, TIME 7.
               My ASL class starts at seven o'clock.

2.   Mike: TIME AGAIN PLEASE?
               Say the time again, please?

      Pat: TIME 7.
               Seven o'clock.

3.   Mike: YOUR ASL CLASS END WHEN?
               When does your ASL class end?

      Pat: MY ASL CLASS END, TIME 8.
               My ASL class ends at eight o'clock.

4.   Mike: OKAY. me-MEET-you, TIME 8.
               Okay. I will meet you at eight o'clock.

      Pat: you-MEET-me WHERE?
               Where will you meet me?

5.   Mike: me-MEET-you HERE.
               I will meet you here.

      Pat: FINE.
               That's fine.

THE MASTER SIGNS

AGAIN

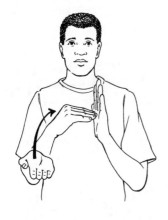

END

FINE

HERE

OKAY/OK

PLEASE

THE MASTER SIGNS

START

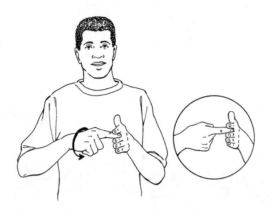

TIME

WHEN

YOUR

Numbers: 6–12 (see Chapter 4, "One Million New Signs" for illustrations for numbers)

WHAT'S IN THE SIGNS (NOTES ABOUT THE GRAMMAR)

1. RULE #5. INFORMATION-SEEKING QUESTIONS

The dialogue uses the signs WHEN and WHERE to ask questions. In these questions, the topic is first described followed by a question sign:

Topic	Question
YOUR ASL CLASS START	WHEN?
YOUR ASL CLASS END	WHEN?
you-MEET-me	WHERE?

What is the appropriate nonmanual signal for information-seeking questions?

2. RULE #1. TOPIC/COMMENT

In the dialogue, a topic/comment format is used to respond to the questions described previously.

Topic	Comment
MY ASL CLASS START,	TIME 7.
MY ASL CLASS END,	TIME 8.
me-MEET-you	HERE.

Another sentence using the topic/comment format is

me-MEET-you,	TIME 8.

3. INDICATING THE TIME

When telling the time that something starts or ends, it is common practice to place the time at the end of the sentence. The following sentences have time at the end of them:

MY ASL CLASS START, TIME 7.
MY ASL CLASS END, TIME 8.
me-MEET-you, TIME 8.

The formula for indicating the time is TIME + #, which yields TIME 7 and TIME 8 in the foregoing sentences. In the translation, a person uses the common English means for saying the time, which could be "My class starts at seven" or "My class starts at seven o'clock."

4. RULE #8. ORDERING OF SIMPLE SENTENCES

The following is an example of a simple sentence requesting information:

TIME AGAIN PLEASE.

WHAT'S IN A SIGN (NOTES ABOUT VOCABULARY)

1. FINE

The sign for FINE is a frequently used sign in ASL. It is most often used alone. Its meaning is often translated in English to "That's fine," "It was fine," "That's okay," "That's all right," and so forth. It is not used to mean the superior quality of material as in "They used a fine cloth to make a cover," nor is it used to mean exceptionally small as in "Read the fine print."

2. MY

The signs ME and MY are distinguished by the index finger pointing for the sign ME and the hand being opened for the sign MY. The open hand is used to indicate the possessive form of all pronouns.

3. YOUR

The sign for YOUR is another example of the open hand being used to indicate the possessive form of a pronoun.

4. me-MEET-you, you-MEET-me

Recall that MEET is a directional verb (see Chapter 6 for information about directional verbs); therefore, the subject and object of the sentence are incorporated into the movement of the sign MEET. For you-MEET-me, the hand that is away from the body moves toward the hand that is held stationary by the chest. See Lesson 1 for an illustration of this sign.

5. ASL SYNONYMS

Some signs can be used to mean other things.

Sign	Also used for
AGAIN	REPEAT
END	CONCLUDE, CONCLUSION, FINISH, TERMINATE
MY	MINE
START	BEGIN, INITIATE, ORIGINAL, ORIGINATE

PRACTICE ACTIVITIES

1. MODEL FOR RULES #1. TOPIC/COMMENT AND #5. INFORMATION-SEEKING QUESTIONS, AND FOR INDICATING THE TIME

Signer A: 1. Describe the topic;
2. ask a question using WHEN.

Topic:	YOUR ASL CLASS START
Question:	WHEN?

Topic:	YOUR ASL CLASS END
Question:	WHEN?

Signer B: 1. Describe the topic;
2. tell the time.

Topic:	MY ASL CLASS START,
Time:	TIME 7.

Topic:	MY ASL CLASS END,
Time:	TIME 8.

Practice

Signer A: YOUR ASL CLASS START WHEN?
Signer B: MY ASL CLASS START, TIME 7.
Signer A: YOUR ASL CLASS END WHEN?
Signer B: MY ASL CLASS END, TIME 8.

More practice: Repeat this exercise using the numbers 6, 9, 10, 11, and 12 for the numbers 7 and 8 in the following phrases:
MY ASL CLASS START, TIME 7.
MY ASL CLASS END, TIME 8.

2. MODEL FOR RULE #8. ORDERING OF SIMPLE SENTENCES

Signer A: 1. Make a request;
2. add the courtesy sign PLEASE.

Request:	TIME AGAIN
Courtesy sign:	PLEASE.

Signer B: 1. Respond to the request.

Response: TIME 7.

Practice

Signer A: TIME AGAIN PLEASE.
Signer B: TIME 7.

3. MODEL FOR RULE #5. INFORMATION-SEEKING QUESTIONS

Signer A: 1. Describe the topic;
                   2. ask a question using the sign WHERE.

Topic: you-MEET-me
Question: WHERE?

Signer B: 1. Repeat the topic;
                   2. answer the question.

Topic: me-MEET-you
Answer: HERE.

Practice

Signer A: you-MEET-me, WHERE?
Signer B: me-MEET-you, HERE.

4. MASTERY LEARNING

When you feel comfortable signing these phrases, practice signing the entire dialogue shown at the beginning of the lesson. Practice the master dialogue using appropriate facial grammar until you can sign the part of each character smoothly.

5. FURTHER PRACTICE

Write three or four sentences stating what time your ASL class starts and ends, what room it is in, and where you will meet someone. Figure out how you will sign each of these sentences; then write the English gloss for your signing. Sign these sentences to a partner who will write down an English translation of what you have signed.

LESSON 7   SIGNS FOR COURSES

LANGUAGE GOALS

The student will
1. **use Rules**   #1. topic/comment and
                     #5. information-seeking questions.
2. **use twenty-three new signs relating to major and minor courses of study in schools, colleges, or universities.**

THE MASTER DIALOGUE

1. Judy: YOU SCHOOL MAJOR WHAT?
            What is your major?

    Pat: ME MAJOR, ALGEBRA.
            My major is algebra.

2. Judy: YOU MINOR WHAT?
            What is your minor?

    Pat: ME MINOR, GEOGRAPHY.
            My minor is geography.

THE MASTER SIGNS

ACCOUNTING

THE MASTER SIGNS

ALGEBRA

ART

BIOLOGY

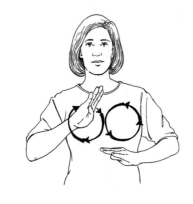

BUSINESS

CHEMISTRY

THE MASTER SIGNS

COMPUTER

DRAMA

ECONOMICS

ENGINEERING

ENGLISH

THE MASTER SIGNS

GEOGRAPHY

HISTORY

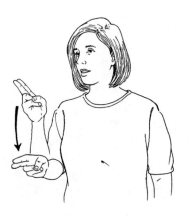

LANGUAGE

MUSIC

LAW

THE MASTER SIGNS

MAJOR

MATH

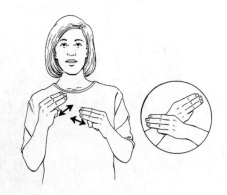

MINOR

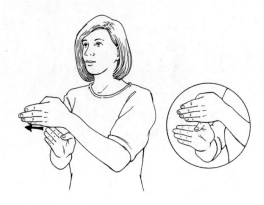

THE MASTER SIGNS

NURSING

PHYSICS

PSYCHOLOGY

SCHOOL

WHAT'S IN THE SIGNS (NOTES ABOUT THE GRAMMAR)

1. RULE #5. INFORMATION-SEEKING QUESTIONS

The dialogue is centered around asking two simple questions:

YOU MAJOR WHAT?

YOU MINOR WHAT?

In both questions the wh-sign comes at the end.

2. RULE #1. TOPIC/COMMENT

The signer responds to both questions describing the topic and then making a comment about it:

ME MAJOR, ALGEBRA.

ME MINOR, GEOGRAPHY.

WHAT'S IN A SIGN (NOTES ABOUT VOCABULARY)

1. COMPUTER

Some signs have many variations. Some of these variations are regional. For example, the state of Michigan has a sign for STORE that is not used in any other state or province. There are a number of ways to make the sign COMPUTER. In fact, it is not uncommon to find two or more variations of the sign COMPUTER used in a single city. The sign COMPUTER selected for this book is a common one, but it is wise to compare the signs you learn in this book with the ones used in your local Deaf community.

2. INITIALIZATION

Some signs are made in the same manner except for their handshapes. The handshape used in these signs is based on the first letter of the sign. This strategy for creating a sign is called *initialization*. ALGEBRA and MATH are signed in the same manner except ALGEBRA is signed with the A handshape and MATH is signed with the M handshape. The same is true for BIOLOGY and CHEMISTRY. Oftentimes, there is a root sign (or base sign) from which the other signs are derived. For BIOLOGY and CHEMISTRY, the root sign is SCIENCE, which is not initialized. The root sign for ECONOMICS is the sign MONEY.

3. ASL SYNONYMS

Some signs can be used to mean other things.

Sign	Also used for
ART	DRAW
ACCOUNTING	COUNTING
DRAMA	ACT, ACTING, THEATER
ENGINEERING	MEASURE, DRAFT
GEOGRAPHY	EARTH
LAW	LEGAL
MAJOR	PROFESSION, CAREER, FIELD (of study)
MUSIC	SING, SONG
SCHOOL	ACADEMIC

PRACTICE ACTIVITIES

1. MODEL FOR RULES #1. TOPIC/COMMENT AND #5. INFORMATION-SEEKING QUESTIONS

Signer A: 1. Describe the topic;
                    2. ask a question about the topic.

Topic:	YOU MAJOR	or	YOU MINOR
Question:	WHAT?	or	WHAT?

Signer B: 1. Describe the topic;
                    2. make a comment about the topic.

Topic:	ME MAJOR	or	ME MINOR
Comment:	ALGEBRA	or	GEOGRAPHY

Practice

Signer A: YOU MAJOR WHAT?
Signer B: ME MAJOR, ALGEBRA.
Signer A: YOU MINOR WHAT?
Signer B: ME MINOR, GEOGRAPHY.

2. MASTERY LEARNING

Practice signing the dialogue until you become familiar with the formation of the signs ALGEBRA and GEOGRAPHY and then substitute these signs with other signs from the master list. Repeat the process until you have mastered all the signs for different school subject matter.

3. FURTHER PRACTICE

Create a dialogue using the format for discussing course work from Lessons 5–7. Write an English translation for each sentence. Then practice signing your dialogue with a partner. When you and your partner feel comfortable signing the dialogue, sign it to a third person and see if that person can interpret it correctly. For example,

Signer A: YOU CLASS, DRAMA?
                 Is your class drama?

Signer B: NO. MY CLASS, HISTORY.
                 No. My class is history.

Signer A: YOU MAJOR, HISTORY?
                 Are you majoring in history?

Signer B: NO. ME MINOR, HISTORY.
                 No. My minor is in history.

Signer A: CLASS START, TIME?
                 What time does class start?

Signer B: CLASS START, TIME 9.
                 Class starts at nine o'clock.

REVIEW OF LESSONS 1–7

For each of the following sentences, translate it to ASL, sign it, and then write the English gloss of the signs you used in your translation.

1. Are you taking geography?

2. The computer class starts at six o'clock.

3. Are you discouraged?

4. How do you feel?

5. When did you learn ASL?

6. I feel lucky, how about you?

7. I am learning ASL numbers now.

8. You're always tired.

9. You go to the business class in the morning.

10. Where is the drama room?

ANSWERS

Note that there may be other ways of translating these sentences than the ones shown here.

1. GEOGRAPHY, YOU TAKE-UP? (Rule #3)

2. COMPUTER CLASS START WHEN? TIME 6. or COMPUTER CLASS START, TIME 6. (Rule #7 or #1)

3. YOU DISCOURAGED? or DISCOURAGED YOU? (Rule #3)

4. FEEL+ YOU? (Rule #5)

5. YOU LEARN ASL, WHEN? (Rule #5)

6. ME FEEL LUCKY, YOU? (Rule #4)

7. NOW, ASL NUMBERS ME LEARN. (Rule #2)

8. YOU TIRED, ALWAYS. (Rule #6)

9. MORNING, BUSINESS CLASS YOU GO-to. (Rules #2 and #6)

10. DRAMA ROOM, WHERE? (Rule #5)

The Deaf Community

After entering the building, they climbed a long steep stairway and proceeded down a dimly lit corridor to an open doorway with a sign beside it announcing the Metro Silent Club. Gloria's heart was beating rapidly—from the climb or nervousness, she wasn't sure which—as they walked through the door. Before her was a big room with a bar at one end and a small makeshift stage at the other. Scattered about the edges were a few round tables and chairs. There were some twenty-five people present with concentrations at strategic locations: a dozen or so at the bar, signing madly; a couple over by a telephone with a machine attached to it, on which one of them was typing, and which she supposed was a TTY; two sets of four at tables, playing cards; and two people by the stage who looked as out of place as she felt. But what struck her most was the eerie silence. Despite all the activity, there was very little noise.

—HARLAN LANE, ROBERT HOFFMEISTER, AND BEN BAHAN
A Journey into the DEAF-WORLD

HOLD THAT SIGN . . .

This passage came from a story that Ben Bahan, a Deaf scholar, tells to illustrate a nondeaf journalist's first foray into a Deaf club. The emphasis on the silence in the club is a poignant observation of how many nondeaf people view the world of the Deaf as a place where people don't hear, where silence is a loud reminder of the difference between the two groups of people. But from the point of view of Deaf people, silence is not the point. What is important is that they obtain a lot of pleasure being with other Deaf people. They enjoy a communication anchored by ASL. They relish the tales about Deaf people's experiences in their world, the Deaf community, and the world of others. They take great pride in their community's activities and the accomplishments of their members. They treat each other with care and understanding almost like they are all members of the same family and in a sense they are. Each of these behaviors is a reason why there is a Deaf community, why Deaf people have their own clubs, sports, organizations, and much more. This chapter introduces you to the Deaf community.

WHO ARE DEAF PEOPLE?

There is no way that you can point to a person sitting and reading a magazine in a lobby whom you have never met before and say, "That person is Deaf." Even if the person is wearing hearing aids, we don't know which community the person identifies with. Wearing a hearing aid has nothing to do with being Deaf, and most Deaf people do not wear them. Similarly, it is not important whether the person is European, African-American, Hispanic, or of some other ethnic origin. Age is not relevant, and neither is the social class or gender of the person. The Deaf community is not shaped by any of these characteristics. In fact, having a hearing loss does not mean that a person is a member of the Deaf community, although it is certainly an important requirement.

The pivotal mark of a Deaf person is how this person communicates. A Deaf person uses sign language, which in America and most of Canada is ASL. This does not mean that the person cannot use other forms of communication such as writing and speaking. Rather, ASL is the linguistic trademark that sets Deaf people apart from the communication behavior of all other groups of people. It is the reason we say that Deaf people represent a linguistic minority. It is also why some people who are deaf do not see themselves as belonging to the Deaf community. We use the lowercase spelling of deaf to refer to a person or a group of people who have a substantial degree of hearing loss. Having a hearing loss does not mean that a person automatically knows how to sign. If a deaf person does not know sign language, then that person will not be able to access the varied cultural experiences associated with the Deaf community. Communication is basic and ASL is the communication of the Deaf community.

Can a nondeaf person who is fluent in ASL be a member of the Deaf community? No, and neither can a nondeaf person who has Deaf parents. Some people describe the Deaf community as including a wide circle of people, Deaf and otherwise. But Deaf people themselves do not view nondeaf people as members of their community because nondeaf people lack a third critical characteristic, which is shared experiences. If you have normal hearing, then you will never have the experiences of a life that is centered around seeing. However, one group of hearing people is often accepted into the Deaf community, but may not be considered part of the Deaf culture, as they are not Deaf themselves. Often referred to as a CODA or a child of Deaf adult, they are brought up in the Deaf community and learn the language and cultural customs because their parents are Deaf and participate in that community.

Who are Deaf people? They are a group of people who have a hearing loss, use a sign language as their primary means of communication, and have shared experiences associated with the hearing loss and the use of sign language.

Let's put all of this in perspective. Let's say you had a young friend who has acquired a hearing loss and was fitted with hearing aids. Would we say that he was Deaf? No, we say that he is hard of hearing because speaking is still his main means of communication. If his hearing continues to deteriorate then we might say that he is becoming deaf, that is, he is acquiring a substantial degree of hearing loss. What if his difficulty with hearing leads him to learn to sign ASL, which becomes his primary language of communication, and he begins participating in some activities in the Deaf community? Would we then say that he is Deaf? We would probably say, "Friend, welcome to the club."

WHERE IS THE DEAF COMMUNITY?

The Deaf community has no geographical boundaries. There are Deaf clubs in many cities, but the clubs are just a part of the larger community of Deaf people. We can talk about the Deaf community in very broad terms like "the Deaf community in America" or we can talk about it in more local terms like "the Deaf community in Phoenix." In both instances we are talking about a group of Deaf people and the things they do in life.

There are communities of Deaf people within the Deaf community. In large urban areas, for example, it is not unusual to find Deaf African-Americans, Deaf Hispanics, or Deaf Asian-Pacifics who have come together because of the common experiences associated not only with being Deaf but also with their ethnicity.

Just as we cannot draw a map outlining the boundaries of the Deaf community, we cannot put our finger on the precise number of Deaf people in the United States. This information does not exist. Estimates though seem to peg this number at about a half million.

What we can say is that most Deaf people are born deaf. A few of them become deaf after birth and some much later in life. This latter group of people are referred to as late-deafened adults. Most people who become deaf later in life and especially after their school years do not readily learn to sign. Therefore, the biggest group of signers are those born deaf or who become deaf early in life. And where do they learn to sign? Only about ten percent of all Deaf people have at least one Deaf parent. These children then have someone who teaches them ASL and helps them develop their cultural identity with the Deaf community. But most Deaf people do not come from Deaf families. Ninety percent of all Deaf people have nondeaf parents, most of whom do not expose their children to people and events in the Deaf community. A majority of nondeaf parents never learn to sign. Therefore, Deaf people who have nondeaf parents will likely have developed their ties with the Deaf community away from home, learning ASL from other Deaf children they meet in school programs and especially in schools for the Deaf.

WHAT'S IMPORTANT IN THE DEAF COMMUNITY?

By coming together and forming their own community, Deaf people have created their own Deaf culture. A *culture* is all that a group of people do and includes their beliefs, values, customs, activities, and language. Many things that Deaf people do are the same as what occurs in nondeaf communities. They work, own homes, get married, raise families, play sports, watch videos, and so forth. They eat, dress up, and celebrate the same kinds of holidays as do most other people in America and Canada. But, we define Deaf culture by looking at what's different in the Deaf community. Deaf people have a strong identity with Deaf culture because they embrace these differences. Descriptions of six important differences follow.

AMERICAN SIGN LANGUAGE

The language Deaf people use is the foremost characteristic of the Deaf community. Knowing ASL opens the doors to meeting other Deaf people and to learning about the Deaf community. ASL cannot be written; therefore, knowledge of it is essential if a person is to learn about the history of a Deaf community, its folklore, its traditions, and as the case might be, its dark secrets. Although there are some written accounts about Deaf culture, experiencing a culture firsthand is much more rewarding and informative than having secondhand knowledge about it. One way the Deaf community is preserving and documenting the linguistic forms of ASL is through several media sources. For instance, Gallaudet University, Washington, DC, has created a video catalog with hundreds of videos of topics ranging from Deaf Culture, History, Video logs (Vlogs), and Sports, which are free to anyone to access and share (*http://videocatalog.gallaudet.edu/userSelectFeed.cfm*). There are also several online resources that provide an outlet for the Deaf community to share their Vlogs, stories, comments, and connect with other Deaf community members such as *http://www.deafvideo.tv/*, *http://www.deafread.com/*, and *http://deafnation.com/*. In addition, social media/networking sites such as Facebook and Twitter, used by scores of people both hearing, Deaf, and hard of hearing, also provide a means for the Deaf community to preserve their language, socialize, connect with other Deaf members, give their opinions, and simply have fun! The possibilities are endless!

SOCIALIZATION

An elderly Deaf man told me about how he would catch a train in the 1940s for a four-hour ride to visit the Deaf club on the weekends. Another Deaf man said that before he got a TTY (a device that allows communication on the phone by typing on a keyboard) in the late 1970s, he and his wife would drive up to three hours to visit their Deaf friends in other cities. They would make the arrangement by exchanging letters but sometimes a visit would be a spur of the moment adventure with no guarantee that their Deaf friends would be home. Whether in Deaf clubs, community events, restaurants, or homes, Deaf people feel a strong need to socialize with each other. They crave the social contact that is absent from their home life, school, and workplace when no one else signs in these places. Even Deaf couples desire to be with other Deaf people in order to enrich their lives. Socializing among themselves keeps Deaf people abreast of news in the Deaf community and gives them much emotional support.

ORGANIZATIONS AND CLUBS

Given the importance of socialization, it is only natural that Deaf people would have their own clubs and organizations. The first known organizations to form in the United States were alumni associations established by graduates of schools for the Deaf. Schools for the Deaf foster a bond between their students and forge strong ties with Deaf people across the state. Alumni associations provide a means for Deaf people to maintain contact with each other as well as to help the schools that brought them together. Deaf clubs are another natural offspring of schools for the Deaf, and many of them are founded in the same city in which the schools are located. There are also associations committed to improving the welfare of Deaf people such as the National Association of the Deaf, and these are discussed in Chapter 12. Other groups are devoted to providing opportunities in the area of sports and recreation, and they also are discussed in that chapter.

SCHOOLS FOR THE DEAF

The hub of many Deaf communities is often a residential school for the Deaf. Almost every state and province has at least one. Children either attend these schools and stay in the dormitories, going home every weekend, or they commute to the school on a daily basis. There are also day schools for the Deaf where all students are commuters. Since the founding of the first school in Hartford in 1817, residential schools have played a prominent role in defining the Deaf community. Children growing up together in a residential setting develop lifelong friendships. Indeed, many Deaf people will say that the older Deaf students and the adults—and especially the Deaf adults—who cared for them in the residences were like family to them. Schools for the Deaf are a haven of Deaf culture offering a lifestyle that cannot be replicated elsewhere.

DEAF WAY

Gallaudet University hosted the first Deaf Way Conference/Celebration in 1989, bringing together more than four thousand Deaf and hard-of-hearing participants. The week of sharing and celebration was an opportunity to examine the unity and the diversity of Deaf life from around the world. The success of this event encouraged the organization of a second gathering in July 2002, which was held at the Washington, DC Convention Center. The weeklong conference and cultural arts festival brought together nearly ten thousand participants comprised of Deaf, hard-of-hearing, deaf-blind, and hearing individuals from 121 countries. Meetings at Gallaudet University offered an exchange of information on a vast array of topics through workshops and presentations by businesses, organizations, schools, and universities from around the world. The underlying message of the conference was that Deaf people can do anything!

DEAF PRIDE

Deaf people live in a world that is largely made for those people who can hear and speak. Consider how you would feel if you were Deaf and had to deal with the following: dialogue in a movie, negotiations with a car salesperson, inspecting a house with a realtor, the weather forecast in the event of an impending storm and having only a radio in the house to learn about it, going through customs at an international airport, filing an accident report with the police, indicating that you were overcharged by a cashier, and giving directions to a person who is lost. These are just a fraction of the situations that Deaf people encounter in their day-to-day interactions in society. The fact is, however, that Deaf people do get along in many of these situations, and it is this success in the face of such strong communication barriers that instills pride in them. Their many responses to these situations may be a result of on-the-spot ingenuity or technological adaptation that you will read about in Chapter 7. Whatever their response, Deaf people are proud of their place in society. They are proud of their history and of their culture, which is how they have adjusted to society. Quite simply, many Deaf people are proud to be Deaf and would want it no other way. This pride is one of the reasons why Deaf people tend to hug one another during greetings and why almost ninety percent of them who get married will marry another Deaf person.

Many other aspects of the Deaf community make Deaf culture a distinctive and desirable choice in life. They are all woven together with the linguistic thread, ASL.

REVIEW EXERCISE

1. What are the three characteristics that best describe members of a Deaf community?

2. How can a person have a hearing loss and not belong to the Deaf community?

3. How do Deaf children who have nondeaf parents usually learn ASL?

4. Describe how the language you speak, the people you hang around with, and the schools you went to influenced your involvement in your community.

5. What does the term "Deaf pride" mean to you?

One Million New Signs

Here is one bold wandering wire and
Now! here are five dancing . . .
     high and low in turns
     with the rhythm of the poles
Five disappearing into one again
And then a crowd,
overlapping . . . quickly and then slowly . . .
So beautiful to the eye and heart,
     one wonders what happens inside . . .
                    —ELLA LENTZ
                    "Eye Music"

HOLD THAT SIGN . . .

In the ASL version of this poem, a Deaf poet, Ella Lentz uses the handshapes for the numbers 1 and 5 to bring to life a poetic rendering of the changing image of telephone lines along the side of the road. In signs, her poem vividly awakens our own memories of watching telephone lines and posts pass by on long car trips. She creates an indelible image wherein the hands with just five fingers are a lens to a multitude of images, as is counting. Counting in ASL is not limited to the sum of the fingers nor is it encumbered by the numbers that the fingers can literally draw in the air. This chapter shows you how numbers are made in ASL, not just one number but millions of them.

THE NUMBERS 1–19

The following illustrations show the signs for the numbers 1–19. Note that the palm faces the body for the numbers 1–5 and is facing away from the body for the numbers 6–9. The palm faces the body again for the numbers 11–15, and then for the numbers 16–19 it is once again facing away from the body.

ONE   TWO   THREE

FOUR   FIVE   SIX

SEVEN   EIGHT   NINE

TEN

ELEVEN

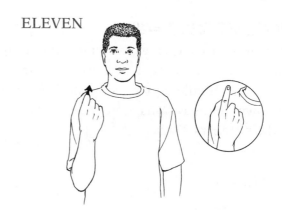

TWELVE

THIRTEEN

FOURTEEN

FIFTEEN

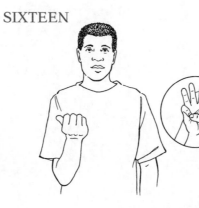

SIXTEEN

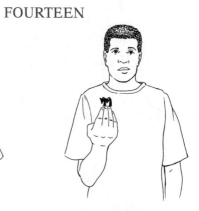

SEVENTEEN

EIGHTEEN

NINETEEN

THE NUMBERS 20–29

There is more than one way to sign some numbers. The L handshape is used to sign the numbers 20–29 in this book because it is a very common handshape and many people find it easier to manipulate than using the 2 handshape to represent the concept of twenty. In the following illustrations, note that the numbers 20–22 are made in a different manner from the numbers 23–29.

TWENTY

TWENTY-ONE

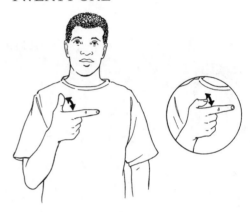

TWENTY-TWO

TWENTY-THREE

TWENTY-FOUR

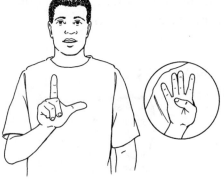

TWENTY-FIVE

TWENTY-SIX

TWENTY-SEVEN

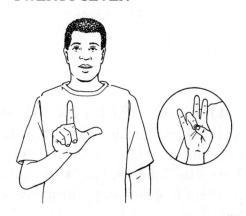

TWENTY-EIGHT

TWENTY-NINE

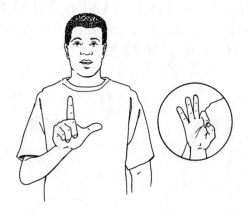

THE NUMBERS 22, 33, 44, . . ., 99

For double digit numbers in which both of the digits are the same, the hand bounces once toward the side of the body. In other words, one number is repeated.

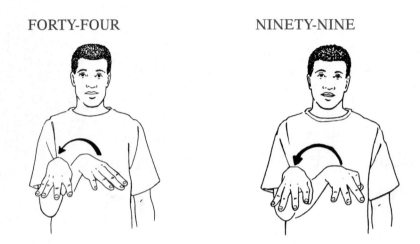

FORTY-FOUR   NINETY-NINE

THE OTHER NUMBERS FROM 30 TO 98

All other numbers from 30 to 98 are made by signing the first digit and then the second digit of the number. The palm of the hand is always facing away from the signer. For numbers 67–69, 76–79, 86–89, and 96–98, the hand twists upward when the second digit is higher than the first digit (e.g., 78) and twists downward when the first digit is higher than the second digit (e.g., 96).

HUNDREDS, THOUSANDS, MILLIONS, AND BEYOND

The following illustrations show the general signs for making the signs HUNDRED, THOUSAND, and MILLION.

HUNDRED   THOUSAND   MILLION

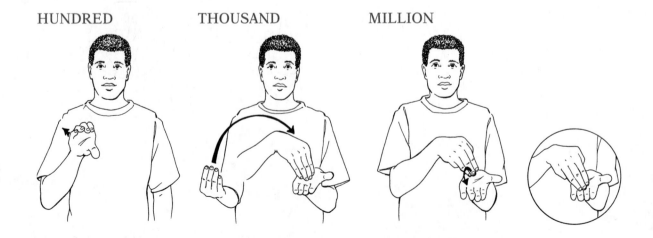

You might have noticed that the sign HUNDRED is made with a C handshape, which is the Latin letter for *hundred*. The sign THOUSAND can also be made with an M handshape, which is the Latin letter for *thousand*. The M handshape is not used in this book because the handshape shown in the previous illustration is a more popular means for signing thousand in ASL. Note that the sign MILLION is simply repeating the sign THOUSAND once, which represents the concept of $1,000 \times 1,000$, which equals 1,000,000.

Would you believe that the sign BILLION is made by repeating the sign THOUSAND twice to get $1,000 \times 1,000 \times 1,000$, which is 1,000,000,000? It is. But this is the end of using the sign THOUSAND to represent numbers. To sign larger numbers that are beyond billions, you must fingerspell the name for the larger number. For example, 3,000,000,000,000 is signed by first signing the number 3 and then fingerspelling T-R-I-L-L-I-O-N.

All numbers signed from 100 and upward are mostly made with the palm facing outward (with the exception of the numbers 11–15). You sign the numbers in the same way that you would say the number in English. Thus, 34,589 will be signed as 34 THOUSAND 5 HUNDRED 89.

Practice

Sign the following numbers.

1. 16; 48; 21; 33; 79; 88; 92; 65; 54; 97; 67; 83; 13; 20; 80

2. 382; 973; 147; 583; 990; 481; 609; 355; 111; 225

3. 9,940; 28,408; 777,594; 17,003; 458,762

4. 3,000,857; 574,389,338; 66,999,515; 478,000,000; 987,488,223

5. 2,385; 13; 74,908; 20,747; 91; 54,893,894; 309,475; 88; 160; 57,081

ADDRESSES AND PHONE NUMBERS

You sign the numbers in addresses and phone numbers in the same manner that you would say them in English. The palm is always facing away from you even when you are signing a number from 1 to 5. The palm faces you, however, whenever you sign 11 to 15 because these numbers cannot be signed in any other manner.

Practice

In the following space write in five phone numbers and practice signing them. For example, 555–0840 and 1–800–555–2431.

1. _____

2. _____

3. _____

4. _____

5. _____

In the following space write out five addresses and practice signing them. Fingerspell all the names. For example, 2531 East 9th Avenue and 4893 Brookside Lane, Suite J-7.

1. _____

2. _____

3. _____

4. _____

5. _____

Everyday ASL

5

VOCABULARY GOALS

The student will
1. create sentences using
    Rules   #3. simple yes/no questions,
                    #5. information-seeking questions, and
                    #8. ordering of simple sentences.
2. use thirty-five new signs related to phrases common to everyday
    conversations.

THE MASTER SIGNS

Sign: **Also used for:**

GOOD-MORNING

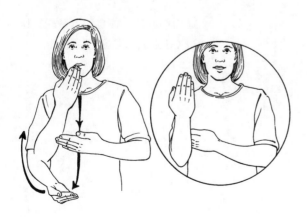

THE MASTER SIGNS

Sign:	Also used for:

GOOD-BYE

BYE, BYE-BYE

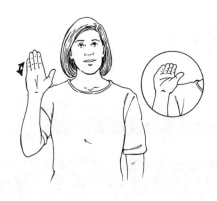

SEE-YOU-LATER

SORRY

APOLOGY, APOLOGIZE, REGRET, REGRETS

THE MASTER SIGNS

Sign: **Also used for:**

OH-I-see

GOOD-LUCK   THAT'S-GOOD

BE-CAREFUL   TAKE-CARE

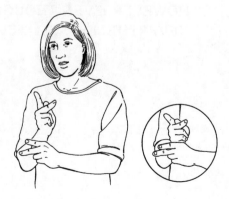

THE MASTER SIGNS

Sign: **Also used for:**

I-LOVE-YOU

DOUBT-it

DOESN'T-MATTER   ANYHOW, ANYWAY, DESPITE,
                                                              HOWEVER, EVEN-THOUGH,
                                                              NEVERTHELESS, WHATEVER

THE MASTER SIGNS

Sign: **Also used for:**

POOR-thing   PITY, MERCY, SYMPATHIZE

KNOW   AWARE

DON'T-KNOW/DIDN'T-KNOW/DOESN'T-KNOW

THE MASTER SIGNS

Sign: **Also used for:**

KNOW-THAT

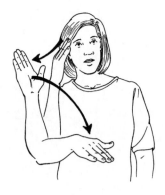

DON'T-CARE   WHO-CARES?

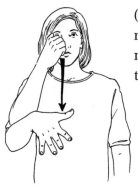

(fingertips of the closed
right hand rest on the
nose and then are
thrown away)

TIME+ (WHAT-TIME?)

THE MASTER SIGNS

Sign: **Also used for:**

LET'S-SEE

WINTER   COLD, CHILLY

SPRING   GROW, PLANT

THE MASTER SIGNS

Sign: **Also used for:**

SUMMER

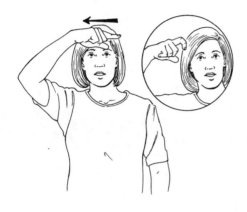

AUTUMN (FALL)   SEPTEMBER

WEATHER

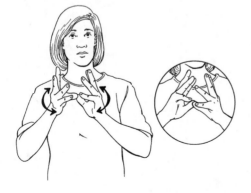

THE MASTER SIGNS

Sign: **Also used for:**

RAIN

SNOW

SUN   SUNSHINE, SUNNY

THE MASTER SIGNS

Sign: **Also used for:**

MOON

STARS

FROST   FREEZE, FROZEN

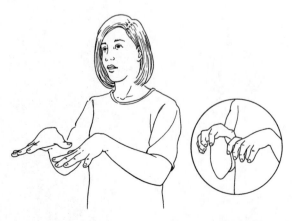

THE MASTER SIGNS

Sign: **Also used for:**

CLOUDS   CLOUDY

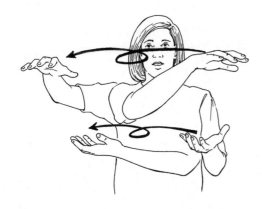

WIND

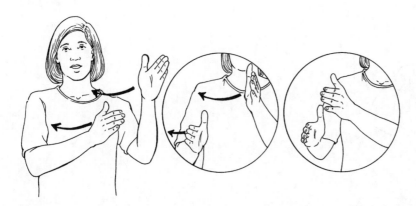

RAINBOW

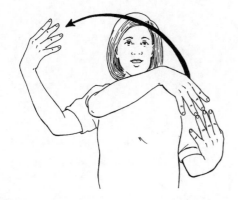

THE MASTER SIGNS

Sign: **Also used for:**

THUNDER

LIGHTNING

WHAT'S IN A SIGN (NOTES ABOUT VOCABULARY)

1. GOOD-MORNING

Although the sign for GOOD-MORNING is a compound derived from the signs GOOD and MORNING, it is made with a single, fluid motion.

2. I-LOVE-YOU

The sign for I-LOVE-YOU is typically used as a gesture of goodwill. It can be used when saying good-bye to someone you are fond of or when waving to a crowd of people to show your appreciation. It can also be used in its intimate sense to mean "I love you very much."

3. TIME+

Repeating the sign TIME and adding the appropriate nonmanual signals for asking an information-seeking question produces "What time is it?"

4. OH-I-see

The sign for OH-I-see is used by itself to indicate that a person understands something. Its translations include "Oh, I see," "Oh, I get it," and "I understand now."

5. POOR-thing

This is a directional verb and therefore the middle finger of the hand should be pointing toward the person to whom it is referring.

6. KNOW-that

This sign is used in an emphatic sense to mean "I know that."

PRACTICE ACTIVITIES

Create dialogues using the signs that you have learned in the first seven lessons with the ones introduced in this one. Use Rules #3. simple yes/no questions, #5. information-seeking questions, and #8. ordering of simple sentences to guide you. Keep your sentences short and pay attention to your facial expressions when signing them. Write the number of the rule beside each sentence. An example of a dialogue follows:

Signer A: GOOD-MORNING. TIME+? (Rule #5)
              Good morning. What time is it?

Signer B: ME DON'T-KNOW. (Rule #8)
              I don't know.

Signer A: FEEL+ YOU? (Rule #5)
              How are you feeling?

Signer B: ME FEEL DEPRESSED. (Rule #8)
              I'm feeling depressed.

Signer A: YOU FEEL DEPRESSED WHY? (Rule #5)
              Why do you feel depressed?

Signer B: ME ALGEBRA TAKE-up. (Rule #8)
              I'm taking up algebra.

Signer A: OH-I-see. POOR-thing. (Rule #8)
              Oh, I see. You poor thing.

Signer B: THANKS. YOU ALGEBRA TAKE-up? (Rule #3)
              Thanks. Are you taking algebra?

Signer A: NO.
              No.

Signer B: YOU LUCKY. (Rule #8)
              You're lucky.

LESSON 9 PRACTICE SIGNING

LANGUAGE GOALS

The student will
1. use Rules #1. topic/comment,
#2. tense with time adverbs, and
#3. simple yes/no questions.
2. use FINISH to indicate that an action has been completed.
3. use ten new signs in a master dialogue.

THE MASTER DIALOGUE

1. Judy: GOOD-MORNING. YOU BIOLOGY STUDY FINISH YOU?
Good morning. Have you finished studying biology?

Pat: YES, YESTERDAY ME BIOLOGY STUDY FINISH.
Yes, I finished studying biology yesterday.

2. Judy: YOU ASL STUDY FINISH YOU?
Have you finished studying ASL?

Pat: NO, ME PLAN STUDY ASL TODAY.
No, I plan to study ASL today.

3. Judy: REALLY? ME STUDY WITH YOU, DON'T-MIND YOU?
Is that so? Do you mind if I study with you?

Pat: ME DON'T-MIND. ME ASL PRACTICE MUST.
I don't mind. I must practice ASL.

4. Judy: ME AGREE. ME PRACTICE MORE, NEED ME.
I agree. I need to practice more.

Pat: START PRACTICE ASL, READY YOU?
Are you ready to start practicing ASL?

5. Judy: ME READY!
I'm ready!

THE MASTER SIGNS

DON'T-MIND

FINISH

MUST

NEED

PLAN

PRACTICE

THE MASTER SIGNS

STUDY

TODAY

WITH

YESTERDAY

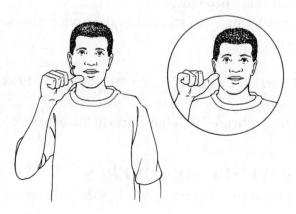

WHAT'S IN THE SIGNS (NOTES ABOUT THE GRAMMAR)

1. RULE #3. SIMPLE YES/NO QUESTIONS

The sign FINISH is often used to ask if an action is completed:

YOU BIOLOGY STUDY FINISH YOU?

Another way of signing this question is to place the FINISH sign before the action sign or verb:

Question	Translation
FINISH STUDY YOU?	Have you finished studying?
YOU BIOLOGY FINISH STUDY YOU?	Have you finished studying biology?

Another yes/no question in the dialogue was

YOU ASL STUDY FINISH YOU?

Notice that the sign YOU is placed at the beginning and end of the question. Although it is not necessary to sign YOU twice in the sentence it is a common practice to do so.

2. USING FINISH TO SHOW THAT AN ACTION IS COMPLETED

The FINISH sign is placed before or after a verb to show that an action is completed.

Before the verb:	ME FINISH STUDY ME.
After the verb:	ME STUDY FINISH ME.

Both phrases mean, "I have finished studying."

To add information about what was studied to the above phrases, you place the information before each phrase:

ME BIOLOGY STUDY FINISH.   or   ME BIOLOGY FINISH STUDY.

A proper translation of both phrases is "I have finished studying biology."

3. RULE #2. TENSE WITH TIME ADVERBS

You place the sign for time at the beginning of a FINISH phrase:

YESTERDAY ME BIOLOGY STUDY FINISH ME.

Placing the sign for time at the beginning of a sentence establishes the tense. Notice that if a signer wishes to emphasize the point that the studying was finished yesterday, then he or she might place the sign YESTERDAY at the end of the phrase to get ME BIOLOGY STUDY FINISH ME, YESTERDAY. This new sentence is an example of a topic/comment sentence structure.

4. RULE #1. TOPIC/COMMENT

The signer describes the topic and then makes a comment about it. The following examples are taken from the dialogue:

Topic	Comment
ME PLAN STUDY ASL	TODAY.
ME ASL PRACTICE	MUST.
ME PRACTICE MORE,	NEED ME.

5. RULE #3. SIMPLE YES/NO QUESTIONS WITH THE SIGNS DON'T-MIND AND READY

Use the signs DON'T-MIND and READY with the formula for creating a yes/no question:

Topic	Question
ME STUDY WITH YOU,	DON'T-MIND YOU?
START PRACTICE ASL,	READY YOU?

WHAT'S IN A SIGN (NOTES ABOUT VOCABULARY)

1. DON'T-MIND

The translation of the sign DON'T MIND depends upon the context in which it is used. By itself or in a sentence it usually means, "I don't mind." As a question, it is commonly translated to "Do you mind?"

2. TODAY/YESTERDAY

The body and the signing space combine to indicate time in ASL. The body itself represents the present time or present tense. That's why the signs TODAY and NOW move in a vertical plane close to the body. To indicate the future, signs move to the front of the body (e.g., TOMORROW). To indicate the past tense, signs move toward the back of the body and YESTERDAY is an example of this.

3. ASL SYNONYMS

Some signs can be used to mean other things.

Sign	Also used for
FINISH	ALREADY, STOP
MUST	HAVE-TO
NEED	NECESSARY, SHOULD
PLAN	ARRANGE, ORDER, PREPARE
PRACTICE	TRAIN, REHEARSE, WORK-ON

PRACTICE ACTIVITIES

1. MODEL FOR RULES #1. TOPIC/COMMENT, #2. TENSE WITH TIME ADVERBS, AND #3. SIMPLE YES/NO QUESTIONS

Signer A: 1. Make a greeting;

2. describe the action;

3. ask a question with the FINISH sign.

Greeting:	GOOD-MORNING.
Action:	YOU BIOLOGY STUDY
Question:	FINISH YOU?

Signer B: 1. Answer the question with the sign YES;

2. establish the time frame of the sentence by using the time adverb YESTERDAY;

3. make a comment.

Response:	YES,
Tense:	YESTERDAY
Comment:	ME BIOLOGY STUDY FINISH.

Signer A: 1. Describe the action;

2. ask a question with the FINISH sign.

Action:	YOU ASL STUDY
Question:	FINISH YOU?

Signer B: 1. Answer the question with the sign NO;

       2. describe a topic;

       3. make a comment about the topic.

       Answer: NO,

       Topic: ME PLAN STUDY ASL

       Comment: TODAY.

Practice

Signer A: GOOD-MORNING. YOU BIOLOGY STUDY FINISH YOU?

Signer B: YES, YESTERDAY ME BIOLOGY STUDY FINISH.

Signer A: YOU ASL STUDY FINISH YOU?

Signer B: NO, ME PLAN STUDY ASL TODAY.

2. MODEL FOR RULES #1. TOPIC/COMMENT AND #3. SIMPLE YES/NO QUESTIONS WITH DON'T-MIND AND READY

Signer A: DON'T-MIND.

       1. Describe the topic for the question;

       2. ask the question about the topic using the DON'T-MIND sign.

       Topic: ME STUDY WITH YOU,

       Question: DON'T-MIND YOU?

Signer B: 1. Answer the question with the DON'T-MIND sign;

       2. describe a topic;

       3. make a comment about the topic.

       Answer: ME DON'T-MIND.

       Topic: ME ASL PRACTICE

       Comment: MUST.

Signer A: 1. Make a remark acknowledging what was just said;

       2. describe the topic;

       3. make a comment about the topic.

       Remark: ME AGREE.

       Topic: ME PRACTICE MORE,

       Comment: NEED ME.

Signer A: READY.
                   1. Describe the topic for the question;
                   2. ask the question about the topic using the READY sign.

                   Topic: START PRACTICE ASL,
                   Question: READY YOU?

Signer B: 1. Answer the question with the READY sign.
                   Answer: ME READY!

Practice

Signer A: ME STUDY WITH YOU, DON'T-MIND YOU?
Signer B: ME DON'T-MIND. ME ASL PRACTICE MUST.
Signer A: ME AGREE. ME PRACTICE MORE, NEED ME.
Signer A: START PRACTICE ASL, READY YOU?
Signer B: ME READY!

3. MASTERY LEARNING

When you feel comfortable signing these phrases, practice signing the entire dialogue shown at the beginning of the lesson. Practice the master dialogue until you can sign the part of each character smoothly using the appropriate facial grammar.

4. FURTHER PRACTICE

Write a short story about taking a class at school and include the following information: the name of the class, the time it starts and ends, your feelings about the class (e.g., ENTHUSIASTIC, BORED), and which room it is in. Translate the story and write it down in English gloss. Sign the story to someone who will then write down what she or he thinks you signed. Compare this story with your original one. You should not only use the signs that you learned in your lessons but also their synonyms. For example, the sign DRAMA also is used for ACT, ACTING, and THEATER (see Lesson 7).

LESSON 10   DISCUSSING TIME

LANGUAGE GOALS

The student will
  1.   use Rules   **#5.** information-seeking questions and
                            #9. conditional sentences.
  2.   use the proper procedures for indicating the time.
  3.   use nine new signs in a master dialogue.

THE MASTER DIALOGUE

1.   Judy: TWO-of-us PRACTICE WHEN?
               When will the two of us practice?

      Pat: TOMORROW AFTERNOON, TIME 3.
               Tomorrow afternoon at three o'clock.

2.   Judy: SUPPOSE ME LATE, DO-what YOU?
               What will you do if I am late?

      Pat: ME WAIT, ASL PRACTICE MYSELF.
               I'll wait and practice ASL by myself.

3.   Judy: SUPPOSE ME FORGET, DO-what YOU?
               What will you do if I forget?

      Pat: ME ASL PRACTICE MYSELF.
               I'll practice ASL by myself.

4.   Judy: TOMORROW AFTERNOON, TIME 3 me-MEET-you HERE.
               I will meet you here tomorrow afternoon at three o'clock.

      Pat: ALL-RIGHT. BYE.
               All right. Bye.

THE MASTER SIGNS

ALL-RIGHT

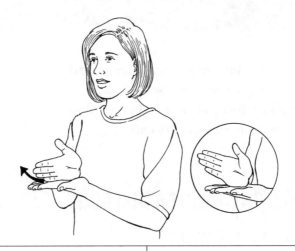

AFTERNOON

DO-what

FORGET

LATE

THE MASTER SIGNS

MYSELF

SUPPOSE

TOMORROW

WAIT

WHAT'S IN THE SIGNS (NOTES ABOUT THE GRAMMAR)

1. RULE #5. INFORMATION-SEEKING QUESTIONS

The rule for creating a wh-question is demonstrated in the dialogue with the sign WHEN. The signer sets up the topic and then asks a wh-question:

topic:	TWO-of-us PRACTICE
wh-question:	WHEN?

The question is asking for information and the proper nonmanual signals are for the signer to (1) *tilt the head forward* and (2) *squeeze the eyebrows together*.

2. RULE #9. CONDITIONAL SENTENCES

A conditional sentence with the sign SUPPOSE can be formed by stating the conditional clause first and then the question:

conditional clause:	SUPPOSE ME LATE,
question:	DO-what YOU?

Another example of this type of conditional sentence follows:

conditional clause:	SUPPOSE ME FORGET,
question:	DO-what YOU?

The proper nonmanual signals for signing the conditional clause are to (1) *raise the eyebrows* and (2) *tilt the head forward slightly*. The proper nonmanual signals for the question consist of (1) *tilting the head forward* and (2) *squeezing the eyebrows together*.

Depending upon the context of the sentence, the sign DO-what has several meanings including the following:

Phrase	Translations
DO-what YOU?	What are you going to do?
	What will you do?
	What do you want to do?
DO-what ME?	What am I going to do?
	What will I do?
	What do I want to do?

In a question, DO-what is placed at the end of the sentence:

SUPPOSE ME LATE, DO-what YOU?
SUPPOSE ME FORGET, DO-what YOU?

3. INDICATING THE TIME

The time phrase, TIME + #, is typically placed after other signs for time:

TOMORROW AFTERNOON, TIME 3.

This translates to "Tomorrow afternoon at three o'clock" or "Three o'clock tomorrow afternoon."

WHAT'S IN A SIGN (NOTES ABOUT VOCABULARY)

1. AFTERNOON

The formation of the sign for AFTERNOON shows the horizon (represented by the horizontal arm) and the sun midway between the zenith and the horizon (represented by the other hand). Lowering the hand that represents the sun will indicate that the time is later in the afternoon.

2. DO-what

The sign for DO-what is often used by itself to mean "What are you going to do about it?" or "What do you want to do about it?" The signer should maintain eye contact with the person to whom she or he is signing.

3. SUPPOSE

The sign for SUPPOSE essentially means "if." It is used to establish a conditional clause. It *does not* have the English meaning "imagine" or "think" as in the sentence "I suppose you would like to walk."

4. TOMORROW

The body and the signing space combine to indicate time in ASL. The body represents the present time or present tense. The signs TODAY and NOW move in a vertical plane close to the body. To indicate the future tense, the sign TOMORROW moves to the front of the body. To indicate the past tense, signs move toward the back of the body (e.g., YESTERDAY).

5. ASL SYNONYMS

Some signs can be used to mean other things.

Sign	Also used for
ALL-RIGHT	OKAY
LATE	NOT-YET
MYSELF	SELF
SUPPOSE	IF

PRACTICE ACTIVITIES

1. MODEL FOR RULE #5. INFORMATION-SEEKING QUESTIONS AND FOR INDICATING THE TIME

Signer A: 1. Describe the topic;

2. ask a question about the topic using the sign WHEN.

Topic: TWO-of-us PRACTICE

Question: WHEN?

Signer B: 1. Respond to the question indicating the time.

Response: TOMORROW AFTERNOON, TIME 3.

Practice

Signer A: TWO-of-us PRACTICE WHEN?

Signer B: TOMORROW AFTERNOON, TIME 3.

2. MODEL FOR RULE #9. CONDITIONAL SENTENCES

Signer A: 1. Describe the conditional clause;

2. ask a question using DO-what.

Conditional clause: SUPPOSE ME LATE,

Question: DO-what YOU?

Signer B:	1. Respond to the question.	
	Response:	ME WAIT, ASL PRACTICE MYSELF.
Signer A:	1. Describe the conditional clause; 2. ask a question using DO-what.	
	Conditional clause: Question:	SUPPOSE ME FORGET, DO-what YOU?
Signer B:	1. Respond to the question.	
	Response:	ME ASL PRACTICE MYSELF.

Practice

Signer A: SUPPOSE ME LATE, DO-what YOU?
Signer B: ME WAIT, ASL PRACTICE MYSELF.
Signer A: SUPPOSE ME FORGET, DO-what YOU?
Signer B: ME ASL PRACTICE MYSELF.

3. MASTERY LEARNING

When you feel comfortable signing these phrases, practice signing the entire dialogue shown at the beginning of the lesson. Practice the master dialogue until you can sign the part of each character smoothly using the appropriate facial grammar.

4. FURTHER PRACTICE

Write five to ten conditional sentences in English, translate them to ASL, and then write the English gloss of the ASL translation. Each conditional sentence should contain the sign SUPPOSE. Sign these to a partner and have your partner write in English a translation of your sentences. Also, have your partner respond to you in signs.

LESSON 11   LEISURE ACTIVITY

LANGUAGE GOALS

The student will
1. use Rules
    - #1. topic/comment,
    - #2. tense with time adverbs,
    - #3. simple yes/no questions,
    - #5. information-seeking questions, and
    - #8. ordering of simple sentences.
2. organize thoughts in the order that they occur to create ASL sentences.
3. use the sign CALLED to name things.
4. use nine new signs in a master dialogue.

THE MASTER DIALOGUE

1. Judy: WHAT'S-UP? YOU ASL STUDY FINISH YOU?
    What's happening? Have you finished studying ASL?

    Pat: YES, ME STUDY FINISH, NOW HOME GO-to.
    Yes, I have finished studying and I am going home now.

2. Judy: TONIGHT, YOU DO-what?
    What are you doing tonight?

    Pat: TONIGHT, ME VIDEO WATCH.
    I am watching a video tonight.

3. Judy: VIDEO CALLED?
    What is the video called?

    Pat: VIDEO CALLED, TITLE "STUDY ASL WITH J-U-D-Y."
    The video's called "Study ASL with Judy."

4. Judy: HA-HA. YOU HUMOR WORK-ON NEED YOU.
    Ha-ha. You need to work on your humor.

    Pat: ME KNOW.
    I know.

THE MASTER SIGNS

CALLED

HA-HA

HOME

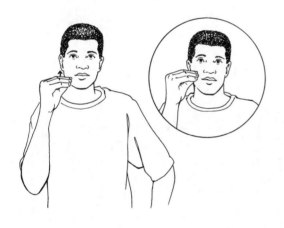

HUMOR

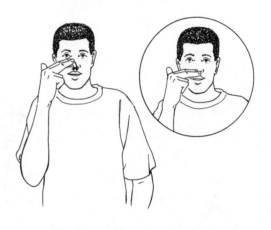

TITLE

TONIGHT

THE MASTER SIGNS

VIDEO

WATCH

WORK-ON

WHAT'S IN THE SIGNS (NOTES ABOUT THE GRAMMAR)

1. RULE #3. SIMPLE YES/NO QUESTIONS

The question

YOU ASL STUDY FINISH YOU?

sets up the topic of the question and then uses the FINISH sign to ask a yes/no question.

2. SEQUENCING THOUGHTS

Sentences can be organized by signing about events and thoughts in the order they occur. In the following sentence, two phrases are linked together in the order in which they occur:

1st event	ME STUDY FINISH,
2nd event	NOW HOME GO-to.

In the translation, the thoughts are joined by the conjunction *and*:

I have finished studying and I am going home now. or
I have finished studying and now I am going home. or
I am done studying and I am going home now. or
I am done studying and now I am going home.

3. RULE #5. INFORMATION-SEEKING QUESTIONS

In the previous lesson, you learned to place the subject pronoun YOU after the sign DO-what. In this lesson, the subject pronoun YOU is placed before the sign DO-what. Both placements are correct. When DO-what is not a sentence by itself, it is commonly placed at the end of the sentence as in

TONIGHT, YOU DO-what?

The English translation of this sentence is "What are you doing tonight?"

4. RULE #8. ORDERING OF SIMPLE SENTENCES

In simple sentences, the verb can be placed before or after the object. That is, the sentence can be SOV (subject-object-verb) or SVO (subject-verb-object):

SOV	ME VIDEO WATCH.
SVO	ME WATCH VIDEO.

Both word orderings are correct, but the SOV ordering is not found in English.

5. NAMING THINGS USING THE SIGN CALLED

The sign CALLED is used to name things or inquire about the names of things. When the name is the title of a video, movie, book, or conference, it is common practice to precede the title with the sign TITLE as in the following:

VIDEO CALLED, TITLE "STUDY ASL WITH J-U-D-Y."

6. RULE #1. TOPIC/COMMENT

The signer describes the topic and then makes a comment about it as in the following sentence from the dialogue:

topic:	YOU HUMOR WORK-ON
comment:	NEED YOU.

WHAT'S IN A SIGN (NOTES ABOUT VOCABULARY)

1. HA-HA

The sign for HA-HA is a variation of fingerspelling H-A several times. The fingerspelling of the letters H and A is not complete. Instead, the sign is made with the thumb up and the index and middle fingers flapping in and out quickly. It has several meanings depending upon the situation in which it is used. In the sentence

HA-HA. YOU HUMOR WORK-ON NEED YOU.

the HA-HA sign is not meant to indicate that something was terrifically funny, and the signer is not laughing. Rather, it is used in good humor to mean

You need to work on your humor.

2. TITLE

This sign TITLE is used to show that the signer is about to give the title of a book, movie, title, conference, or something else that has a proper title. It is signed before the title is given, and in a written English translation it usually appears as quotation marks. It can be used to refer to a title as in the following:

YOUR CLASS TITLE WHAT?
Translation: What is the title of your class?

MY CLASS TITLE, COMPUTER SCIENCE.
Translation: My class title is "Computer Science."

3. TONIGHT

You have learned that the body and the signing space combine to indicate time in ASL. The sign TONIGHT, like the signs TODAY and NOW, moves in a vertical plane close to the body to represent the present time.

4. WATCH

There are many signs to describe the many different ways of looking at something. Different signs are used to show that someone is staring, glaring, scanning, watching, seeing, and so forth. The handshape is typically the V handshape with the two fingers representing the eyes. In the sign WATCH, the V handshape is horizontal and is moved forward firmly once. There are also variations of the sign WATCH.

5. ASL SYNONYMS

Some signs can be used to mean other things.

Sign	Also used for
CALLED	NAMED
HUMOR	COMEDY, FUNNY
TITLE	QUOTE, QUOTATION
VIDEO	VIDEOTAPE
WORK-ON	PRACTICE, REHEARSE

PRACTICE ACTIVITIES

1. MODEL FOR RULE #3. SIMPLE YES/NO QUESTIONS

Signer A: 1. Describe the topic;
                   2. ask a question using the FINISH sign.

          Action: YOU ASL STUDY
          Question: FINISH YOU?

Signer B: 1. Answer the question affirmatively with the sign YES;
                   2. describe what action was finished;
                   3. add a follow-up comment.

          Affirmative answer: YES,
          Describe action finished: ME STUDY FINISH,
          Follow-up comment: NOW HOME GO-to.

Practice

Signer A: YOU ASL STUDY FINISH YOU?
Signer B: YES, ME STUDY FINISH, NOW HOME GO-to.

2. MODEL FOR RULES #5. INFORMATION-SEEKING QUESTIONS, #2. TENSE WITH TIME ADVERBS, AND #8. ORDERING OF SIMPLE SENTENCES

Signer A: 1. Describe the time relating to the DO-what question;
                   2. ask the question using the DO-what sign.

          Time: TONIGHT,
          Question: YOU DO-what?

Signer B: 1. Repeat the time;
                   2. describe the activity that responds to the DO-what question
                      using an SOV sentence.

          Time: TONIGHT,
          Response: ME VIDEO WATCH.

Practice

Signer A: TONIGHT, YOU DO-what?
Signer B: TONIGHT, ME VIDEO WATCH.

3. MODEL FOR USING THE SIGN CALLED

Signer A: 1. Describe an object;
                2. ask for its name using the sign CALLED.

Description:	VIDEO
Question:	CALLED?

Signer B: 1. Repeat the question;
                2. state the title.

Question:	VIDEO CALLED,
Title:	TITLE "STUDY ASL WITH J-U-D-Y."

Practice

Signer A: VIDEO CALLED?
Signer B: VIDEO CALLED, TITLE "STUDY ASL WITH J-U-D-Y."

4. MODEL FOR RULE #1. TOPIC/COMMENT

Signer A: 1. Use the sign HA-HA to make a remark on someone's attempt at
                   humor;
                2. describe the topic;
                3. make a comment about it.

Remark:	HA-HA.
Topic:	YOU HUMOR WORK-ON
Comment:	NEED YOU.

Signer B: 1. Respond to the comment.

Response:	ME KNOW.

Practice

Signer A: VIDEO CALLED?

Signer B: VIDEO CALLED, TITLE "STUDY ASL WITH J-U-D-Y."

Signer A: HA-HA. YOU HUMOR WORK-ON NEED YOU.

Signer B: ME KNOW.

5. MASTERY LEARNING

When you feel comfortable signing these phrases, practice signing the entire dialogue shown at the beginning of the lesson. Practice the master dialogue until you can sign the part of each character smoothly using appropriate facial grammar.

6. FURTHER PRACTICE

Write five to ten sentences that ask a yes/no question using the sign FINISH. The FINISH sign is typically used to indicate that an action is completed. Translate each sentence to ASL and then write the English gloss of the ASL translation. Sign these to a partner and have your partner write in English a translation of your sentences. Also, have your partner respond to you in signs.

6

Directional Verbs and Communicating

Directional Verbs That Change the Meanings of Sentences in Space

Journalists say that when a dog bites a man that is not news, but when a man bites a dog that is news. This is the essence of the language instinct: language conveys news. The streams of words called "sentences" are not just memory prods, reminding you of man and man's best friend and letting you fill in the rest; they tell you who in fact did what to whom.

—STEVE PINKER
The Language Instinct

HOLD THAT SIGN . . .

In American Sign Language, certain verbs tell us who did what to whom, without any help from nouns or pronouns. In English you rely on words to identify the who (subject) and the whom (object) of a sentence. In the sentence "He contacted her" three words are spoken, and there is no doubt as to who contacted whom. In ASL, only the sign CONTACT is made to give us the ASL sentence, he-CONTACT-her. Three ASL characteristics make this possible. The first is that nouns can be established in the signing space, and after they are established, these nouns can be used to refer to someone or something. The second characteristic is that certain verbs can move in different directions to tell us who did what to whom. The third characteristic is the orientation of the hand(s) during the signing.

The orientation also tells us about the subject and the object of a sentence. Therefore, to understand what a verb is telling us, we must know what action the verb is describing, and we must also map its movement. This chapter describes the rules for using verbs in space.

BOB point-right, LYNN point-left

This phrase is an example of Rule #6 on pronominalization. The signer establishes two reference points in the signing space for two people. In the signing space, Bob is placed to the right of the signer; Lynn is placed to the left. After this is done, the signer merely points to the right to refer to Bob and points to the left when talking about Lynn. In the following sentence the signer is telling us which sports Bob and Lynn play:

HE-point-right PLAY SOCCER, SHE-point-left PLAY BASEBALL.

The signer points to the right for HE and to the left for SHE. This sentence translates to "He plays soccer and she plays baseball."

Let's keep the same positions in the signing space for Bob and Lynn and look at the ASL translation of the sentence "She gives the book to him":

BOOK she-GIVE-him.

The sign she-GIVE-him is made by moving the sign GIVE from the left side of the signing space to the right side or from the position of SHE to the position of HIM. This is shown in the following diagram.

BOOK   she-GIVE-him

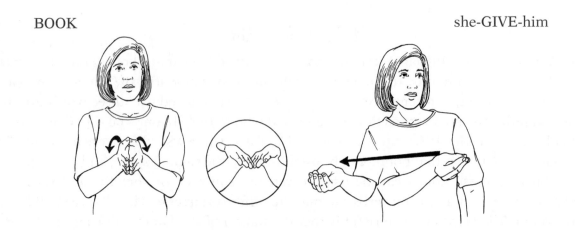

Notice that it is not necessary to sign the subject and object of the sentence because they are already incorporated into the movement of the sign. Although she-GIVE-him is just one sign, it shows Lynn (who) doing something to Bob (whom). That is, Lynn is giving the book to Bob. In the following diagram, the neutral sign for GIVE is shown.

In a neutral sign, the subject and object of a sentence are not indicated.

Verbs that can move about in space to indicate who is doing what to whom are called *directional verbs*. Not all verbs are directional verbs. This chapter provides a listing of many of the common directional verbs used in ASL (derived in part from the work of Baker and Cokely, *American Sign Language: A Teacher's Resource Text on Grammar and Culture*).

THE FOUR ASPECTS OF DIRECTIONAL VERBS

a. she-GIVE-him
b. you-PICK-ON-me

Directional verbs can inflect for source, subject, object, or goal. The *source* is the beginning location of the verb. The *goal* is the end location of the verb. The *subject* is the doer of the action described by the verb. The *object* is the recipient of the action. Subject and source are typically in the same location and object and goal are also usually in the same location.

In sentence a the source is the position in the signing space where the sign GIVE begins, which is where "she" has been established. The subject is the person represented by "she." The object is the person representing "him." The goal is the end position of the sign GIVE, which is the location in the signing space of the person represented by "him."

In sentence b the source is the position in the signing space where the sign PICK-ON begins, which is where "you" is placed. The subject is the person represented by "you." The object is the signer who is represented by "me." The goal is the end position of the sign PICK-ON, which is the location in the signing space of the person represented by "me."

Using these four aspects, we can now further explore how verbs show the relationship between the subject and object of a sentence.

A.   VERBS THAT INDICATE THE SUBJECT AND THE OBJECT

   a. he-BLAME-me, ALWAYS. (He's always blaming me.)
   b. NEXT-WEEK she-HELP-you. (She will help you next week.)
   c. he-ASK-them, NAME. (He asked them their names.)

In each of these sentences only one sign is used for the verb. The following illustrations show the direction of movement of each verb relative to the signer.

he-BLAME-me   she-HELP-you

he-ASK-them

The source or starting position for all directional verbs indicates the subject of the sentence. The goal or ending position for these verbs is the object of the sentence. Before the verb can be signed as they are in these illustrations, the signer must first establish a position for each person referred to by the pronouns. Only the pronouns ME and YOU do not have to be established because the persons they represent are present. Notice that the verb he-ASK-them is a sweeping movement. This is because the pronoun THEM is made by sweeping the index finger either on the right side or the left side of the signing space depending where the signer has placed the people who are represented by THEM.

List of Verbs That Indicate the Subject and Object

Following is a list of verbs whose movements indicate the subject and object of a sentence.

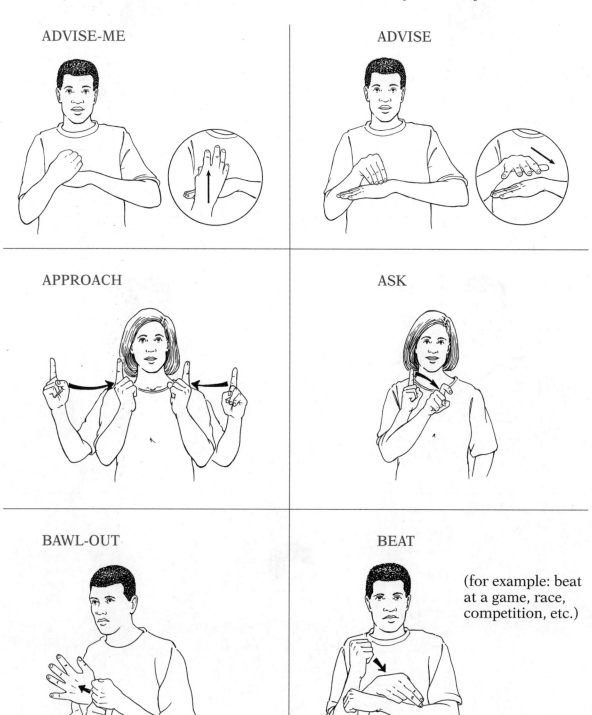

ADVISE-ME

ADVISE

APPROACH

ASK

BAWL-OUT

BEAT

(for example: beat at a game, race, competition, etc.)

BLAME

BORROW

FORCE

GIVE

LEND

HELP

HONOR

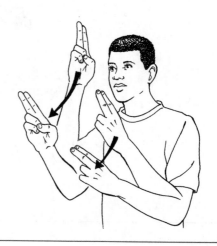

FINGERSPELL

HATE

INFLUENCE

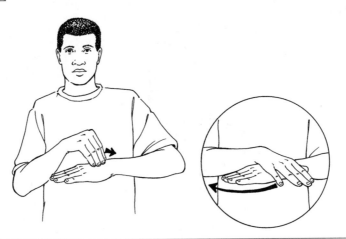

INFORM

INSULT

INTERROGATE

KICK

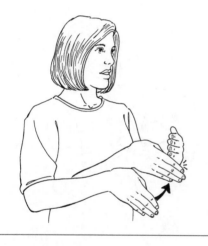

KILL

LOOK

ORDER/COMMAND

PARTICIPATE/JOIN

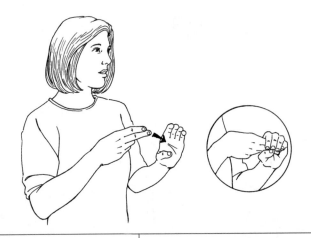

OVERCOME

PAY

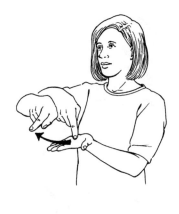

PAY-ATTENTION

PICK

PITY

PREACH

QUIT

RESPECT

RIDICULE

SCOLD

SELL

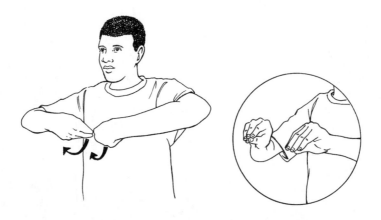

SEND

SHOOT

SHOW

STEAL

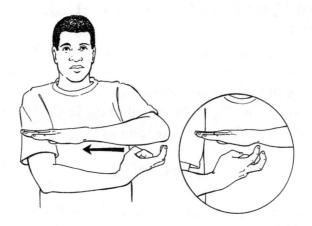

TEACH

B. THE ROLE OF THE DOMINANT HAND AND NONDOMINANT HAND IN VERBS THAT INDICATE THE SUBJECT AND OBJECT OF A SENTENCE

There are more verbs that indicate the subject and the object of a sentence. The principle for using them is the same as for the verbs listed previously with one exception: the nondominant hand is placed in front of the referent for the object of the sentence while the dominant hand moves toward it. Thus, placement of the hands is critical where one of the hands moves and the other one does not. The sentence

he-PICK-ON-me.

means "He is picking on me." The neutral sign for PICK-ON is shown in the following illustration.

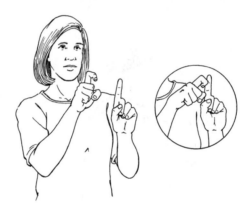

In this sign, the right hand moves while the left hand does not. We call the hand that moves the dominant hand and the hand that does not move the nondominant hand. Let's look at an illustration of the sign for you-PICK-ON-me.

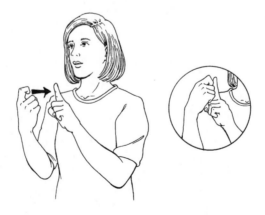

In this sign, the left hand is the nondominant hand, and it is held stationary in front of the signer's body. This hand indicates the object of the sentence. The right hand is the dominant hand, and it is moved toward the nondominant hand. This configuration of the hands shows "who is doing what to whom." The dominant hand moves from the subject or the position of "you" in the signing space toward the signer. The signer is represented by "me" in the sentence.

Because of the presence of the nondominant hand in the position of the object of a sentence, it is difficult to sweep the hand to indicate pronouns for more than one person such as THEY, THEM, and the plural form of YOU. Thus, instead of a sweep, the signer simply repeats the sign while moving it to the side. This is shown in the following illustration of the sign me-CONTACT-them.

This example is typical of the relationship between the dominant hand and the non-dominant hand in directional verbs. The orientation of the hands is also important. The drawings for the verbs listed in this chapter are for the neutral position of the verb. Yet, when signing, the orientation of the hands will change depending upon where the subject and object of the sentence are placed in the signing space. For this reason, beginning signers are advised to seek out a skilled signer or an ASL instructor to demonstrate both the orientation and the movement of the hands for directional verbs.

List of Directional Verbs That Use a Nondominant Hand to Indicate the Object of a Sentence

ARREST

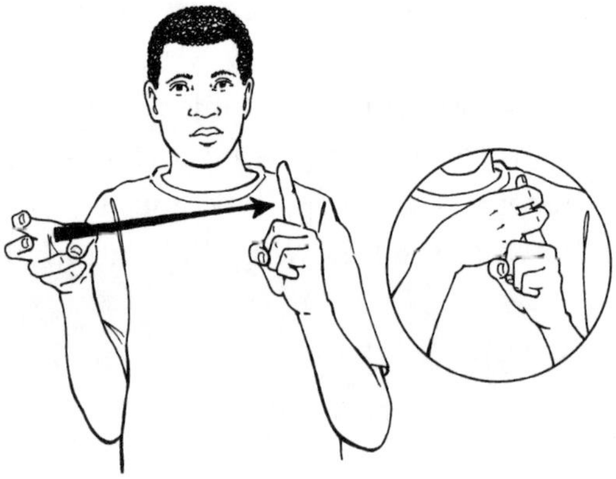

BEAT-UP

BOTHER

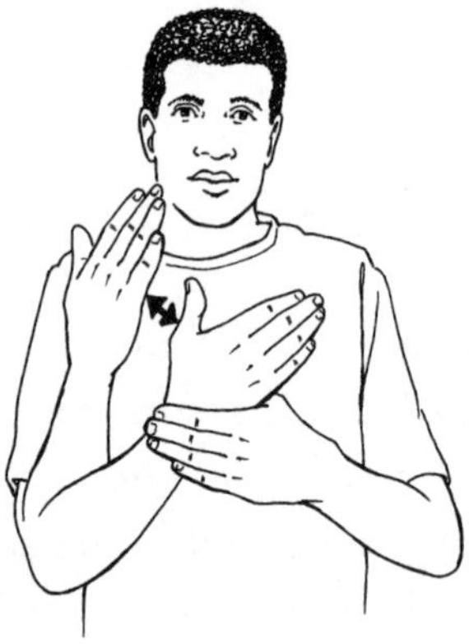

BRIBE

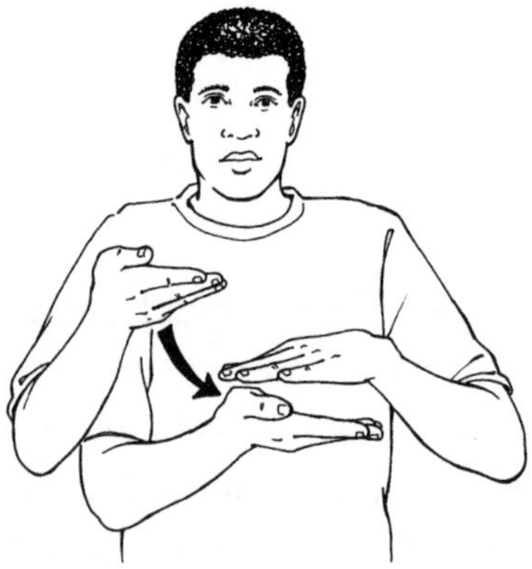

CHALLENGE

COLLIDE

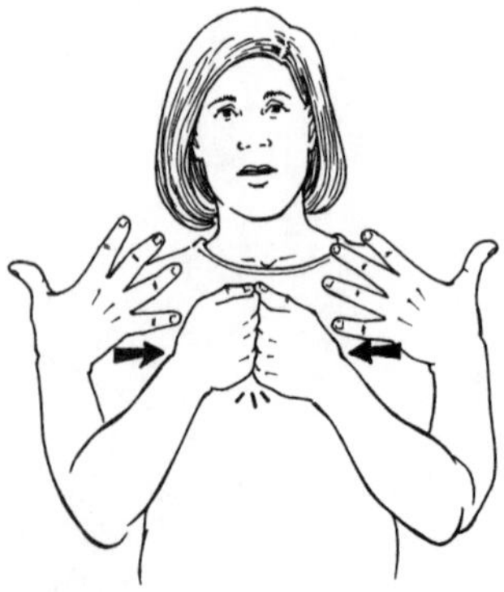

CONFRONT

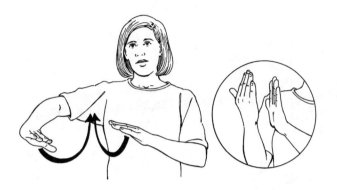

COPY

CRITICIZE

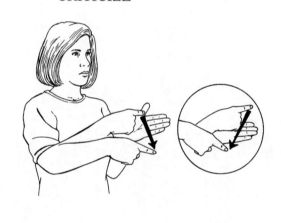

DECEIVE/FOOL/CON

FLATTER

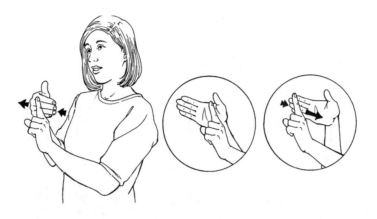

GET-EVEN-WITH

HIT

MOOCH-FROM

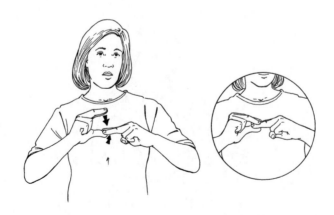

KISS

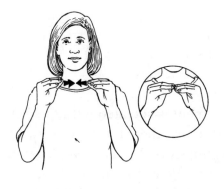

PICK-ON

SUMMON/CALL

SUPPORT

TOUCH/CONTACT

C. VERBS THAT INDICATE THE MOVEMENT FROM A SOURCE TO A GOAL

a. me-FLY-to LOS-ANGELES. (I fly to Los Angeles.)
b. SANDWICHES she-BRING-here. (She brings the sandwiches here.)
c. YESTERDAY, HOME you-GO-to. (You went home yesterday.)

The movement of some action verbs shows the movement associated with this verb. In sentence a the sign FLY-to begins where the subject ME is and then moves outward. In sentence b the sign she-BRING-here begins where the subject SHE has been placed in the signing space and then moves to a place in front of the signer to represent the concept "here." In sentence c the sign you-GO-to begins where the addressee (i.e., YOU) is and then moves away. Each of these signs is shown in the following illustrations.

me-FLY-to   she-BRING-here   you-GO-to

Oftentimes, the action verb is moving to a place that has not yet been identified. In this instance the signer moves the verb to a neutral position and then identifies the place. This principle is illustrated in sentences a and b.

List of Verbs That Indicate the Movement from a Source to a Goal

ARRIVE

ATTEND

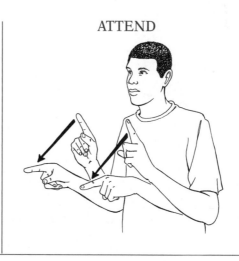

BRING

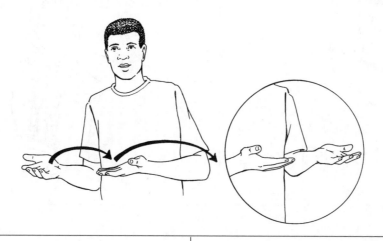

CARRY

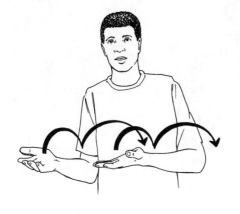

COME

DRIVE

ENTER

FLY

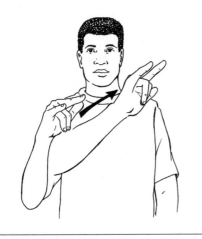

JUMP

GO-to

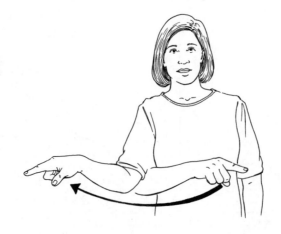

MOVE

PATRONIZE

RIDE-IN

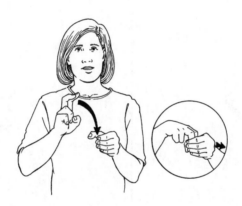

RIDE-ON

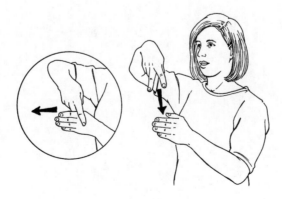

RUN

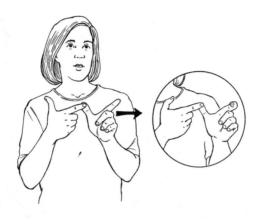

TRANSFER

WALK

D. RECIPROCAL VERBS

   a. they-LOOK-each-other. (They looked at each other.)
   b. TOMORROW, they-INFORM-each-other. (We will inform each other tomorrow.)
   c. LAST-NIGHT they-PITY-each-other. (They pitied each other last night.)

Some verbs can be modified to indicate that two people, two things, or two groups are performing a particular action to one another. These verbs are called *reciprocal verbs*. Their movements are linked to the location in the signing space of the two people, two things, or two groups. Reciprocal verbs are signed differently than the verbs when signed in a neutral manner. The illustrations for the neutral sign for the verbs LOOK, INFORM, and PITY were shown earlier. Below are examples of how these verbs are made when they are used as reciprocal verbs in sentences a, b, and c.

they-LOOK-each-other

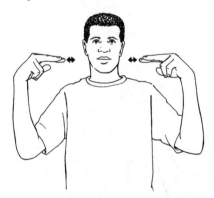

they-PITY-each-other

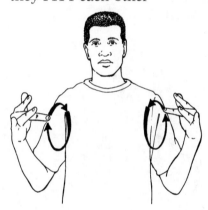

they-INFORM-each-other

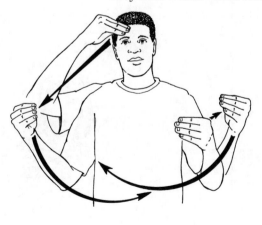

List of Reciprocal Verbs

AGREE

APPROACH

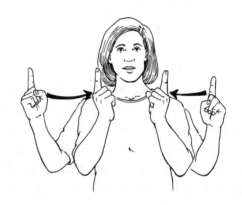

ARGUE

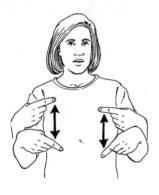

CHALLENGE

CLASH

COLLIDE

CONFLICT

CONFRONT

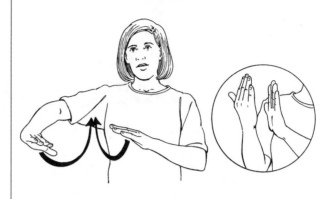

CORRESPOND

DISAGREE

EXCHANGE

INFORM

INSULT

LOOK

MEET

PITY

TEACH

REVIEW EXERCISE

Place a check mark in the column to indicate whether the main characteristic of the following verbs (a) can indicate the subject and object of a sentence, (b) uses a nondominant hand to indicate the object of a sentence, (c) can indicate the movement from a source to a goal, or (d) marks them as reciprocal verbs. Although some verbs have more than one of the following characteristics, select only the main one.

	Indicate subject and object	Nondominant hand shows the object	Movement from source to goal	Reciprocal verbs
1. BOTHER				
2. LOOK				
3. TRANSFER				
4. PAY				
5. ARGUE				
6. SUPPORT				
7. RUN				
8. INFORM				
9. QUIT				
10. DRIVE				

ANSWERS

	Indicate subject and object	Nondominant hand shows the object	Movement from source to goal	Reciprocal verbs
1. BOTHER		X		
2. LOOK				X
3. TRANSFER			X	
4. PAY	X			
5. ARGUE				X
6. SUPPORT		X		
7. RUN			X	
8. INFORM				X
9. QUIT		X		
10. DRIVE			X	

LESSON 12 THE DEAF TEACHER

LANGUAGE GOALS

The student will
1. use Rules   #3. simple yes/no questions,
                   #5. information-seeking questions,
                   #6. pronominalization,
                   #7. rhetorical questions, and
               #10. negation.
2. use the AGENT-sign to create a noun from a verb sign.
3. use eight new signs in a master dialogue.

THE MASTER DIALOGUE

1. Mike: YOU TEACH COMPUTER SCIENCE YOU?
            Do you teach computer science?

    Jenny: NO, ME STUDENT. SCHOOL TEACHER SHOW-UP NOT-YET.
            No, I'm a student. The school teacher hasn't shown up yet.

2. Mike: TEACHER YOU MEET FINISH YOU?
            Have you met the teacher?

    Jenny: MEET (shake head) NOT-YET ME.
            No, I haven't met her yet.

3. Mike: ME HEARD, TEACHER point-right, SHE-point-right DEAF.
            I heard that the teacher's deaf.

    Jenny: REALLY? SHE-point-left DEAF?
            Oh, really? She's deaf?

4. Mike: (nod head) SHE-point-right DEAF. YOU DIDN'T-KNOW?
            Yes, she is deaf. You didn't know that?

    Jenny: (shake head) ME DIDN'T-KNOW.
            No, I didn't know.

THE MASTER SIGNS

AGENT-sign

DEAF

HEARD

NOT-YET

SHE

(SHE-point-right)

THE MASTER SIGNS

(SHE-point-left)

SHOW-UP

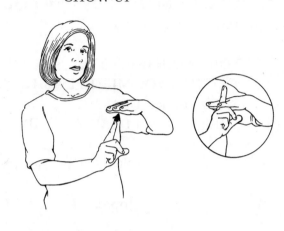

STUDENT

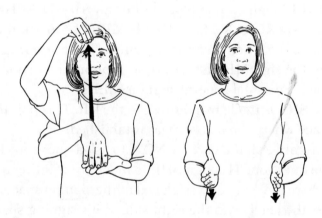

TEACHER

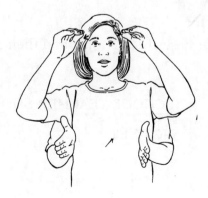

WHAT'S IN THE SIGNS (NOTES ABOUT THE GRAMMAR)

1. RULE #3. SIMPLE YES/NO QUESTIONS

Four yes/no questions were asked:

  a. YOU TEACH COMPUTER SCIENCE YOU?
  b. TEACHER YOU MEET FINISH YOU?
  c. SHE-point-left DEAF?
  d. SHE-point-right DEAF, YOU DIDN'T-KNOW?

In sentence a the sign YOU can be used to ask a yes/no question as shown in the following:

topic:	YOU TEACH COMPUTER SCIENCE
question:	YOU?

Repeating the pronoun in a sentence is a common ASL grammatical device.

In sentence b the FINISH sign can be placed after a verb—TEACHER MEET FINISH YOU?—or before a verb—TEACHER YOU FINISH MEET?—to ask if an action has been completed. The meaning of both sentences is the same: "Have you met the teacher?" Note that in this variation of the sign MEET there is no pronoun incorporated into its movement. Instead, the signer makes the general sign for MEET.

In sentence c the sign SHE is made by pointing to the left. This pointing is referring to a place in the signing space where the teacher was established.

Sentence d uses the negative sign DIDN'T-KNOW to ask a question. The negative sign is placed at the end of the question. The sign SHE is made by pointing to the right in order to be consistent with where the teacher was placed in the signing space. That is, in the dialogue, Mike first placed the teacher to the right side of his signing space in the sentence, ME HEARD, TEACHER point-right, SHE-point-right DEAF. Therefore, when he signs SHE again he must point to the same spot. More about pronominalization is found below.

2. RULE #10. NEGATION

To negate a thought, you first describe the topic and then add the appropriate negative sign.

topic:	SCHOOL TEACHER SHOW-UP
negative:	NOT-YET.

The sign NOT-YET does not always need to be placed at or near the end of a sentence. In the sentence

MEET (shake head) NOT-YET ME.

it would also be correct to sign

ME NOT-YET MEET.

The meaning in both cases is the same. The nonmanual signals that accompany the use of NOT-YET depend upon the situation. Sometimes, the signer will shake the head while signing NOT-YET to emphasize the negative. If the signer is exasperated that someone has not shown up, then she or he might open the mouth slightly while wrinkling the nose.

3. RULE #6. PRONOMINALIZATION

Pointing with the index finger is critical to the identification of pronouns in ASL. It can be used when a person is not present as long as the pronoun to which it refers has been established in the signing space. After a signer points to a spot to refer to someone or something then that spot becomes a referent point for that person or thing:

TEACHER point-right, SHE-point-right DEAF.

The dialogue has indicated to point to the right side; however, this was an arbitrary choice. The point can also be to the left side, and the meaning of the sentence will remain the same. A notation was made to "point-right" after the first occurrence of the pronoun SHE to remind you on which side of the signing space the teacher was placed. After a signer locates a person in the signing space then the other signer can refer to that person by simply pointing to the same location. When the pointing instruction stands alone as in the above signed sentence, then it is made in addition to the sign that precedes it. That is, in the phrase, TEACHER point-right, there are two hand gestures—TEACHER and a point to the right. But when the pointing gesture is linked to the pronoun as in SHE-point-right then there is only one hand gesture—the point to the right, which is the sign for SHE.

Note that if Mike points to his right side and Jenny wants to talk about the teacher, she would point to the same side, *which would be her LEFT side* if she and Mike are facing each other. Think of the signers Mike and Jenny as being mirror images of each other when trying to picture what the signing space looks like.

WHAT'S IN A SIGN (NOTES ABOUT VOCABULARY)

1. DEAF
The sign DEAF can be made either by moving the index finger from the mouth to the ear, as shown in the illustration in this book, or by moving the index finger from the ear to the mouth.

2. DIDN'T-KNOW
In Lesson 8, you learned the sign KNOW and DIDN'T KNOW. To form the sign DIDN'T-KNOW, the sign KNOW is turned away from the body. This characteristic of turning the hand away is referred to as *negative incorporation*. The sign DIDN'T-KNOW is the same as the signs "DON'T KNOW" and "DOESN'T KNOW."

3. AGENT-sign
The AGENT-sign is shown in the following diagram and is used to make a noun out of a verb using the formula VERB + AGENT-sign = NOUN:

LEARN + AGENT-sign = LEARNER or STUDENT
TEACH + AGENT-sign = TEACHER

Compare the signs for LEARN and TEACH with the signs for STUDENT (LEARNER) and TEACHER and you will note that the verb signs are not formed in precisely the same manner when the noun is made. Their movements are slightly modified to accommodate the formation of the AGENT-sign.

4. TRUE
The sign TRUE can be interpreted in many different ways, but the basic meaning is that something or someone is a reality.

5. ASL SYNONYMS
Some signs can be used to mean other things.

Sign	Also used for
NOT-YET	LATE
SHE	HE, HER (nonpossessive form), HIM, IT
SHOW-UP	APPEAR, POP-UP
TEACHER	INSTRUCTOR, PROFESSOR
TRUE	ACTUAL, CERTAIN, REAL, REALLY, REALITY, SURE

PRACTICE ACTIVITIES

1. MODEL FOR RULE #3. SIMPLE YES/NO QUESTIONS

| Signer A: | 1. Describe the topic; |
| | 2. sign YOU at the end of the sentence. |

| Topic: | YOU TEACH COMPUTER SCIENCE |
| Question: | YOU? |

| Signer B: | 1. Answer the question with the sign NO; |
| | 2. describe who you are. |

| Topic: | NO, |
| Description: | ME STUDENT. |

Practice

Signer A: YOU TEACH COMPUTER SCIENCE YOU?
Signer B: NO, ME STUDENT.

2. MODEL FOR RULES #3. SIMPLE YES/NO QUESTIONS AND #10. NEGATION

| Signer A: | 1. Describe the topic; |
| | 2. shake the head and add the appropriate negative sign (NOT-YET). |

| Topic: | SCHOOL TEACHER SHOW-UP |
| Negation: | NOT-YET. |

| Signer B: | 1. Describe the topic; |
| | 2. ask a yes/no question using the sign FINISH. |

| Topic: | TEACHER YOU MEET |
| Question: | FINISH YOU? |

| Signer A: | 1. Describe the action related to the topic; |
| | 2. shake head and use the sign NOT-YET to negate the action. |

| Action: | MEET |
| Negation: | (shake head) NOT-YET ME. |

Practice

Signer A: SCHOOL TEACHER SHOW-UP NOT-YET.
Signer B: TEACHER YOU MEET FINISH YOU?
Signer A: MEET (shake head) NOT-YET ME.

3. MODEL FOR RULE #6. PRONOMINALIZATION

Signer A:

1. Sign the noun TEACHER;
2. point to the right side (or left side) of the signing space after making the noun sign;
3. point again to the same spot to indicate the pronoun SHE;
4. describe the teacher.

Noun:	TEACHER
Locate the noun:	point-right,
Pronoun:	SHE-point-right
Description:	DEAF.

Signer B:

1. Respond to Signer A's comment about the teacher;
2. point to the location where the TEACHER was placed in the signing space by Signer A;
3. ask a yes/no question with the sign DEAF.

Response:	REALLY?
Pronoun:	SHE-point-left
Question:	DEAF?

Signer A:

1. Answer the question affirmatively by nodding your head;
2. point to the location where TEACHER was placed in the signing space;
3. describe her;
4. ask a yes/no question.

Answer:	(nod head)
Pronoun:	SHE-point-right
Description:	DEAF.
Question:	YOU DIDN'T-KNOW?

Signer B:

1. Respond to the question.

Response:	(shake head) ME DIDN'T-KNOW.

Practice

Signer A: TEACHER point-right, SHE-point-right DEAF.

Signer B: REALLY? SHE-point-left DEAF?

Signer A: (nod head) SHE-point-right DEAF, YOU DIDN'T-KNOW?

Signer B: NO, ME DIDN'T-KNOW.

4. MASTERY LEARNING

When you feel comfortable signing these phrases, practice signing the entire dialogue shown at the beginning of the lesson. Practice the master dialogue until you can sign the part of each character smoothly while using the appropriate facial grammar.

5. FURTHER PRACTICE

Use the following dialogue to review signs for descriptive terms introduced in Lesson 4.

Signer A: TEACHER-point-right, SHE-point-right DEAF.

Signer B: REALLY? SHE-point-left DEAF?

Signer A: (nod head) SHE DEAF.

LESSON 13   THE INTERPRETER

LANGUAGE GOALS

The student will
1.   use Rules   #5. information-seeking questions,
                        #6. pronominalization, and
                        #7. rhetorical questions.
2.   use the sign FINALLY at the end of a sentence.
3.   demonstrate how a temporal aspect of ASL can be shown by repeating a
      verb sign to indicate its progressive form.
4.   use ten new signs in a master dialogue.

THE MASTER DIALOGUE

1.   Mike: TEACHER SHOW-UP, FINALLY!
               The teacher has finally shown up!

      Jenny: WOMAN THERE, WHO SHE?
               Who is that woman?

2.   Mike: WOMAN THERE, SHE INTERPRETER.
               That woman is an interpreter.

      Jenny: INTERPRETER, DO-what?
               What does an interpreter do?

3.   Mike: DEAF HEARING COMMUNICATE HOW? INTERPRETER INTERPRET.
               Deaf and hearing people communicate because an interpreter interprets.

      Jenny: OH-I-see, SHE INTERPRET.
               I get it, she interprets.

4.   Mike: (nods head) LEARN+ YOU, FINALLY!
               Yes, you are finally learning.

      Jenny: SILLY YOU. ME LEARN ALWAYS.
               You are being silly. I am always learning.

THE MASTER SIGNS

COMMUNICATE

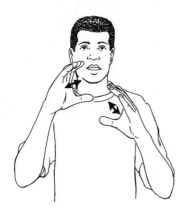

HEARING

FINALLY (while signing, mouth the sound, "Pah!")

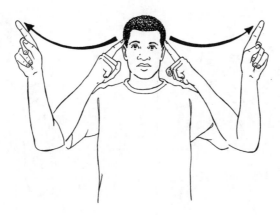

HOW

INTERPRET

THE MASTER SIGNS

INTERPRETER

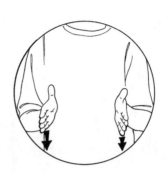

SILLY

THERE

WHO

WOMAN

WHAT'S IN THE SIGNS (NOTES ABOUT THE GRAMMAR)

1. USE OF THE SIGN FINALLY

The sign for FINALLY can be used alone to mean "It's about time" or "It finally happened" or some other close approximation to these meanings. It can also be used after an action to show that the action has finally taken place. It typically follows the action to which it is referring:

TEACHER SHOW-UP, FINALLY!

The sign FINALLY is often made with the signer mouthing the expression "Pah!"

2. RULE #5. INFORMATION-SEEKING QUESTIONS

The signer describes the topic and then signs the wh-question.

Topic	Wh-question
WOMAN THERE	WHO SHE?
INTERPRETER,	DO-what?

3. RULE #6. PRONOMINALIZATION

When a person is present, pronouns can be signed by directly pointing to that person. This pointing behavior is represented by the sign THERE. In the dialogue, the Deaf teacher and the interpreter are visible to the two signers. Therefore, to talk about the woman interpreter, the signer uses the sign THERE to point directly at her. Because the woman is now placed in the signing space, the signer can point to this place when referring to the woman with the pronoun SHE. In the following two sentences:

WOMAN THERE, WHO SHE?
WOMAN THERE, SHE INTERPRETER.

the signs THERE and SHE are made in exactly the same manner.

4. RULE #7. RHETORICAL QUESTIONS

In the rhetorical question

DEAF HEARING COMMUNICATE HOW? INTERPRETER INTERPRET.

HOW is not directly translated into English. Rather, it is translated to the conjunction *because*. One translation of this sentence is "Deaf and hearing people communicate because an interpreter interprets." When signing HOW, (1) *the head tilts forward* and (2) *the eyebrows are raised* because the question is a rhetorical one.

5. SILLY YOU

The translation of SILLY YOU is "You are being silly." It can be used with other phrases or by itself. The face should relay the feelings of the signer who is signing this phrase.

6. TEMPORAL ASPECT: PROGRESSIVE FORM OF A VERB

The progressive form of some verbs can be indicated by repeating the sign. This repetition is indicated by the plus sign (+) placed after the sign. Thus, we have the following:

progressive form:	LEARN+
translation:	learning

WHAT'S IN A SIGN (NOTES ABOUT VOCABULARY)

1. FINALLY

A nonmanual signal that often accompanies the sign FINALLY is *a voiceless expression of the syllable "Pah" with the mouth held open for a few seconds while the final position of the sign is also held.* This signal along with holding the hands in the final position of the sign helps to emphasize the relief that a person feels when something has finally taken place.

2. HEARING

The sign for HEARING refers to a hearing person. This sign is not used to refer to the act of hearing. This sign is also used for SAY and SPEAK. The connection in the meaning of the sign stems from the fact that a hearing person normally speaks, which distinguishes him or her from a deaf person, who normally uses sign language.

3. INTERPRET/INTERPRETER

Some verbs can be made into a noun by adding the AGENT-sign at the end of the verb sign. Thus, INTERPRET + AGENT-sign = INTERPRETER.

4. OH-I-see

The sign for OH-I-see can be translated to "Oh, I see what you mean," "I get it," "Now I understand," and other close approximations to these meanings. It is often used to indicate to another signer that someone is following or understanding what's being said. A nonmanual signal that is suitable to this sign is to (1) *tilt the head back slightly* and (2) *raise the eyebrows slightly.*

5. ASL SYNONYMS

Some signs can be used to mean other things.

Sign:	HEARING
Also used for:	PRONOUNCE, SAY, SPEAK

PRACTICE ACTIVITIES

1. MODEL FOR RULES #5. INFORMATION-SEEKING QUESTIONS AND #6. PRONOMINALIZATION

Signer A: 1. Describe the topic of the question;
             2. ask a wh-question using the sign WHO.

             Topic: WOMAN THERE,
             Question: WHO SHE?

Signer B: 1. Respond to the question by indicating the subject (you must select an imaginary place in the signing space when signing THERE);
             2. describe the subject.

             Subject: WOMAN THERE,
             Identity: SHE INTERPRETER.

Practice

Signer A: WOMAN THERE, WHO SHE?
Signer B: WOMAN THERE, SHE INTERPRETER.

2. MODEL FOR RULES #5. INFORMATION-SEEKING QUESTIONS AND #7. RHETORICAL QUESTIONS

Signer A: 1. Describe the subject of the sentence;
2. ask a question with the DO-what sign.

Subject:	INTERPRETER,
Question:	DO-what?

Signer B: 1. Begin the rhetorical question by describing a topic;
2. end the rhetorical question by asking a question with the sign HOW;
3. answer the question.

Topic:	DEAF HEARING COMMUNICATE
Question:	HOW?
Answer:	INTERPRETER INTERPRET.

Practice

Signer A: INTERPRETER, DO-what?

Signer B: DEAF HEARING COMMUNICATE HOW? INTERPRETER INTERPRET.

3. FURTHER PRACTICE SENTENCES

Signer A: OH-I-see, SHE INTERPRET.

Signer B: (nods head) LEARN+ YOU, FINALLY!

Signer A: SILLY YOU, ME LEARN ALWAYS.

4. MASTERY LEARNING

When you feel comfortable signing these phrases, practice signing the entire dialogue shown at the beginning of the lesson. Practice the master dialogue until you can sign the part of each character smoothly using the appropriate facial grammar.

5. FURTHER PRACTICE

The following dialogue is to help you practice fingerspelling. Substitute a fingerspelled name, occupation, or descriptive term for the italic word.

Signer A: WOMAN THERE, WHO SHE?

Signer B: WOMAN THERE, SHE *R-E-P-O-R-T-E-R*.

Signer A: SHE *R-E-P-O-R-T-E-R*?

Signer B: YES, SHE *R-E-P-O-R-T-E-R*.

LESSON 14   UNDERSTANDING COMMUNICATION

LANGUAGE GOALS

The student will
1. use Rules
   - #2. tense with time adverbs,
   - #5. information-seeking questions,
   - #6. pronominalization, and
   - #9. conditional sentences.
2. review the directional qualities of the sign PICK-UP to indicate the pronouns ME and YOU.
3. use ten new signs in a master dialogue.

THE MASTER DIALOGUE

1. Jenny: DEAF TEACHER THERE, SHE SIGN FINGERSPELL FAST.
   The Deaf teacher signs and fingerspells fast.

   Mike: SHE SIGN, YOU UNDERSTAND SHE?
   Do you understand her signing?

2. Jenny: NO, ME UNDERSTAND LITTLE-BIT.
   No, I just understand a little bit.

   Mike: SUPPOSE YOU SKILL SIGNER, YOU UNDERSTAND SHE?
   If you were a skilled signer, would you understand her?

3. Jenny: ME SKILL SIGNER, ME UNDERSTAND EASY.
   If I were a skilled signer, I would understand easily.

   Mike: SUPPOSE YOU INEPT SIGNER, DO-what YOU?
   What would you do if you were an inept signer?

4. Jenny: ME INEPT SIGNER, ME SIGN PRACTICE.
   If I were an inept signer, I would practice my signing.

   Mike: RIGHT! TOMORROW, DO-what YOU?
   Right! What are you doing tomorrow?

5. Jenny: TOMORROW, YOU ME SIGN PRACTICE.
   You and I will practice signing tomorrow.

   Mike: ALL-RIGHT. TOMORROW me-PICK-UP-you.
   Okay. I will pick you up tomorrow.

6. Jenny: GOOD. SEE YOU TOMORROW.
   That's good. I will see you tomorrow.

   Mike: BYE.
   Bye.

THE MASTER SIGNS

EASY

FINGERSPELL

FAST

THE MASTER SIGNS

INEPT

LITTLE-BIT

me-PICK-UP-you

THE MASTER SIGNS

SEE

SIGNER

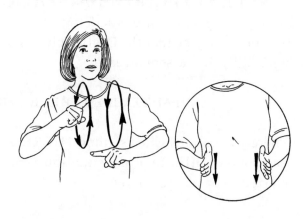

SKILL

UNDERSTAND

WHAT'S IN THE SIGNS (NOTES ABOUT THE GRAMMAR)

1. RULE #6. PRONOMINALIZATION

In this dialogue, you are practicing how to create a pronoun when the person is present. You must imagine that the Deaf teacher is present so that you can point to her when signing THERE in the sentence:

DEAF TEACHER THERE, SHE SIGN FINGERSPELL FAST.

Where you pointed when signing THERE is exactly the same place to point when signing the pronoun SHE. In a real situation, where you point will change if the person being referred to by pointing moves.

2. RULE #9. CONDITIONAL SENTENCES

The dialogue contains two sentences with conditional clauses with the sign SUPPOSE and two sentences where the nonmanual signals are the clue that the clause is conditional. The sign SUPPOSE is placed at the beginning of the sentence, followed by the condition, and then either a question or a comment related to the condition.

Conditional clause	Question/comment
SUPPOSE YOU SKILL SIGNER,	YOU UNDERSTAND SHE?
SUPPOSE YOU INEPT SIGNER,	DO-what YOU?
ME SKILL SIGNER,	ME UNDERSTAND EASY.
ME INEPT SIGNER,	ME SIGN PRACTICE.

When translating, the conditional clause can be placed at the beginning or the end of the sentence.

Translation: Conditional clause at the beginning of the sentence:

If you were a skilled signer, would you understand her?
If you were an inept signer, what would you do?
If I were a skilled signer, I would understand easily.
If I were an inept signer, I would practice signing.

Translation: Conditional clause at the end of the sentence:

Would you understand her if you were a skilled signer?
What would you do if you were an inept signer?
I would easily understand if I were a skilled signer.
I would practice signing if I were an inept signer.

3. RULE #5. INFORMATION-SEEKING QUESTIONS

When asking a wh-question using the DO-what sign, place the sign for the time adverb at the beginning of the sentence:

TOMORROW DO-what YOU?

A translation for this is "What are you doing tomorrow?"

4. RULE #2. TENSE WITH TIME ADVERBS

Placing a sign for indicating time at the beginning of a sentence is a common way for showing tense in ASL. Note the placement of the sign TOMORROW in each of the following sentences and the corresponding translation:

Sentence indicating time	Translation
TOMORROW DO-what YOU?	What are you doing tomorrow?
TOMORROW, YOU ME SIGN PRACTICE.	You and I will practice signing tomorrow.
TOMORROW me-PICK-UP-you.	I will pick you up tomorrow.

However, in common expressions of departure such as "See you later," "See you in a while," and "See you tomorrow," the sign for time comes at the end of the sentence:

| SEE YOU TOMORROW. | I will see you tomorrow. |

WHAT'S IN A SIGN (NOTES ABOUT VOCABULARY)

1. SHE/HER

When "her" is used as the objective form of she, it is signed in the same manner as SHE. This is the way it is signed in the dialogue. When it is used as the possessive form of SHE, then it is signed with an open hand. The English gloss for the objective form is SHE and for the possessive form it is HER.

2. INEPT

The sign for INEPT should be accompanied by a facial expression that emphasizes the awkwardness or lack of skill of the person being described. A common facial expression is to puff the cheeks while making the sign.

3. SEE

There are many signs to describe the different ways of looking at something. The hand-shape is typically the V handshape with the two fingers representing the eyes.

4. SIGNER

The sign for SIGNER is made by making the AGENT-sign after SIGN. The AGENT-sign changes the meaning of a verb to a noun.

5. PICK-UP

PICK-UP is a directional verb. In the phrase me-PICK-UP-you, the signer reaches toward the addressee and makes the sign.

6. ASL SYNONYMS

Some signs can be used to mean other things.

Sign	Also used for
FAST	QUICK, RAPID
FINGERSPELL	SPELL
INEPT	INCOMPETENT
LITTLE-BIT	TINY
SKILL	EXPERT, PROFICIENT
UNDERSTAND	COMPREHEND

PRACTICE ACTIVITIES

1. MODEL FOR RULES #3. SIMPLE YES/NO QUESTIONS AND #6. PRONOMINALIZATION

Signer A:
1. Describe the person;
2. sign THERE by pointing to the person or pointing ahead to the left side (or the right side) as if the person is present;
3. point again to the same spot to indicate the pronoun SHE;
4. make a comment about the person.

Description:	DEAF TEACHER
Point:	THERE (point ahead to the left side),
Pronoun:	SHE (point ahead to the left side)
Comment:	SIGN FINGERSPELL FAST.

Signer B:
1. Point in the same direction that Signer A did when placing the Deaf teacher in the signing space;
2. describe an action for the subject pronoun SHE;
3. ask a yes/no question.

Pronoun:	SHE (point in the same direction that Signer A did)
Action:	SIGN,
Question:	YOU UNDERSTAND SHE?

Signer A:
1. Respond to the question by signing NO;
2. make a follow-up comment to the negative response.

Negative:	NO,
Comment:	ME UNDERSTAND LITTLE-BIT.

Practice

Signer A: DEAF TEACHER THERE, SHE SIGN FINGERSPELL FAST.
Signer B: SHE SIGN, YOU UNDERSTAND SHE?
Signer A: NO, ME UNDERSTAND LITTLE-BIT.

2. MODEL FOR RULE #9. CONDITIONAL SENTENCES

Signer A:
1. Ask a question with a conditional clause (introduce the conditional clause by signing SUPPOSE);
2. state the condition;
3. make a question about the condition.

a. Introduce:	SUPPOSE
Condition:	YOU SKILL SIGNER,
Question:	YOU UNDERSTAND SHE?

b. Introduce:	SUPPOSE
Condition:	YOU INEPT SIGNER,
Question:	DO-what YOU?

Signer B:
1. State the condition;
2. make a comment about the condition.

a. Condition:	ME SKILL SIGNER,
Comment:	ME UNDERSTAND EASY.

b. Condition:	ME INEPT SIGNER,
Comment:	ME SIGN PRACTICE.

Practice

Signer A: SUPPOSE YOU SKILL SIGNER, YOU UNDERSTAND SHE?
Signer B: ME SKILL SIGNER, ME UNDERSTAND EASY.
Signer A: SUPPOSE YOU INEPT SIGNER, DO-what YOU?
Signer B: ME INEPT SIGNER, ME SIGN PRACTICE.

3. MODEL FOR RULE #2. TENSE WITH TIME ADVERBS

Signer A:
1. Indicate the time;
2. ask a DO-what question.

Time:	TOMORROW,
Question:	DO-what YOU?

Signer B:
1. Indicate the time;
2. make a comment.

Time:	TOMORROW,
Comment:	YOU ME SIGN PRACTICE.

Signer A:	1. Make a remark;	
	2. indicate the time;	
	3. make a comment.	

	Remark:	ALL-RIGHT.
	Time:	TOMORROW
	Comment:	me-PICK-UP-you.

Signer B:	1. Make a remark;	
	2. make a comment;	
	3. indicate the time.	

	Remark:	GOOD.
	Comment:	SEE YOU
	Time:	TOMORROW.

Practice

Signer A: TOMORROW, DO-what YOU?

Signer B: TOMORROW, YOU ME SIGN PRACTICE.

Signer A: ALL RIGHT. TOMORROW me-PICK-UP-you.

Signer B: GOOD. SEE YOU TOMORROW.

4. MASTERY LEARNING

When you feel comfortable signing these phrases, practice signing the entire dialogue shown at the beginning of the lesson. Practice the master dialogue until you can sign the part of each character smoothly while making the appropriate nonmanual signals.

5. FURTHER PRACTICE

Create a dialogue with conditional sentences similar to the ones shown in this lesson. Keep the sentences and dialogue short. Write the English gloss and the English translations for your ASL sentences. Practice signing the dialogue with a partner.

REVIEW OF LESSONS 8–14

Translate each of the following sentences to ASL, sign it, and then write the English gloss of the signs you used in your translation.

1. I don't care if you have finished studying.

2. It snowed yesterday.

3. I will meet you here tomorrow afternoon at one o'clock.

4. What are you doing if it snows tomorrow?

5. How do I contact you if I forget your name?

6. What's the name of the video?

7. Must I practice ASL?

8. He hasn't shown up for class yet.

9. The interpreter signs in ASL.

10. She's a skillful signer.

ANSWERS

Note that there may be other ways of translating these sentences than the ones shown here.

1. YOU STUDY FINISH? ME DON'T-CARE.

2. YESTERDAY, SNOW.

3. TOMORROW AFTERNOON, TIME ONE, me-MEET-you HERE.

4. SUPPOSE TOMORROW SNOW, DO-what YOU?

5. SUPPOSE YOUR NAME ME FORGET, me-CONTACT-you HOW?

6. VIDEO NAME?

7. ASL PRACTICE, ME MUST?

8. HE CLASS SHOW-UP, NOT-YET.

9. INTERPRETER SIGN HOW? ASL.

10. SIGN, SHE SKILL.

The Deaf Way

Technology and Other Adaptations: The Deaf Way

Many of the technological advances for the majority in our society have penalized Deaf people. This irony emerges most clearly in telecommunications. The invention of the telephone made it difficult for Deaf people to compete in the labor market. Radio became an important means of broadcasting information, whether commercial, political, governmental, or whatever, further cutting off Deaf people from the larger society surrounding them. Television did little to improve the situation, though it embraced the technology that could have (and to some extent does) include Deaf people. Talking pictures were a blow to the entertainment and education of Deaf people; they could enjoy the "silents" on a par with the rest of the audience. But Deaf people and their supporters have not passively accepted the status quo. They have taken steps to reduce the handicap the new technologies have imposed.

—Jerome Schein
At Home Among Strangers

HOLD THAT SIGN . . .

Only in recent years have there arisen technological developments that help rather than hamper the lives of Deaf people. I am reminded of this each time I stay in a hotel. In the past, when I had to wake up early in order to catch a flight home, I would ask the hotel staff to come into my room at a certain time and turn the light on. One morning, I happened to wake up thirty minutes after the time I had asked to be awaken. I noticed a sheet of paper that had been slipped under the door with the message, "It is 4:30 A.M., time to wake up. The hotel management." More amazing is the fact that I had heard the same story from other Deaf people and so I had warned the staff about the necessity of actually turning on the light. Today when I stay at a hotel, I set an alarm that vibrates under my pillow. I make calls on a TTY to confirm that my flight is leaving as scheduled. I answer the door or the telephone when a light flashes in the room. I hope the flashing light for the fire alarm never goes off. I then nod off to sleep watching a late-night movie that is fully captioned. All these little wonders are provided at no extra charge by the hotel. These little wonders are the subject of this chapter.

TELECOMMUNICATION TECHNOLOGY

TTY

Telecommunication technology had its first major impact on the Deaf community with the introduction of the *teletypewriter*. Known as a TTY, this device was invented in the 1960s by Robert Weitbrecht, a Deaf physicist and electrical engineer. The principle of the TTY is that signals are sent over a normal phone line that are translated to letters and symbols that can be read either off a scroll of paper and/or an LCD display. The TTY itself looks like a keyboard similar to that used with a computer but smaller. A regular telephone handset is rested on a coupler on top of the TTY. Pressing the keys produces a series of tones, which are the signals that are received and sent after a number has been dialed and a connection with another TTY is made. The simplicity of the TTY is in contrast to its value to Deaf people. It allows Deaf people to make their own calls rather than relying on the voice and ears of a nondeaf person. When Weitbrecht invented the TTY, he started off by manually assembling them and demonstrating to other people how to use them. Today, several companies make TTYs, which range from basic models with only an LCD readout to complex ones with built-in answering machines, memory, and automatic redial.

The creation of the TTY posed a problem; to be workable both parties must have a TTY. Thus, although it provides a certain degree of liberty over the phone lines, its use is still restricted by the number of people who own it. As a casual perusal of a phone book will show you, many state and government agencies have a dedicated TTY number, as do some private businesses such as airline offices and agencies that provide services to Deaf people. A Deaf person can use a TTY to call 911, and an increasing number of pay phones are now equipped with a TTY.

Still, the overall number of TTYs in use is minute compared to the number of telephones available. How does a Deaf person call the doctor's office, an air-conditioning repair service, a catalog company, or a nondeaf cousin? How would a Deaf person phone in their vote for the answer to a survey question that has appeared on television? The answer to all these questions is the *relay service*, which is also known as the message relay service. The Americans with Disabilities Act that passed in 1990 mandates that all states must provide a link between a person using a TTY and another person using a voice telephone. This link is called a relay service because it consists of a third party, the relay operator, who is able to receive or send messages by TTY or voice. For instance, a Deaf person wishing to reserve seats at a theater would call the relay service phone number and then give the phone number for the theater. The relay operator would then dial the number and type everything the person at the theater says and voice everything that the Deaf person types on the TTY.

Videophones are the next generation of telecommunication access for Deaf people. These systems have a camera mounted on top of a screen so that two people can communicate in signs. Although just in its infancy, it is a safe bet to say that it will not be long before it is a household item.

VRS

The current generation of telecommunication access for Deaf people involves the Video Relay System (VRS), which is a form of the Telecommunication Relay Service (TRS). These services assist people with hearing loss to communicate with the hearing community through video equipment and a TRS operator, thus enabling Deaf or hard-of-hearing people to communicate through visual and sign modes, rather than through a typed text. With this system, the Deaf person calls the TRS operator using a television or computer with a video camera device and Internet connection. The TRS operator makes the call to the hearing person and relays the conversation to each person in either sign language (to the Deaf person) or voice (to the hearing person). With the use of the VRS, Deaf people can communicate in their own language, rather than having to type their messages. Several service providers offer equipment free of charge for Deaf or hard-of-hearing people.

There are additional means for Deaf people to communicate face-to-face with other videophones, webcams, and Skype. Further, the latest technology allows video conferencing through some new cell phones, which enable Deaf people to communicate "on the go," rather than in their home, through the VRS or videophone.

VRI

Another form of communication technology is Video Remote Interpreting (VRI). This is used when a deaf person and a hearing person are in the same room with a TV and video equipment connected to a high speed Internet service. An interpreter from a remote call center appears on the TV and the deaf person signs to the interpreter as the interpreter voices the message to the hearing person. The key difference is that with a VRS call, the interpreter is interpreting a normal telephone call made by one party to the other. VRI is useful for emergencies or whenever in-person interpreter contact is not available.

The Captioned Telephone (CapTel) is a telephone with a screen that displays every word the other party says throughout the conversation. It is used by Deaf and hard-of-hearing persons who speak well. CapTel users can listen to the caller, and can also read written captions in the CapTel display window.

CAPTIONED FILMS AND TV

Another telecommunication technology device that has had a significant impact on the lives of Deaf people is *captioning* of television programs and videos. Captioning allows viewers to read the spoken dialogue on a television or a video. To read the captions, however, the captioning option on a television set must first be turned on, which is why this technology is often referred to as closed-captioning or closed-captions. In the past, a special decoder unit had to be attached to a television for the closed-captions to be made visible on the screen. In 1993, Congress passed the Television Decoder Circuitry Act, which requires all televisions with a screen thirteen inches or larger to have the capacity to display captioning. The captioning itself is usually done prior to being shown on television or placed on a video. Real-time captioning also occurs and is used with major sports programs and other live broadcasts. A number of companies are in the captioning business, and together they caption all prime-time network programs, many daytime and late-night programs including news, various sports programs, State of the Union addresses, major movies that come out on videos, and many other programs.

ALERTING DEVICES

Alerting devices make Deaf people aware of sounds that are in the environment. There are various types of alerting devices, and they all operate on the principle of making the occurrence of sounds visible (e.g., lights flashing) or tactile (e.g., vibration). The first and most popular types of alerting devices are those adaptations where lights flash when a doorbell or telephone rings, an alarm goes off, a baby cries, a dog barks, or some other sound signal occurs. The advancement of this technology is such that an entire house can be wired for Deaf people. This setup allows a Deaf person to control where in the house the lights will flash when, for example, the phone rings. Obviously, a light flashing in the living room is of no use to a person who is sleeping in an upstairs bedroom or is downstairs in the workshop. Schools for the Deaf and institutions such as Gallaudet University and the National Technical Institute for the Deaf have visible fire alarms throughout their campuses.

The alerting principle of a flashing light has been applied to tactile technology. Bed alarms that vibrate a gadget placed under a pillow are available. A tactile signal such as a vibration is especially useful for pagers. Another type of tactile signal is air blowing from a fan. This type of signal is used by deaf-blind people.

COMPUTER TECHNOLOGY

Deaf people are riding the wave of advances in computer technology. The major benefit they receive from this technology is the same that nondeaf people receive—convenience. Fax machines remove the need for using a TTY or a relay service. Correspondence via e-mail diminishes the necessity of using the telephone. Indeed, I rarely use a TTY anymore to contact Deaf people and anyone else who has an e-mail address. The Internet too provides greater access for Deaf people to reach out to one another. Simple and affordable video cameras allow people to send an online video of themselves. This is a boon to those people who wish to use ASL to converse with someone online. This technology still must improve before the online video is fast enough to transmit signing in a smooth, real-time manner; nevertheless, it is available. Another example of the value of the Internet is seen by the fact that the 1997 World Games for the Deaf in Copenhagen, Denmark, had its own website. This allowed Deaf people and others all over the world to get daily updates on medal standings and winnings in the various events. The value of this website is magnified by the fact that over 60 countries and 3,500 athletes participated in the Games.

SIGN LANGUAGE INTERPRETING

A sign language interpreter transmits messages from ASL to English and from English to ASL. To do this, interpreters must be fluent in both languages. They must also understand the culture of the speakers of both languages. Their work is indispensable to facilitating the interactions between Deaf and nondeaf people. Sign language interpreting just became a profession with the formation of the Registry of Interpreters for the Deaf in 1964. Since this time, the availability of interpreters has given Deaf people better access to communication in many places that nondeaf people have always taken for granted. Such places include public schools, training facilities for jobs, the workplace, medical and dental offices, courts of law, tours on cruise ships, national park lectures, and many more.

Sign language interpreting is an adaptation to a nondeaf world. Or, if we look at it from the Deaf perspective, it is an adaptation by nondeaf people that allows them access to the Deaf world. It is included in this chapter because the day is rapidly approaching when some interpreters will work without leaving the confines of their homes or offices. In fact, this is already happening on a small scale. For example, a Deaf person or an agency with a videophone dials an interpreter who also has one. The videophone transmits sounds in addition to videos. Thus, a Deaf and a nondeaf person sit in front of the videophone where the Deaf person signs to the camera and the nondeaf person speaks to a microphone. The interpreter at the other end of the line interprets what is being signed or spoken.

REAL-TIME REPORTING

The technology of court reporters is being used in classrooms and meetings to provide Deaf people with a transcription of all that is being said. The technology setup requires a stenographic machine, a laptop computer, and software to convert stenographic symbols to print on the screen. The real-time reporter types everything being said, and the Deaf person is able to read this on the computer screen. Modification of this setup includes using television monitors with the words being printed against the background of a video of the speaker, including that of the Deaf person when she or he is talking. A recent development called C-print has been created where a regular keyboard on a laptop can be used instead of a stenographic machine. Whatever the setup, real-time has given Deaf people another option for accessing spoken information that can be used in place of sign language interpreters or alongside of them.

TELEPHONE TECHNOLOGIES

Technology provided at least a partial solution to the frequent and familiar complaints about people on cell phones talking too loudly and their use at inappropriate times. Since necessity is the mother of invention, industry found a solution in the form of text messaging and instant messaging to use when it is inconvenient to talk on the phone. Serendipitously, they have provided an invaluable tool for the deaf and a silent, convenient, and more confidential means of communication for all. Short Message Service (SMS) or text messaging is similar to having e-mail on your mobile phone. Shortly after text messaging ("texting") became available in the late 1990s, it spread through the Deaf community very quickly and has become a way of life for most Deaf members. Texting has become one of the primary means of convenient and fast communication, opening up communication access for socializing, conducting business, emergencies, and so on, for Deaf and hard-of-hearing people. Also available is a service that provides text-based relay calls from the Deaf person's cell phone to a relay operator, who then voices the text to a hearing person.

Keeping in touch with peers is of primary importance to Deaf and hearing adolescents; therefore having a "cell" has become a tool for socialization. Technology that may have been developed for a particular reason has in fact served as a means of enhancing the lives of many Deaf individuals. With this device a Deaf person can make, break, or change appointments or even conduct personal business at any time without the intervention of an interpreter or other third party. Similarly, videophones yield visual conversations for those wishing to communicate in sign language. These technologies allow one to see who's available to exchange messages whenever and wherever they happen to be.

OTHER TECHNOLOGIES

Assistive listening devices (ALD) amplify sounds and include hearing aids, telephone amplifiers, and infrared transmitters and FM transmitters used to amplify sounds without interference from extraneous environmental noise. Although they are a part of Deaf culture, they are not crucial to a person functioning or socializing in the Deaf community. Their value stems only from the access to sounds that they provide some Deaf people wherever they might be. What is important to know about ALD is that they do not make a Deaf person hear normally in a way that eyeglasses help many people see normally. Hearing aids help some people hear some sounds but the benefit is highly individual and most Deaf people do not use them. The major group of people who use ALD are hard-of-hearing people and late-deafened adults.

SIGNING ONLINE

Signing Online (*www.signingonline.com*) is a series of four courses on the Web teaching basic skills and signs needed to become fluent in ASL.

Stewart and Winn built this innovative instructional program for learning how to sign using advanced computer video technology. The student is able to review videos as often as needed, which is one of the key features of the entire program. Lessons are accompanied by notes about Deaf culture and the lives of Deaf and hard-of-hearing people. Upon completion the student will have learned over 800 signs and will know how to put them together to carry on meaningful conversations in ASL.

Originally created for people who had little or no time to attend classes or with little or no access to instructors, the courses are rapidly being incorporated into high school and college curriculums while still available as an individual/self-paced learning option.

COCHLEAR IMPLANTS

A cochlear implant is an electronic device that is implanted into a person's head to deliver a sensation of hearing for profoundly Deaf persons who do not benefit from regular high-powered hearing aids.

The first cochlear implant system was created in the 1970s. Today thousands of people in the world use cochlear implants. Although originally intended for late-deafened adults, cochlear implantation rates continue to explode and infants as young as six months old are now using implants. Unlike hearing aids and assistive listening devices that amplify sounds, a cochlear implant does not make sounds louder. Instead, it directly stimulates the surviving auditory nerve fibers in the cochlea enabling the individual to perceive sound. The device consists of a receiver, a thin cord, and a transmitting coil that acts like the hair cells of the cochlear. The speech processor of the implant codes the sounds picked up from the environment by a microphone worn outside the body. A cochlear implant does not restore normal hearing; it provides an artificial form of hearing. The sounds people with cochlear implants hear can be quite different from sounds they might *remember* hearing before becoming Deaf.

The following websites will provide you with additional information about cochlear implants

National Institute for Deafness and Other Communication Disorders
http://www.nidcd.nih.gov/health/hearing/coch.asp

U.S. Department of Health and Human Services: Food and Drug Administration
http://www.fda.gov/MedicalDevices/ProductsandMedicalProcedures/ ImplantsandProsthetics/CochlearImplants/default.htm

Gallaudet University: Cochlear Implant Information Center
http://clerccenter.gallaudet.edu/Clerc_Center/Information_and_Resources/
Cochlear Implant_Education_Center.html

American Speech, Language and Hearing Association
http://www.asha.org/public/hearing/treatment/cochlearimplant.htm

University of Texas-Dallas: Cochlear Implant Lab
http://www.utdallas.edu/~loizou/cimplants/tutorial/

U.S. National Library of Medicine: National Institute of Health
http://www.nlm.nih.gov/medlineplus/cochlearimplants.html

It's All Relative

8

LESSON 15   OPPOSITES

VOCABULARY GOALS

The student will
1.   use Rules   #1. topic/comment and
                      #5. information-seeking questions.
2.   use twenty-one pairs of opposites to describe people, places, and courses.

THE MASTER DIALOGUE

DIALOGUE A—MODEL FOR DESCRIBING PEOPLE

Signer A: YOUR TEACHER, DEAF HEARING WHICH?
              Is your teacher deaf or hearing?

Signer B: MY TEACHER, DEAF.
              My teacher is deaf.

MASTER SIGNS: OPPOSITES FOR DESCRIBING PEOPLE

DEAF

HEARING

SHORT-1

TALL

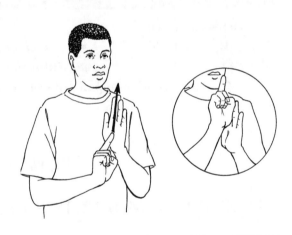

THIN

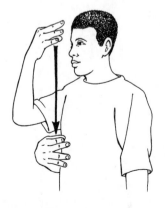

THICK

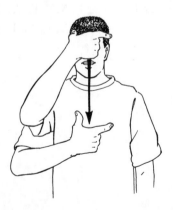

MASTER SIGNS: OPPOSITES FOR DESCRIBING PEOPLE

YOUNG

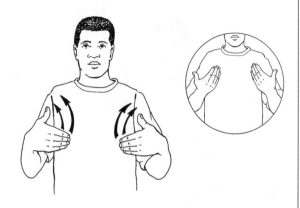

OLD

BEAUTIFUL

UGLY

SKILLED

INEPT

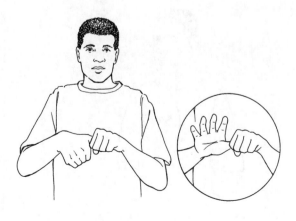

MASTER SIGNS: OPPOSITES FOR DESCRIBING PEOPLE

RICH

POOR

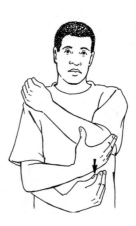

KIND

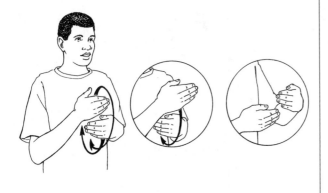

MEAN

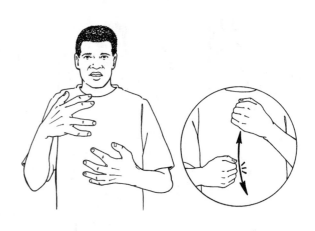

POLITE

RUDE

MASTER SIGNS: OPPOSITES FOR DESCRIBING PEOPLE

STRONG

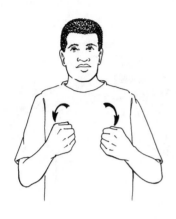

WEAK

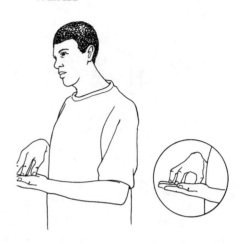

DIALOGUE B—MODEL FOR DESCRIBING A ROOM

Signer A: YOUR ROOM, SMALL LARGE WHICH?
             Is your room small or large?

Signer B: MY ROOM, LARGE.
             My room is large.

MASTER SIGNS: OPPOSITES FOR DESCRIBING A ROOM

SMALL

LARGE

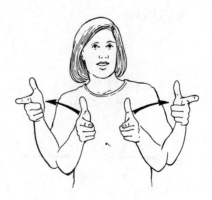

MASTER SIGNS: OPPOSITES FOR DESCRIBING A ROOM

QUIET

NOISY

EMPTY

FULL

NARROW

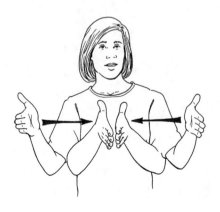

WIDE

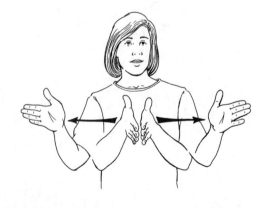

MASTER SIGNS: OPPOSITES FOR DESCRIBING A ROOM

BRIGHT

DARK

CLEAN

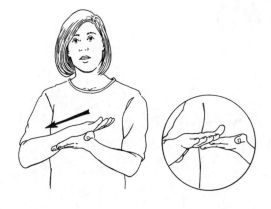

DIRTY

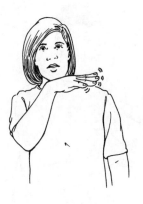

DIALOGUE C—MODEL FOR DESCRIBING A COURSE

Signer A: YOUR ASL COURSE, FASCINATING DULL WHICH?
             Is your ASL course fascinating or dull?

Signer B: MY ASL COURSE, FASCINATING.
             My ASL course is fascinating.

MASTER SIGNS: OPPOSITES FOR DESCRIBING A COURSE

EASY

DIFFICULT

SLOW

FAST

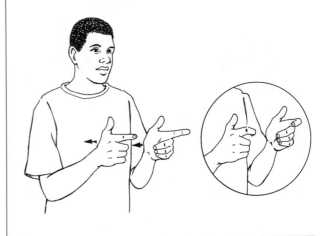

IMPORTANT

WORTHLESS

MASTER SIGNS: OPPOSITES FOR DESCRIBING A COURSE

SHORT-2

LONG

FASCINATING

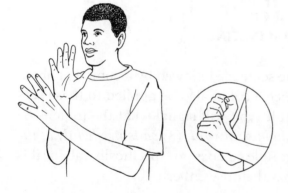

DULL

WHAT'S IN THE SIGNS (NOTES ABOUT THE GRAMMAR)

1. RULE #5. INFORMATION-SEEKING QUESTIONS

The sign WHICH can be used to present a choice of answers to a question. It is particularly helpful when the choice involves opposites as in the following sentences:

YOUR TEACHER, DEAF HEARING WHICH?

YOUR CLASS ROOM, SMALL LARGE WHICH?

YOUR ASL COURSE, FASCINATING DULL WHICH?

The subject is first identified, followed by the descriptive terms (the adjectives), and then the sign WHICH.

2. RULE #1. TOPIC/COMMENT

You can describe things in the following manner:

MY TEACHER, DEAF.

MY ROOM, LARGE.

MY ASL COURSE, FASCINATING.

The topic or the subject is at the beginning of the sentence followed by a comment about it. Note that Rule #8 (ordering of simple sentences) could also be applied to these sentences. However, by using the topic/comment rule, you will signal what the topic is by (1) *raising the eyebrows* and (2) *tilting the head slightly forward*, (3) *pausing slightly at the end of the topic*, and then (4) *signing the comment*. Rule #8 does not specifically call for this use of nonmanual signals, although it does not bar their use either.

WHAT'S IN A SIGN (NOTES ABOUT VOCABULARY)

1. SHORT-1

The meaning of the SHORT-1 sign refers to a physical characteristic of something—height.

2. SHORT-2

The sign for SHORT-2 refers to the length of time and cannot be used interchangeably with the sign SHORT-1.

3. ASL SYNONYMS
Some signs can be used to mean other things.

Sign	Also used for
SHORT-1	DIMINUTIVE, LITTLE, SMALL
THIN	GAUNT, LEAN, LANK, SKINNY, SLIM
YOUNG	YOUTH
OLD	AGE
BEAUTIFUL	GORGEOUS, HANDSOME, LOVELY, PRETTY
SKILLED	ADEPT, COMPETENT, EXPERT, PROFICIENT
INEPT	INEXPERIENCED
RICH	AFFLUENT, FORTUNE, WEALTH, WEALTHY
POOR	POVERTY
MEAN	CRUEL
KIND	BENEVOLENT, GENEROUS, HUMANE
POLITE	COURTEOUS, COURTESY, GENTLE, MANNERS
RUDE	CURT, DISCOURTEOUS, IMPOLITE, MEAN
STRONG	STRENGTH, POWERFUL
SMALL	LITTLE, MINIATURE, TINY
LARGE	BIG, GIGANTIC, HUGE, IMMENSE, MASSIVE
QUIET	CALM, SERENE, SILENT, TRANQUIL
NOISY	LOUD
EMPTY	AVAILABLE, BARE, NAKED, NUDE, VACANT
WIDE	BROAD
BRIGHT	BRILLIANT, CLEAR
CLEAN	NICE
DIRTY	FILTHY, POLLUTED
EASY	EFFORTLESS, SIMPLE
DIFFICULT	HARD
FAST	QUICK, RAPID, SWIFT

Sign	Also used for
IMPORTANT	CRITICAL, CRUCIAL, VALID, VALUABLE, WORTHWHILE, WORTHY
WORTHLESS	IRRELEVANT, POINTLESS, USELESS
SHORT-2	BRIEF, BREVITY, FLEETING, TEMPORARY
FASCINATING	APPEALING, ATTRACTIVE
DULL	BORING, TEDIOUS, TIRESOME

PRACTICE ACTIVITIES

1. MASTERY LEARNING

Practice asking and answering questions by substituting signs from the list of opposites in the model shown in the master dialogue. Be sure to use the correct nonmanual signals associated with asking a wh-question and forming a topic/comment sentence.

2. FURTHER PRACTICE

Write ten sentences that use the sign WHICH to ask a question. Sign these sentences to a partner who must then answer them.

LESSON 16   RELATIONS AND PLACES

LANGUAGE GOALS

The student will

1. use Rules   #1. topic/comment,
   - #3. simple yes/no questions,
   - #5. information-seeking questions,
   - #6. pronominalization, and
   - #8. ordering of simple sentences.
2. use the directional qualities of the sign TEACH to indicate the subject and object of a sentence.
3. use eight new signs in a master dialogue.

THE MASTER DIALOGUE

1. **Kate:** YOU STUDENT YOU?
   Are you a student?
   Bob: YES, ME STUDENT. YOUR CLASS, ME TAKE-UP.
   Yes, I am a student. I am taking your class.

2. **Kate:** NAME YOU?
   What is your name?
   Bob: ME NAME, B-O-B.
   My name is BOB.

3. **Kate:** YOU LEARN ASL HOW?
   How did you learn ASL?
   Bob: MY BROTHER point-left, HE DEAF. ME SMALL, he-TEACH-me.
   My brother's deaf and he taught me when I was little.

4. **Kate:** YOUR BROTHER LIVE WHERE?
   Where does your brother live?
   Bob: HE LIVE BOSTON.
   He lives in Boston.

5. **Kate:** YOUR BROTHER LIVE BOSTON?
   Your brother lives in Boston?
   Bob: YES, HE ENGINEER.
   Yes, he's an engineer.

6. **Kate:** MY BROTHER, ENGINEER ALSO.
   My brother is an engineer, too.
   Bob: NEAT!
   Hey, that's neat!

THE MASTER SIGNS

ALSO

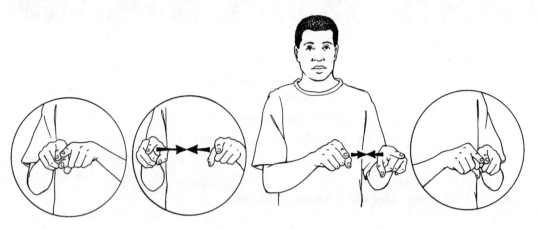

BOSTON

BROTHER

ENGINEER

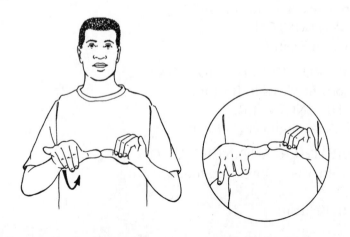

THE MASTER SIGNS

he-TEACH-me

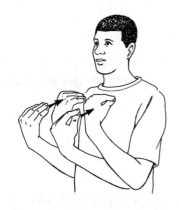

LIVE

NEAT, COOL

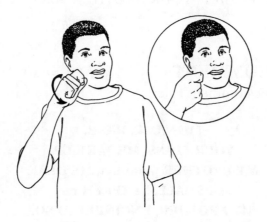

SMALL

WHAT'S IN THE SIGNS (NOTES ABOUT THE GRAMMAR)

1. RULE #3. SIMPLE YES/NO QUESTIONS

   a. YOU STUDENT YOU?
   b. YOUR BROTHER LIVE BOSTON?

The sign YOU is often used to ask a simple yes/no question as shown in question a. The question "Are you a student?" could also be asked as follows:

YOU STUDENT?

STUDENT YOU?

In both examples, the nonmanual signals for asking a yes/no question will typically accompany the last sign. However, with a short sentence a signer could send the proper nonmanual signals throughout the sentence.

In question b, a topic is described, YOUR BROTHER, followed by a question about the topic, LIVE BOSTON?

2. RULE #1. TOPIC/COMMENT

Five sentences use the topic/comment rule:

ME NAME, B-O-B.

YOUR CLASS, ME TAKE-UP.

MY BROTHER point left, HE DEAF.

ME SMALL, he-TEACH-me.

MY BROTHER, ENGINEER ALSO.

3. RULE #5. INFORMATION-SEEKING QUESTIONS

When asking a wh-question, you set up the topic and then use the wh-sign.

Topic	Wh-sign
YOU LEARN ASL	HOW?
YOUR BROTHER LIVE	WHERE?

4. RULE #6. PRONOMINALIZATION

In the sentence

MY BROTHER point-left, HE DEAF.

where do you point to sign HE? You point to the left because that is where BROTHER was placed in the signing space.

5. RULE #8. ORDERING OF SIMPLE SENTENCES

The sentences

HE LIVE BOSTON.

HE ENGINEER.

are examples of a simple sentence structure.

WHAT'S IN A SIGN (NOTES ABOUT VOCABULARY)

1. BROTHER

An older sign for brother and one that is still used in many places is a compound sign where the signs BOY and SAME are combined. The illustration for BROTHER shown in this lesson is a more common sign. To illustrate the difference between the two types of signs, the next lesson shows the sign SISTER being made by signing GIRL and SAME. You should, however, select one handshape for signing BROTHER and SISTER and use it consistently.

2. LIVE

These are two common signs for LIVE. In this book illustration the sign is made with double A handshapes. The sign is also made with double L handshapes. The use of the L handshape to form a sign is called *initialization* because the handshape is determined by the initial letter of the sign. Initialization is a linguistic device that is sometimes used to help clarify the intended meaning of a sign.

3. NEAT

The NEAT sign is used to mean one of the following or something similar: "That's neat," "That's cool," and "That's super." It is not to be used to mean tidy (e.g., "a neat room"), simple and elegant (e.g., "a neat outfit"), or brief (e.g., "a neat response").

4. BOSTON

Many name signs for cities will use the handshape for the initial letter of the city's name.

5. SMALL

The sign SMALL is used in the sense of a young child. The signer is indicating the height of a child rather than the size of an object.

6. he-TEACH-me

TEACH is a directional verb. The sign originates in the location where the pronoun HE is placed in the signing space. The fingertips are turned toward the signer to indicate whom is being taught.

7. ASL SYNONYMS

Some signs can be used to mean other things.

Sign	Also used for
ALSO	TOO
ENGINEER	DRAFTING, MEASURE
LIVE	ADDRESS
TEACH	EDUCATE, EDUCATION, INSTRUCT, INSTRUCTION

PRACTICE ACTIVITIES

1. MODEL FOR RULES #1. TOPIC/COMMENT AND #3. SIMPLE YES/NO QUESTIONS

Signer A: 1. Describe the topic;
2. ask the question using the sign YOU.

Topic: YOU STUDENT
Question: YOU?

Signer B: 1. Respond to the question with the sign YES;
2. repeat the topic;
3. describe a topic;
4. make a comment about the topic.

Response:	YES,
Topic:	ME STUDENT.
Topic:	YOUR CLASS,
Comment:	ME TAKE-UP.

Practice

Signer A: YOU STUDENT YOU?

Signer B: YES, ME STUDENT. YOUR CLASS, ME TAKE-UP.

2. MODEL FOR ASKING FOR THE NAME OF SOMEONE

Signer A: 1. Sign the topic;

2. sign the pronoun YOU.

Topic:	NAME
Pronoun:	YOU?

Signer B: 1. Repeat the topic;

2. fingerspell your name.

Topic:	ME NAME,
Name:	B-O-B.

Practice

Signer A: NAME YOU?

Signer B: ME NAME, B-O-B.

3. MODEL FOR RULES #1. TOPIC/COMMENT, #5. INFORMATION-SEEKING QUESTIONS, AND #6. PRONOMINALIZATION

a. HOW

Signer A: 1. Describe the topic;

2. ask a question using the sign HOW.

Topic:	YOU LEARN ASL
Question:	HOW?

Signer B:	1. Describe the topic;
	2. make a comment about the topic.

Topic:	MY BROTHER point-left,
Comment:	HE DEAF.

Topic:	ME SMALL,
Comment:	he-TEACH-me.

Practice

Signer A: YOU LEARN ASL HOW?
Signer B: MY BROTHER, HE DEAF. ME SMALL, he-TEACH-me.

b. WHERE

Signer A:	1. Describe the topic;
	2. ask a wh-question with the sign WHERE.

Topic:	YOUR BROTHER LIVE
Comment:	WHERE?

Signer B:	1. Repeat the topic;
	2. name the place where the person lives.

Topic:	HE LIVE
City:	BOSTON.

Practice

Signer A: YOUR BROTHER LIVE WHERE?
Signer B: HE LIVE BOSTON.

4. MODEL FOR RULES #1. TOPIC/COMMENT AND #3. SIMPLE YES/NO QUESTIONS

Signer A:	1. Describe the topic;
	2. ask a yes/no question about the topic.

Topic:	YOUR BROTHER
Question:	LIVE BOSTON?

Signer B:	1. Respond affirmatively to the yes/no question,
	2. describe the subject.

Response:	YES,
Description:	HE ENGINEER.

Signer A:	1. Describe the topic;
	2. make a comment about the topic.

	Topic:	MY BROTHER,
	Comment:	ENGINEER ALSO.

Signer B:	1. Make a remark relating to what Signer B has just said.

	Remark:	NEAT!

Practice

Signer A: YOUR BROTHER LIVE BOSTON?
Signer B: YES, HE ENGINEER.
Signer A: MY BROTHER, ENGINEER ALSO.
Signer B: NEAT!

5. MASTERY LEARNING

When you feel comfortable signing these phrases, practice signing the entire dialogue shown at the beginning of the lesson. Practice the master dialogue until you can sign the part of each character smoothly while using the appropriate nonmanual signals.

6. FURTHER PRACTICE

With a partner, place two people in your signing space and describe them using signs learned in Lesson 15. Then ask a question about a person you have just described and see if your partner can answer it. For example,

Signer A:	MY BROTHER point-left, MY TEACHER point-right.
	HE-point-left LITTLE, SHE-point-right GENEROUS.
	SHE-point-right WHAT?
Signer B:	SHE-point-left GENEROUS.
Signer A:	LITTLE WHO?
Signer B:	HE-point-right LITTLE.

When signer B answers the question, he or she must use the same location that Signer A used to establish the people in the signing space. For example, if both signers are facing each other, then when Signer A points to his or her right to indicate the teacher, Signer B must point to his or her left in order to refer to this teacher. That is, both signers point to the same spot in space.

LESSON 17   RELATIONS, CITIES, AND OCCUPATIONS

VOCABULARY GOALS

The student will
1. learn thirteen new signs that describe family relations.
2. learn twenty-one new name signs for cities.
3. learn thirteen new signs for occupations.

PRACTICE ACTIVITIES

1. MASTERY LEARNING

The master dialogue for this lesson is taken from Lesson 16 except the sign for a family relation (BROTHER), a city (BOSTON), and occupation (ENGINEER) are replaced with the signs for other family relations, cities, and occupations. Proceed slowly through each sentence and each new sign. The purpose of this exercise is to use a sentence structure that will allow you to become familiar with new signs for family relations, cities, and occupations. There are no new ASL sentence structures introduced in the dialogue. Do not try to learn all the signs listed here in a single day. Select a few to learn every day until you have gone through all the lists. You can also refer to this lesson on a need-to-know basis, especially for signs for cities that you do not use in your daily conversations. Do practice the sentences until you feel comfortable signing them. As always, remember to use your non-manual signals.

Family Relations

1. Reb: YOU LEARN ASL HOW?
   Rachel: MY SISTER, SHE DEAF. ME SMALL, she-TEACH-me.

2. Reb: YOUR SISTER LIVE WHERE?
   Rachel: SHE LIVE BOSTON.

3. Reb: YOUR SISTER LIVE BOSTON?
   Rachel: YES, SHE ENGINEER.

4. Reb: MY SISTER, ENGINEER TOO.

THE MASTER SIGNS

AUNT

COUSIN

FATHER

GRANDFATHER

GRANDMOTHER

MOTHER

THE MASTER SIGNS

WIFE

HUSBAND

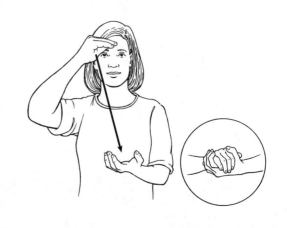

NEPHEW

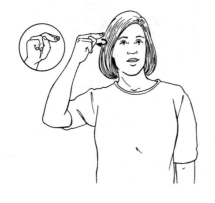

NIECE

THE MASTER SIGNS

RELATIVES

SISTER	UNCLE

may also be made with L-handshapes
as in BROTHER (page 25)

Cities

1.   Reb: YOUR SISTER LIVE WHERE?
     Rachel: SHE LIVE CHICAGO.

2.   Reb: YOUR SISTER LIVE CHICAGO?
     Rachel: YES, SHE ENGINEER.

THE MASTER SIGNS

ATLANTA

BALTIMORE

CHICAGO

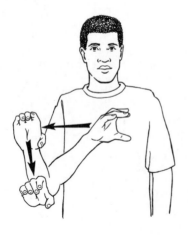

CITY

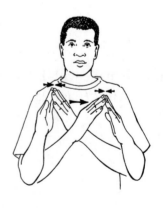

THE MASTER SIGNS

DETROIT

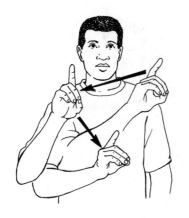

EDMONTON

HOUSTON

LOS-ANGELES

MIAMI

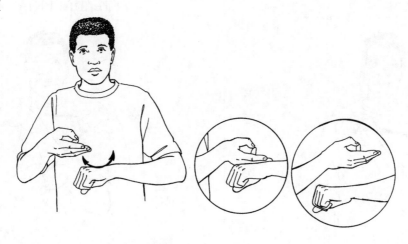

THE MASTER SIGNS

MONTREAL

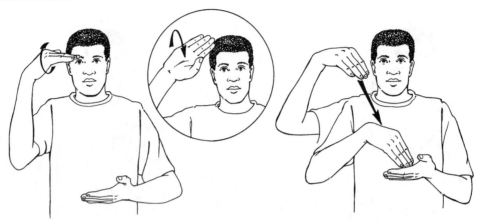

NEW-ORLEANS

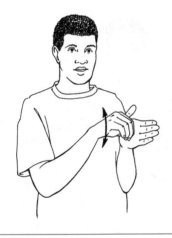

NEW-YORK

OTTAWA

PHILADELPHIA

THE MASTER SIGNS

PITTSBURGH

ROCHESTER

SAN-FRANCISCO

SEATTLE

TORONTO

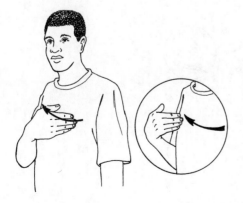

VANCOUVER

THE MASTER SIGNS

WASHINGTON, D.C.

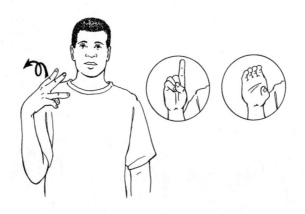

Occupations

1.   Reb: YOUR SISTER LIVE CHICAGO?
     Rachel: YES, SHE PLUMBER.
     Reb: MY SISTER, PLUMBER ALSO.

THE MASTER SIGNS

CARPENTER

THE MASTER SIGNS

COMPUTER-ANALYST

DOCTOR

NURSE

FARMER

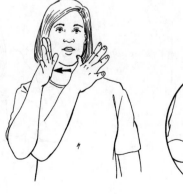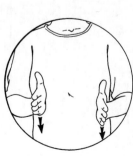

THE MASTER SIGNS

JANITOR

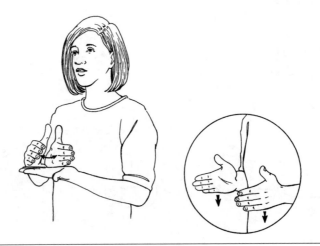

LAWYER

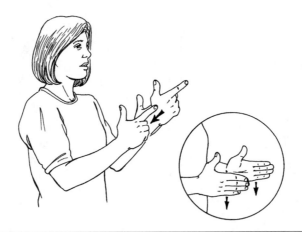

OCCUPATION

PILOT

THE MASTER SIGNS

PLUMBER/MECHANIC

POLICE-OFFICER

SCIENTIST

SECRETARY

2. FURTHER PRACTICE

Create a dialogue that uses signs from Lessons 15–17. In your dialogue, have one person ask another person about his or her relatives, their occupations, and where they live.

Body- and Gaze-Shifting— Personalizing the Message

Another common device that is used in ASL to show "who does what" is *body and gaze shifting.* For example, the Signer may move his/her body to the left or to the right "into" a location that represents someone. While "in" that location, everything the Signer says or does reflects what that person says or does. When this kind of body shifting into a location (and looking *from* that location) is used, the Signer also tends to take on other affective or characteristic traits of the person (e.g., smiling or sighing when signing LOVE). This is because the message has become "personalized." The Signer has essentially assumed the role of that person and is signing as if s/he were that person.

—CHARLOTTE BAKER AND DENNIS COKELY
American Sign Language

HOLD THAT SIGN . . .

The imagination is a great asset in ASL. To become someone else while signing, you must be able to create an image in your mind of what it is like to be this person. If you are repeating something that this person has said, then you try to say it the way it was originally said. Even though repeating something might just mean repeating the signs, there are times when you will want to mimic the body movements and facial expressions that accompanied the original message. In this way, you personalize the message—you let people know that this is how someone else acted.

IT ALL STARTS WITH AN IMAGE

Body- and gaze-shifting help indicate "what was said" and "who said it" or "what was done" and "who did it." This is accomplished through movement on the horizontal or vertical plane and the direction of a signer's gaze. The basic principle of this technique is that what a signer says or does is a direct reflection of what someone else has said or done. By shifting the body into a particular position, a signer becomes a certain person where the identity of this person is derived from the context of the conversation. To do this you must have an image of what a person said and how this person acted. Read the following and imagine how you might sign it:

**LONG-AGO ME CHILD, MY MOTHER she-SCOLD-me WHY?
ME WATCH TV TOO-MUCH.
SHE SAY, "YOU TV WATCH++ YOUR EYES DETERIORATE."
ME LISTEN, REFUSE.**

One way of signing this story is to turn the shoulders to the right and gaze slightly upward while signing she-SCOLD-me. You look upward because you have become the child you once were, and you are portraying your mother as being taller than you at that time. Because your mother was taller, you sign she-SCOLD-me with your index finger coming down toward your head as if your mother were shaking her finger at you. When you looked to the right, you placed your mother in the right side of your signing space. Therefore, you turn the shoulders to the left (because you are to the left of her in the signing space) and gaze slightly downward (because your mother was taller than you when you were a child) when saying what your mother said. To sign the last phrase, you sign LISTEN while leaning your head slightly to the right to indicate to whom you were listening (your mother). Finally, to demonstrate your act of defiance, you look to the left and sign REFUSE. You have now personalized the story—you assumed the role of yourself as a child and of your mother during that time.

THE FOUR TECHNIQUES OF BODY- AND GAZE-SHIFTING

There are four basic techniques that will help you master the art of shifting your body and eyes when you are personalizing your signing.

1. MOVEMENT ALONG THE HORIZONTAL PLANE

Movement to the right or left along the horizontal plane typically identifies "who" is talking. This movement can be made by

a. turning the shoulders and head to the right or left,
b. turning the head in either direction,
c. turning the whole body to the right or left, or
d. gazing to the right or left.

In the following story, the image is of a woman who is looking at a doctor holding a needle and becomes dizzy:

> **WOMAN point-left, she-LOOK-right DOCTOR NEEDLE HOLD.**
> **SHE DIZZY.**

To sign this story, you turn the shoulder to the right while signing she-LOOK-right DOCTOR NEEDLE HOLD because the woman has been placed in the left side of the signing space. You return to a normal pose with eye contact with the addressee when signing the rest of the sentence. To top off this story, you should also look dizzy when signing DIZZY.

2. MOVEMENT ALONG THE VERTICAL PLANE

Movement of the head and gazing up and down illustrate the different height or status of a person, and the different height of an object.

> **WOMAN point-left, she-LOOK-up BUILDING TALL.**
> **SHE DIZZY.**

This story is similar to the previous one except this time instead of looking at a doctor holding a needle, the woman is looking up at a tall building. To sign this, you should look to the right and gaze upward while signing she-LOOK-up BUILDING TALL. You should return to a normal signing position and look at the addressee when signing SHE DIZZY.

In the story about the mother and child who watched too much TV, we saw that the signer would look down when saying what his mother had said to him as a child. The signer looked down to convey the image of a mother looking down at her shorter child.

3. POSITIONS RELATING TO DIRECTIONAL MOVEMENTS

Directional movements are related to the use of directional verbs, which you learned about in Chapter 6. The directional movement refers to the movement of a sign that indicates the subject and object of a sentence. When signing a directional verb, your head and eyes should look in the direction that the verb is moving. You may also want to turn your body in that direction depending upon the amount of emphasis you wish to give to the sentence you are signing.

But gazing with directional verbs also depends on whether a signer is going to personalize a story. With the sentence "He asked her to please help him study," we get the following translation:

> **he-ASK-her, STUDY she-HELP-him PLEASE.**

If you are not going to personalize this sentence, there is no need to shift the body. You can simply gaze in the direction that the directional verbs move. The sign he-ASK-her moves from wherever the person represented by "he" was placed in the signing space to wherever the person represented by "her" was placed. If "he" is on the left side and "her" is on the right, then the sign moves from the left to the right side, and you should gaze toward the right side. The right side is also referred to as the goal of the directional verb; therefore, gazing toward the goal is a good rule of thumb when using directional verbs. Similarly, you should gaze to the left for she-HELP-him. In the final part of the sentence, you can continue gazing to the right or you can resume a normal position with eye contact with your addressee.

Now, let's change this sentence to "He asked her, 'Will you please help me with my homework?' " which we can translate to

he-ASK-her, STUDY you-HELP-me PLEASE?

If you keep the same placements in the signing space for the two pronouns, you shift your body to the right when signing he-ASK-her. Then, you will personalize the question by continuing to face the right side while signing the entire question. Because you have become the person referred to by the pronoun *he*, you sign you-HELP-me from the right side toward yourself.

4. COMPARISON

The visual and spatial qualities of ASL provide a convenient means of making comparisons. This is done by locating objects in the signing space and then using body- and gaze-shifting to establish a comparison. A signer in the process of comparing two dogs might place one of them in the right side of the signing space and the other in the left side. Then, for example, by gazing downward to the right and smiling, the signer indicates some degree of affection or feelings toward that particular dog. A downward gaze to the left accompanied with a frown would make it obvious that the signer is not as pleased with that dog as with the other.

REVIEW EXERCISE

Beside each sentence write the direction in which you might shift your body and gaze when signing. Remember that, unless otherwise stated, it does not matter whether you select the right or left side of the signing space as long as you remember where you have placed people or objects in the signing space. For example,

> She told her little brother, "Don't eat chips in bed." *look to the right and downward*
> But he responded back to her, "Go away." *look to the left and upward*

1. I looked and saw a police officer standing outside my car window. He didn't look happy.

2. "Look. Can you see the bird on the roof?"

3. The teacher told John, "Thank you for doing such fine work."

4. The child asked the teacher, "Can I be a frog in the play?" The teacher responded, "No, because you were a frog last year."

5. I watched the kite fly in the air.

6. I was shocked when I saw him standing beside me.

7. I was lying on the ground when my aunt came up and said, "The grass is wet, please stand up."

8. The game is canceled for tomorrow.

9. I told my dog, "Sit and I will feed you."

10. I looked over my shoulder and saw my classmate.

ANSWERS

1. Look to the left (i.e., look outside the driver's side of the car).

2. Look up to the right (or left).

3. Imagine that John is sitting down and the teacher is standing up; then look down and to the left (or right).

4. When signing what the child is asking, look up to the right (or left). When signing what the teacher responds, look down and to the left (or right).

5. Look up toward the sky as if watching a kite fly.

6. Look directly to the left (or right) side.

7. Look down in front of you.

8. Keep your eyes on the addressee because there is no need to shift your gaze.

9. Look down in front of yourself (or to the right or left).

10. Look over your right (or left) shoulder.

Talking About Time

LESSON 18   THE TIME LINE

LANGUAGE GOALS

The student will
1.   use Rules   #2. tense with time adverbs and
              #5. information-seeking questions.
2.   use one technique for indicating time in ASL.
3.   use twenty-one new signs in three master dialogues.

THE MASTER DIALOGUES

PAST TENSE: DIALOGUE

Jenny: YESTERDAY, DO-what YOU?
                What did you do yesterday?

Michael: YESTERDAY, ME BOOK READ.
                I read a book yesterday.

THE MASTER SIGNS

BEFORE

LONG-TIME-AGO

PAST (BEFORE)

RECENTLY

THE MASTER SIGNS

UP-TILL-NOW

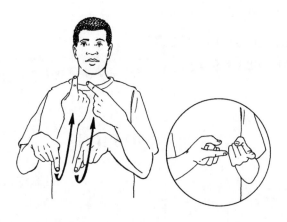

YESTERDAY

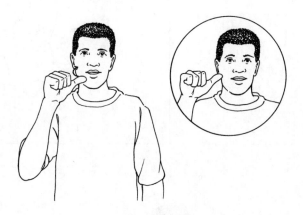

PRESENT TENSE: DIALOGUE

Michael: TODAY, DO-what YOU?
          What are you doing today?

Jenny: TODAY, ME STORY WRITE.
          I am writing a story today.

THE MASTER SIGNS

NOW

PRESENT

TODAY

FUTURE TENSE: DIALOGUE

Jenny: TOMORROW, DO-what YOU?
            What are you doing tomorrow?

Michael: TOMORROW, ME PICTURE DRAW.
            I will draw a picture tomorrow.

THE MASTER SIGNS

FUTURE

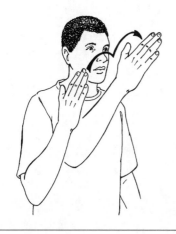

LATER

TOMORROW

FROM-NOW-ON

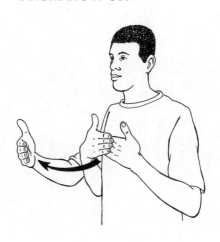

THE MASTER SIGNS

IN-A-WHILE

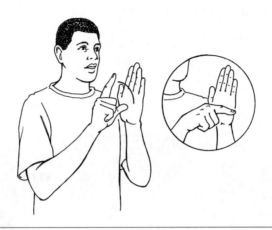

AFTER

OTHER MASTER SIGNS

BOOK

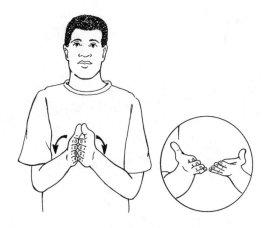

DRAW

PICTURE

READ

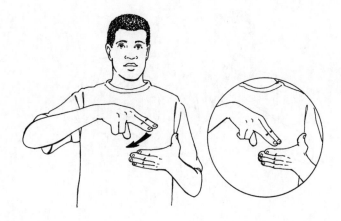

OTHER MASTER SIGNS

STORY

WRITE

POETRY

MAGAZINE

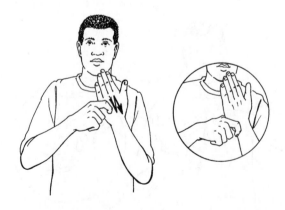

OTHER MASTER SIGNS

NEWSPAPER

WHAT'S IN THE SIGNS (NOTES ABOUT THE GRAMMAR)

1. THE TIME LINE

The body and the signing space combine to indicate time in ASL. The body represents the present time. Movement of signs to the back of the body represents action and events that took place in the past or the past tense. Movement to the front of the body represents action and events that have yet to occur or the future. Thus, the time line runs from the front to the back of the body. The position of signs for time adverbs illustrates their relationship to the time line.

2. RULE #2. TENSE WITH TIME ADVERBS

Signs in ASL are not marked for time. You indicate time by first signing a time adverb, which establishes the time for the forthcoming sentences. After you sign the time adverb, the tense remains the same until it is changed. The master dialogue has the following time adverbs:

YESTERDAY, ME BOOK READ.

TODAY, ME STORY WRITE.

TOMORROW, ME PICTURE DRAW.

3. RULE #5. INFORMATION-SEEKING QUESTIONS

The wh-questions in this lesson take into account Rule #2, because each one of them begins with a time adverb at the beginning of the question, which establishes the tense for the question. The three wh-questions in the dialogue are

YESTERDAY, DO-what YOU?

TODAY, DO-what you?

TOMORROW, DO-what YOU?

4. FACIAL GRAMMAR

Nonmanual signals can clarify the intended time frame. One set of signals is used to indicate that something happened close in time. These signals include *raising the shoulders and moving them forward a bit*, *tightening the muscles around the mouth* (either with or without the mouth open), and *tilting the head to the side or forward*. These signals would be appropriate if you used the sign RECENTLY to indicate that something just happened a few moments ago. It would not be correct to use these signals to talk about something that happened recently in a more general sense such as "She recently moved into her new home."

   Another set of nonmanual signals is used to show that something happened or will happen in the distant past or future. These signals are *the puffed cheeks* with *the eyebrows either raised or squeezed together*. Examples of sentences in which these signals can be used are "It was a long time ago when the buffaloes roamed freely across the prairie" and "It will be in the very distant future before people are able to travel outside our solar system."

WHAT'S IN A SIGN (NOTES ABOUT THE VOCABULARY)

1. BEFORE

Two signs for "before" are shown in this lesson. The sign BEFORE that is shown in the illustration refers to an event or action that occurred or will occur before a specific point in time. Examples of when it is used are "I arrived there before she did," "Dinosaurs inhabited the earth before human beings," and "I will arrive there before 5:00 this afternoon."

   The other sign for "before" is made in the same manner as the sign PAST. It refers to something that occurred in the past as illustrated in the sentences "I have met you before" and "I can't remember where I used to put my books before."

2. AFTER

The sign AFTER refers to an event or action that occurred or will occur after a specific point in time. Thus, it refers to something that happened after something else did. Examples of how it is used are "I will meet you after the game" and "The school closed after the blizzard came."

3. ASL SYNONYMS
Some signs can be used to mean other things.

Sign	Also used for
DRAW	ART, ARTISTIC, ILLUSTRATE, ILLUSTRATION
MAGAZINE	ARTICLE, BROCHURE, CATALOG, PAMPHLET
NEWSPAPER	PRINT
PAST	AGO, BEFORE, FORMER
PICTURE	PHOTO, PHOTOGRAPH
POETRY	POEM
PRESENT	CONTEMPORARY, CURRENT, CURRENTLY, PRESENTLY
NOW	AT-ONCE, IMMEDIATE
IN-A-WHILE	SHORTLY
STORY	NARRATIVE, NOVEL, PARABLE, PHRASE, PROSE, TALE

PRACTICE ACTIVITIES

1. MASTERY LEARNING
Practice signing the three dialogues substituting signs from the master sign list. When signing the questions, be sure to use the appropriate nonmanual signals.

2. FURTHER PRACTICE
Use selected directional verb signs from Chapter 6 to create ten sentences that include signs for time adverbs learned in this lesson. Write an English translation for each of your sentences. Sign your sentences to a partner. Recall that the illustrations for directional verbs in this book are for the neutral position of the sign. In the following examples, the subject and object of the sentence are incorporated into the movement of the verb sign. Check with a teacher to ensure that you are making the sign in the correct manner. Examples follow:

a. TODAY, TEACHER (point-right) BOOK you-GIVE-her.
   Give the book to the teacher today.
b. LONG-TIME-AGO, B-E-T-T-Y (point-left) she-INFORM-me SCHOOL, SHE ENJOY.
   A long time ago, Betty informed me that she enjoyed school.
c. NEXT-WEEK, YOU ME SIGNS, TEACH-each-other.
   Next week, you and I will teach each other signs.

LESSON 19   TALKING ABOUT TIME

LANGUAGE GOALS

The student will

1.   **use Rules**   **#1. topic/comment,**

#2. tense with time adverbs,

#3. simple yes/no questions,

#4. long yes/no questions,

#5. information-seeking questions,

#7. rhetorical questions,

#8. ordering of simple sentences, and

#10. negation.

2.   **use fourteen new signs in a master dialogue.**

THE MASTER DIALOGUE

Reb: FINALLY! ME WAIT, ONE HOUR.
          Finally. I waited for one hour.

Rachel: YOU WAIT WHY? YOU ARRIVE EARLY.
          You waited because you arrived early.

Reb: TRUE. SUNDAY ACCOMPANY-me MOVIE WANT YOU?
          That's true. Do you want to come with me to a movie on Sunday?

Rachel: CAN'T. THIS WEEK, ME BUSY.
          I can't. I'm busy this week.

Reb: NEXT MONTH, YOU BUSY?
          Are you busy next month?

Rachel: NO. NEXT MONTH, MY SCHEDULE EMPTY.
          No. Next month my schedule is empty.

Reb: YOU LUCKY. THIS YEAR, MY SCHEDULE FULL.
          You're lucky. This year my schedule is full.

Rachel: YOU AVAILABLE WHEN?
          When are you available?

Reb: NEXT-WEEK ME CAN'T. IN-THREE-WEEKS MONDAY?
          I can't next week. How about on a Monday in three weeks?

Rachel: GOOD. SEE YOU IN-THREE-WEEKS.
          Good. I will see you in three weeks.

THE MASTER SIGNS

ACCOMPANY-me

AVAILABLE (EMPTY)

BUSY

HOUR

IN-THREE-WEEKS

MONTH

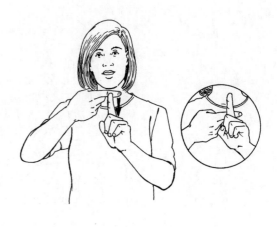

THE MASTER SIGNS

NEXT

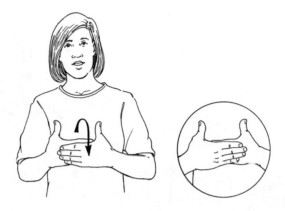

MONDAY

NEXT-WEEK

SCHEDULE

THE MASTER SIGNS

SUNDAY

THIS

WEEK

YEAR

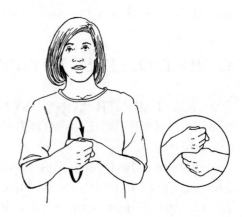

WHAT'S IN THE SIGNS (NOTES ABOUT THE GRAMMAR)

1. RULE #1. TOPIC/COMMENT

The dialogue illustrates how the topic/comment sentence structure can be used to talk about time:

    a. ME WAIT, ONE HOUR.
    b. THIS WEEK, ME BUSY.
    c. NEXT MONTH, MY SCHEDULE EMPTY.
    d. THIS YEAR, MY SCHEDULE FULL.

In each of these sentences, the time adverb is placed at the beginning of the sentence. This strategy also establishes the tense in sentences b, c, and d. Using the topic/comment structure for these sentences places the emphasis on the comment that is made in each one of them. Because time in the dialogue is important, the nonmanual signals associated with the topic/comment sentence structure are used to highlight the time adverbs.

In sentence a, the time adverb ONE HOUR is used to make a comment about how long Reb waited for Rachel to show up.

2. RULE #2. TENSE WITH TIME ADVERBS

    a. NEXT MONTH, YOU BUSY?
    b. IN-THREE-WEEKS MONDAY?

In sentence a the topic is first described (NEXT MONTH) followed by a yes/no question about it (YOU BUSY?). In sentence b all the signs are used to ask a question about a particular time. There is no need to include movie in the question because the dialogue is about finding a day to go and see a movie.

3. RULE #4. LONG YES/NO QUESTIONS

Time, topic, and question are combined in the following yes/no question:

time:	SUNDAY
topic:	ACCOMPANY-me MOVIE
question:	WANT YOU?

4. RULE #5. INFORMATION-SEEKING QUESTIONS

The wh-question in the dialogue places the sign WHEN at the end of the sentence:

YOU AVAILABLE WHEN?

5. RULE #7. RHETORICAL QUESTIONS

The following rhetorical question was used to explain why Reb had waited for one hour:

YOU WAIT WHY? YOU ARRIVE EARLY.

The question is first asked and then an answer is given immediately.

6. RULE #8. ORDERING OF SIMPLE SENTENCES

A common salutary remark when departing is illustrated in the sentence

SEE YOU IN-THREE-WEEKS.

The signed phrase SEE YOU is followed by the time adverb IN-THREE-WEEKS. Another simple sentence in the dialogue was

YOU LUCKY.

7. RULE #10. NEGATION

The dialogue provides three examples of negation. In two of the instances, Rachel signs CAN'T or NO in response to a question. When responding to a yes/no question, a simple YES or NO or another negative sign is often sufficient. In the second instance, Reb explains that she can't do something next week:

NEXT-WEEK ME CAN'T.

The negative sign CAN'T is placed at the end of the sentence.

WHAT'S IN A SIGN (NOTES ABOUT THE VOCABULARY)

1. NEXT-WEEK
The sign for NEXT-WEEK uses the time line to represent the concept of one week from now. The sign WEEK is made and then the hand moves forward beyond the stationary hand (i.e., into the future).

2. IN-THREE-WEEKS
This is an example of how numbers are incorporated into a sign. The sign NEXT-WEEK is made with the 3 handshape. This is a common linguistic device in ASL.

3. ASL SYNONYMS
Some signs can be used to mean other things.

Sign	Also used for
NEXT-WEEK	IN-ONE-WEEK, a-WEEK-from-now

PRACTICE ACTIVITIES

1. MODEL FOR RULES #1. TOPIC/COMMENT AND #7. RHETORICAL QUESTIONS

Signer A: 1. Initiate the conversation with a remark;
2. describe a topic;
3. make a comment about the topic.

Remark:	FINALLY!
Topic:	ME WAIT,
Comment:	ONE HOUR.

Signer B: 1. Ask a rhetorical question;
2. answer the question.

| Rhetorical question: | YOU WAIT WHY? |
| Answer: | YOU ARRIVE EARLY. |

Practice

Signer A: FINALLY! ME WAIT, ONE HOUR.
Signer B: YOU WAIT WHY? YOU ARRIVE EARLY.

2. MODEL FOR RULES #1. TOPIC COMMENT, #4. LONG YES/NO QUESTIONS, AND #10. NEGATION

Signer A:
    1. Make a remark about a previous comment;
    2. establish the time frame by signing a time adverb;
    3. describe the topic;
    4. ask a yes/no question about the topic.

Remark:	TRUE.
Time:	SUNDAY
Topic:	ACCOMPANY-me MOVIE
Question:	WANT YOU?

Signer B:
    1. Respond to the yes/no question with a negative;
    2. describe a topic;
    3. make a comment about the topic.

Response:	CAN'T.
Topic:	THIS WEEK,
Comment:	ME BUSY.

Practice

Signer A: TRUE. SUNDAY ACCOMPANY-me MOVIE WANT YOU?
Signer B: CAN'T. THIS WEEK, ME BUSY.

3. MODEL FOR RULES #1. TOPIC/COMMENT, #3. SIMPLE YES/NO QUESTIONS, AND #8. ORDERING OF SIMPLE SENTENCES

Signer A:
    1. Describe a topic;
    2. ask a yes/no question about the topic.

Topic:	NEXT MONTH,
Question:	YOU BUSY?

Signer B:
    1. Respond to the yes/no question with a negative;
    2. describe a topic;
    3. make a comment about the topic.

Response:	NO.
Topic:	NEXT MONTH,
Comment:	MY SCHEDULE EMPTY.

Signer A:

1. Make a remark using a simple sentence structure;
2. describe a topic;
3. make a comment about the topic.

Remark:	YOU LUCKY.
Topic:	THIS YEAR,
Comment:	MY SCHEDULE FULL.

Practice

Signer A: NEXT MONTH, YOU BUSY?

Signer B: NO. NEXT MONTH, MY SCHEDULE EMPTY.

Signer A: YOU LUCKY. THIS YEAR, MY SCHEDULE FULL.

4. MODEL FOR RULES #3. SIMPLE YES/NO QUESTIONS, #5. INFORMATION-SEEKING QUESTIONS, #8. ORDERING OF SIMPLE SENTENCES, AND #10. NEGATION

Signer A:

1. Describe the topic;
2. ask a wh-question about the topic.

Topic:	YOU AVAILABLE
Question:	WHEN?

Signer B:

1. Describe the topic;
2. sign a negative about the topic;
3. ask a new question by proposing a new date of when you will be available.

Topic:	NEXT-WEEK
Negative:	ME CAN'T.
Question:	IN-THREE-WEEKS MONDAY?

Signer A:

1. Make a remark about what Signer B asked;
2. describe an action;
3. state a time adverb.

Remark:	GOOD.
Action:	SEE YOU
Time:	IN-THREE-WEEKS.

Practice

Signer A:	YOU AVAILABLE WHEN?
Signer B:	NEXT-WEEK ME CAN'T. IN-THREE-WEEKS MONDAY?
Signer A:	GOOD. SEE YOU IN-THREE-WEEKS.

5. MASTERY LEARNING

When you feel comfortable signing these phrases, practice signing the entire dialogue shown at the beginning of the lesson. Practice the master dialogue until you can sign the part of each character smoothly while using the appropriate facial grammar.

6. FURTHER PRACTICE

Create five time-related sentences. Write the English gloss for the ASL sentences and the English translations. Sign your sentences to a partner who will write down the English translation to compare with your translations. Two examples are

a. IN-THREE-WEEKS, SCHOOL FINISH.
   School is finished in three weeks. *or* In three weeks, school will be finished.
b. me-HELP-you WHEN? ONE MONTH AGO?
   When did I help you? Was it one month ago?

Remember that there is usually more than one way to translate an ASL sentence into English. However, although the wording of the translations might be different, the meaning of all translations should be the same.

LANGUAGE GOALS

The student will

1.   use various ASL grammar rules to create a dialogue.
2.   use the plural forms of time adverbs.
3.   incorporate the numbers 1–9 into time adverbs.
4.   use twenty new signs for time adverbs in a self-created dialogue.

THE MASTER SIGNS

1. DAYS OF THE WEEK

The most correct way to sign the days of the week (except SUNDAY) are with the palm in—facing the body. However, they are pictured palm out so that the student can see them better.

SUNDAY

MONDAY

THE MASTER SIGNS

TUESDAY

WEDNESDAY

THURSDAY

FRIDAY

SATURDAY

2. PAST AND FUTURE FORM

The following signs use the time line to refer to time that is either in the past (the hand moves toward the back of the shoulder) or future (the hand moves to the front of the body).

LAST-WEEK

LAST-YEAR

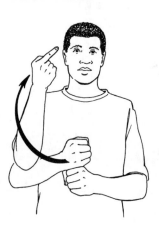

NEXT-WEEK

NEXT-YEAR

3. ADVERBIAL FORM -LY

To create the adverb form -LY, the movement of the dominant hand is repeated in HOUR, WEEK, and MONTH. The sign YEARLY is made by repeating the sign for NEXT-YEAR. The sign DAILY is made by repeating the sign for TOMORROW.

HOURLY

DAILY

MONTHLY

WEEKLY

YEARLY

4. INCORPORATING NUMBERS INTO HOURS, DAYS, WEEKS, AND MONTHS

The numbers 1–9 can be used with the signs for HOUR, DAY, WEEK, and MONTH, to represent the concepts one hour, two hours, . . ., nine hours; one day, two days, . . ., nine days; one week, two weeks, . . ., nine weeks; and one month, two months, . . ., nine months. Some people also use this technique to sign one year, two years, and so forth, while others first sign the number and then the sign YEAR—in other words, they do not incorporate the number into the sign for year.

1–9 HOURS (see illustrations for THREE-HOURS & SEVEN-HOURS)
1–9 DAYS (see illustrations for FOUR-DAYS & SIX-DAYS)
1–9 WEEKS (see illustrations for FIVE-WEEKS & NINE-WEEKS)
1–9 MONTHS (see illustrations for TWO-MONTHS & EIGHT-MONTHS)

3 HOURS

7 HOURS

4 DAYS

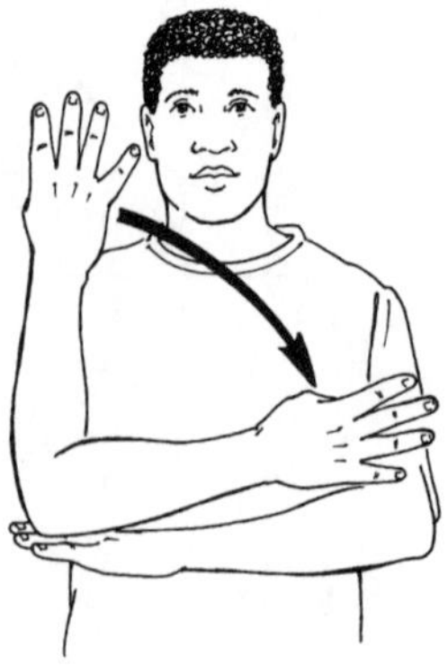

6 DAYS

5 WEEKS

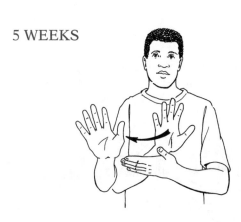

9 WEEKS

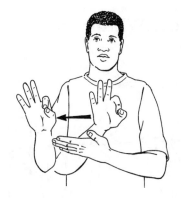

2 MONTHS

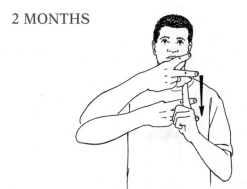

8 MONTHS

The signs for 1–9 WEEKS can be incorporated into the signs for

a. NEXT-WEEK to give
    IN-ONE-WEEK, IN-TWO-WEEKS, . . ., IN-NINE-WEEKS
b. LAST-WEEK to give
    ONE-WEEK-AGO, TWO-WEEKS-AGO, . . ., NINE-WEEKS-AGO

5. MORE TIME ADVERBS

OFTEN

SOMETIMES

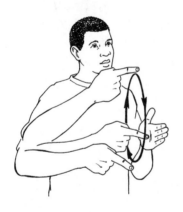

NOON

DAY

NIGHT

DURING

UNTIL

PRACTICE ACTIVITIES

Select signs learned in any of the previous lessons to create dialogues that incorporate the signs learned in this lesson. Use any or all the ASL grammar rules. Keep your sentences short, and write the rule number next to each one. An example of a dialogue is provided for you.

Signer A: HELLO P-E-T-E-R, SCHOOL START WHEN? (Rule #5)
                      Hello Peter, when does school start?

Signer B: SCHOOL START, IN-FOUR-WEEKS TUESDAY. (Rule #1)
                      School starts on Tuesday in four weeks.

Signer A: NEXT-WEEK THURSDAY, STUDY YOU WANT? (Rule #4)
                      On Thursday next week, do you want to study?

Signer B: NEXT-WEEK THURSDAY FINE. SEE-you-LATER. (Rule #8)
                      Next week on Thursday is fine with me. See you later.

REVIEW OF LESSONS 15–20

Translate each of the following sentences to ASL by writing the English gloss of the signs used in the translation and signing it.

1. Can I borrow your book?

2. I study ASL every day because my sister is deaf.

3. I start working at seven o'clock Monday morning.

4. Do you feel hot or cold?

5. I live in Philadelphia.

6. My cousin is a computer analyst.

7. My room is dark and quiet.

8. What time did you finish writing the poem?

9. What is the name of your uncle?

10. Is that woman over there an engineer or secretary?

ANSWERS

Note that there may be other ways of translating these sentences than the ones shown here.

1. YOUR BOOK, you-BORROW-me?

2. EVERY DAY ME STUDY ASL WHY? MY SISTER, DEAF.

3. MONDAY MORNING, ME START WORK, TIME 7.

4. YOU FEEL HOT COLD WHICH?

5. ME LIVE WHERE? PHILADELPHIA.

6. MY COUSIN, SHE COMPUTER-ANALYST.

7. MY ROOM, DARK QUIET.

8. YOU POEM WRITE FINISH, TIME?

9. YOUR UNCLE, NAME?

10. WOMAN THERE, SHE ENGINEER SECRETARY WHICH?

Classifiers and the World Games for the Deaf

11

Classifiers: The Paintbrush of ASL

One sign technique that is relatively easy to understand and incorporate in ASL . . . is the use of ASL "classifiers." These "classifiers" are various hand shapes that represent a noun and show *location* and also possible *action* of that noun. For example, the vertically raised index finger of the fisted hand shape could represent a person who could move from one spot to another, go up or downstairs or in an elevator, or meet another person (when the two identical fisted handshapes with index's raised are brought together). Another one of many possibilities might be to use the "classifier" shape to represent telephone poles zipping by outside a bus or train window. The speed of the train or bus could be represented by the speed of movement of the hand (as the poles go by the window). Still another "classifier" of this type is the 3 handshape that represents a motorized land or water vehicle (car, bus, truck, van, or boat). For example, "The car stopped and backed into the parking spot" could all be communicated with the 3 handshape held in a horizontal position. Similarly, a boat could be represented as it moves forward through choppy water.

—BERNARD BRAGG AND JACK OLSON
Meeting Halfway in American Sign Language

HOLD THAT SIGN . . .

Classifiers are not unique to ASL or any other sign language. The spoken language, Navajo, uses classifiers in ways almost identical to ASL. Japanese uses classifiers when counting people, objects, and events. But native speakers of English may find classifiers difficult because English has no classifier system. This chapter introduces some common ASL classifiers. These classifiers and others can be used to outline the shape of a building, pattern of a dress, flow of tap water, ray of sunbeam, limp of a hurt athlete, scattering of many ants, and so forth. We might even say that classifiers have a sense for the dramatic. At the very least, your knowledge of classifiers will help you paint images in the air.

WHAT ARE CLASSIFIERS AND HOW DO WE REPRESENT THEM IN PRINT?

Classifiers are a set of signs used to describe (a) a physical characteristic of a noun, and/or (b) the movement or location of a noun. Classifiers make signing more artlike. They do this by representing an object's size, shape, depth, texture, movement, and/or location.

The important feature of a classifier is the handshape. In this text, signs that serve as classifiers are identified in three parts. The first part is the symbol cl-, which denotes that the sign is a classifer.

The second part gives the handshape of a number or letter. If only one letter or number is shown such as cl-F or cl-2, then only the dominant hand is used to make the sign. If a specific hand is to be used, then it will be specified using the term *right* or *left* to indicate which hand is used to make the classifier. In cl-F(right), for example, the right hand is used. If a double letter or double number is shown such as cl-LL or cl-33, both hands are classifiers.

The third part tells us what characteristic or action of a noun the classifier is representing. Although a classifier is representing a characteristic or action of a noun, it is *not* the sign for that noun. An example of a classifier is shown in the following illustration.

The handshape of the classifier cl-1:go-past-me, tells us that the signer is referring to a person or an animal because the 1 handshape is used to represent a person or animal. The movement of the handshape relative to the signer shows a person or animal going past the signer.

The classifier by itself does not identify the subject or object of a sentence. This must be done by adding more information, as in the following sentences:

a. MY NEPHEW cl-1:go-past-me.
b. YOUR HORSE cl-1:go-past-me.

In sentence a we know that the signer is talking about his or her nephew going past him or her. In sentence b the subject is the addressee's horse. More information can be added to these phrases to indicate the time that both events occurred.

c. ONE HOUR AGO, MY NEPHEW cl-1:go-past-me.
    My nephew went past me an hour ago.
d. YESTERDAY, YOUR HORSE cl-1:go-past-me.
    Yesterday, your horse went past me.

In sentences a–d, the classifier cl-1:go-past-me describes an action associated with the subject of the sentence. The classifier is not in fact the sign for go.

A BASIC RULE FOR USING CLASSIFIERS

a. RED PEN cl-1:on-shelf.
    The red pen is on the shelf.

RED   PEN   cl-1:on-shelf

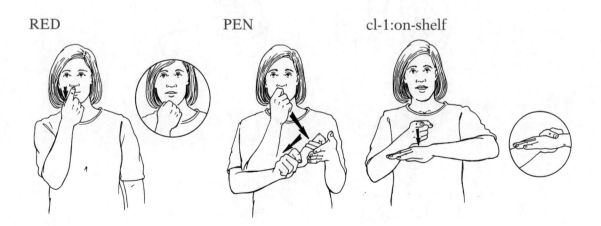

b. STEAK cl-LL:large.
    The steak is large.

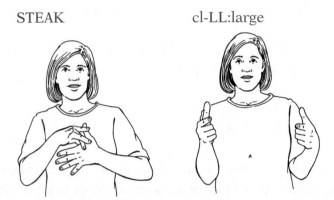

STEAK   cl-LL:large

It must be clear what a classifier is representing before it can be used. Thus, the basic sentence pattern for using classifiers is

noun(s)/classifier

In the first part of the sentence, the signer identifies the subject, object, or both. Examples of how the noun(s)/classifier rule is used follow:

a. There are lots of people going to the movie.

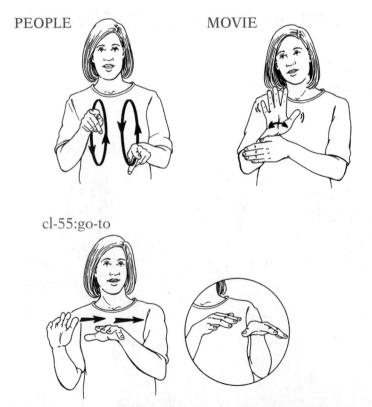

PEOPLE   MOVIE

cl-55:go-to

b. There is a little bit of milk in the glass.

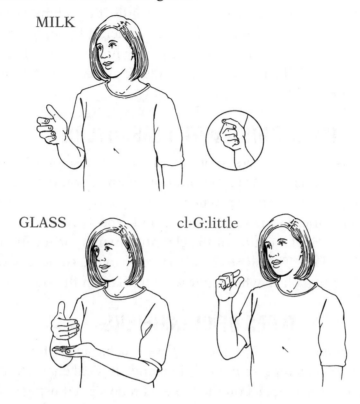

MILK

GLASS   cl-G:little

c. Bob followed Ted.

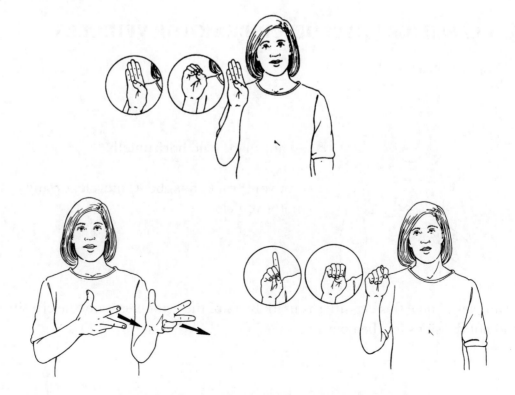

In all three examples, the nouns in the sentences are signed first; then a classifier is used to represent the noun. In sentence a the classifier for indicating a horde of people moving in a particular direction is used to represent the movement of people. In sentence b the classifier for indicating a small quantity is used to show how much milk is left in a glass. In sentence c both the right and left hands are used as classifiers representing one motor vehicle passing another one.

POSITIONING WITH CLASSIFIERS

The movement of a classifier for a person or an animal in the signing space is not a random event. Each movement is a clear representation of an action that someone or something has done, is doing, or will be doing. When watching a signer, you must pay attention to the location of the classifier in the signing space and especially to where the movement of the classifier ends. The final location of the classifier marks the location of the subject or object in the signing space. The signer can later refer to the subject or object of a sentence simply by pointing to a place where they were marked in the signing space.

TYPES OF CLASSIFIERS

Following is a list of common classifiers and the physical characteristic of a noun that they represent. Most classifiers can represent more than one physical characteristic. For example, the phrase "a small, round object on the table" can be signed using a single classifier that describes the size (small), shape (round), and location (on the table).

A. CLASSIFIERS THAT DESCRIBE MOTOR VEHICLES

1. Motor vehicle (cl-3)

3 handshape held horizontally

Car, van, truck, bus, boat, bicycle, or any other type of motor vehicle

Examples of how this classifier is used: In all of the examples, only the classifier is shown and not the signs for the nouns.

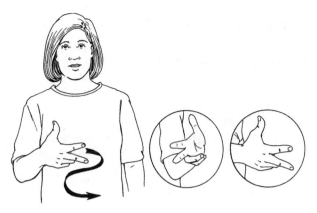

A car going up a hill   A boat weaving

2. Two motor vehicles (cl-33)

Both 3 handshapes held horizontally

Two cars, two vans, two buses, two boats, or two of any other type of motor vehicle

Examples of how this classifier is used:

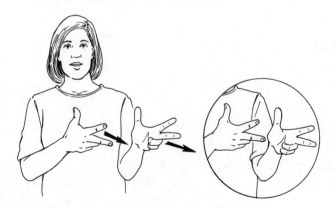

One car following another car   Two trucks driving toward each other

B. CLASSIFIERS THAT SHOW THE ACTION OF PEOPLE OR THINGS

3. Person or animal (cl-1)

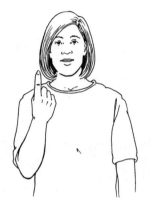

1 handshape held vertically

Person, animal

Examples of how this classifier is used:

A person turning away

A person falling down

4. Two people or two animals (cl-11 or cl-2)

Both 1 handshapes held vertically

Two people, two animals

cl-11

2 handshape held vertically

Two people, two animals

cl-2

Examples of how these classifiers are used:

One person turning away from
another person

Two people moving forward

5. Many people in a line (cl-44)

Both 4 handshapes held vertically

A stream of people or animals

Examples of how this classifier is used:

Stream of people moving past   A long lineup

6. Large quantity of things moving in a specific direction (cl-55)

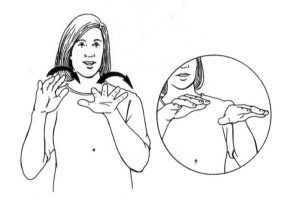

Both 5 handshapes held with palms down

Hordes of people, animals, bicycles, cars, and so forth moving toward a common place

Examples of how this classifier is used:

Horde of people coming together   Horde of animals moving backward

7. Person standing or walking (cl-V)

V handshape held upside down

Person standing or walking

Examples of how this classifier is used:

A person falling off of a platform

A person walking up a spiral staircase

8. Chair, person, or animal seated (cl-bent V)

Bent V handshape held horizontally

A chair, a person sitting, an animal sitting

Examples of how this classifier is used:

A person sitting next to a tree

A person sitting on a platform

C. CLASSIFIERS THAT SHOW THE SIZE AND SHAPE OF THINGS

9. Cylindrical objects (cl-1/)

Finger pointing or 1 handshape held horizontally or upright

Pen, pencil, straw, log, telephone pole

Examples of how this classifier is used:

A pen on top of a table

A straw in a cup

10. Flat objects (cl-B)

B handshape with thumb next to index finger

Bed, sheet of paper, kite, tile, board, leaf

Examples of how this classifier is used:

A leaf falling off a tree

A person lying on a bed

11. Small, flat, and round objects (cl-F)

F handshape held horizontally or vertically

Coin, button, medal, pendant, watch

Examples of how this classifier is used:

A button on a shirt

A small badge on the chest

12. Large, flat, and round (cl-LL)

Two L handshapes forming the outline of a horizontal circle

Plate, steak, large hole, frisbee, discus

Examples of how this classifier is used:

The size of a child-size Frisbee

The size of an adult-size Frisbee

13. Small container-like objects (cl-C)

C handshape held horizontally

Glass, bottle, vase, can, cup, pencil holder

Examples of how this classifier is used:

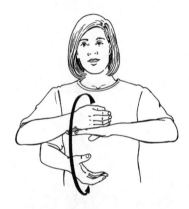

A glass falling off a shelf

Raising a bottle above the head

14. Larger size container-like objects (cl-CC)

Two C handshapes forming the outline of a container

Paint can, garbage can, large bowl, melon, pumpkin

Examples of how this classifier is used:

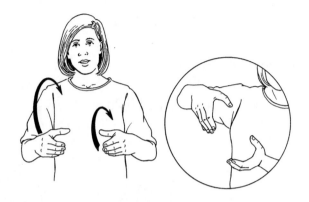

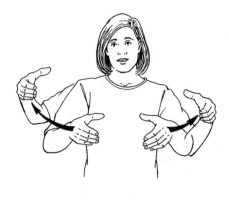

Pouring from a large bowl   A pumpkin growing larger

15. Flat surfaces (cl-BB)

Two B handshapes held horizontally and pulled apart

Tabletop, stage, shelf, floor

Examples of how this classifier is used:

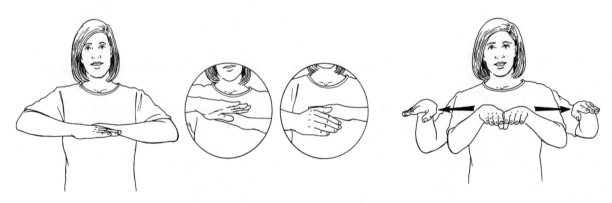

A wavy floor   A long table

D. CLASSIFIERS THAT SHOW THE AMOUNT

16. Small amount (cl-G)

G handshape

Small amount of liquid or solid, small height of a stack of things, small insect

Examples of how this classifier is used:

The amount of water in a container

Comparing the height of two piles of paper

17. Medium amount (cl-L)

L handshape

Medium amount of liquid or solid, medium height of a stack of things or something that grows

Examples of how this classifier is used:

The height of grass

The height of a stack of paper on a shelf

18. Large amount (cl-BB/)

Two B handshapes with one held above the other

Large amount of liquid or solid, high height of a stack of things or something that grows

Examples of how this classifier is used:

The increasing height of a stack of books

How high something has grown

E. CLASSIFIERS THAT SHOW A STATIONARY OBJECT

19. Stationary object (cl-A)

A handshape held with the thumb up

House, vase, lamp, building, statue, grain bin

Examples of how this classifier is used:

Two houses side by side

Two lamps apart from each other

F. CLASSIFIERS THAT SHOW THE FLOW OF THINGS

20. Flow of liquid (cl-4>)

4 handshape held vertically with fingers pointed to the side, hand moves up and down

Indicates the flow of liquid, bleeding nose, running tap, running water

Examples of how this classifier is used:

A bleeding nose   A running tap

21. Flow of objects (cl-44/)

Two 4 handshapes, hands move back and forth to the side. Can also be done with one palm facing up and the other palm facing down.

Indicates the flow of objects moving along a conveyor belt or assembly line, logs moving down a river

Examples of how this classifier is used:

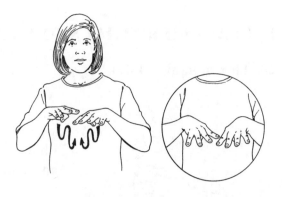

Long line of objects moving along   Logs moving down a river

PLURALS

Many classifiers that represent a person, animal, or thing can be moved to indicate plurality. Often, both hands are used when the plural form of a classifier is being made. The following illustrations show the plural form of three classifiers. Compare each of them with the singular form of the classifier shown in the preceding section.

Many coins   Many houses   Many chairs in a half circle

Notice that in the illustration of many chairs in a half circle the classifier describes the object (chair), the number of objects (many), and the location of the objects relative to each other (aligned in a half circle).

REVIEW EXERCISE

Write the symbol for the classifier that is most appropriate for representing each of the following phrases.

1. a herd of deer

2. a large leak in a water pipe

3. a pedestrian crossing the street

4. the size of a barrel

5. the stillness of a calm sea

6. the waves of a rough ocean

7. two bottles of pop

8. a fallen telephone pole

9. two people standing side by side

10. three lamps in a row

11. a lineup of people

12. a one-inch stack of paper

13. a large pothole

14. a kite in the air

15. a boat rocking from side to side

ANSWERS

1. cl-55

2. cl-4>

3. cl-1

4. cl-CC

5. cl-BB

6. cl-BB

7. cl-C

8. cl-1

9. cl-11

10. cl-A

11. cl-44

12. cl-G

13. cl-LL

14. cl-B

15. cl-3

LESSON 21   INTRODUCTION TO CLASSIFIERS: PERSON

LANGUAGE GOALS

The student will
1. use Rules   #3. simple yes/no questions and
                #8. ordering of simple sentences.
2. demonstrate the use of the classifier cl-1: in a sentence and recognize how it is used to represent relationships between the subject and object of a sentence.
3. use the directional verb LOOK/WATCH.
4. use one new classifier and five new signs in a master story.

THE MASTER STORY

YESTERDAY, MAN cl-1:WALK-past-me.
Yesterday, a man walked past me.

ME WATCH-go-past. ME KNOW HIM?
I watched him as he went past. Did I know him?

ME CALL-OUT, P-E-T-E!
I called out, "Pete!"

cl-1:he-TURN-TOWARD-me, cl-1:CAME-UP-to-me. me-LOOK-at-him.
He turned and came up to me. I looked at him.

MISTAKE ME. ME DON'T-KNOW HIM.
I had made a mistake. I didn't know him.

ME SAY, ME MISTAKE SORRY.
I said, "I am sorry, I have made a mistake."

cl-1:he-TURN-AWAY, cl-1:he-MOVE-AWAY.
He turned and went away.

THE MASTER CLASSIFIERS

Main classifier cl-1: (upright 1 handshape to refer to a person in the story)

Classifier action

CAME-UP-to-me

he-MOVE-AWAY

he-TURN-AWAY

WALK-past-me

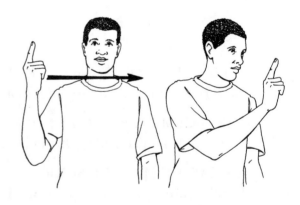

THE MASTER SIGNS

CALL-OUT

HIM	MAN

me-LOOK-at-him	MISTAKE

THE MASTER SIGNS

SAY

WATCH-go-past

WHAT'S IN THE SIGNS (NOTES ABOUT THE GRAMMAR)

1. TELLING A STORY

You tell a story in ASL by stringing thoughts together in the order that they occur. In the master story, a sequence of events is used to describe a case of mistaken identity. The first sign of the story is YESTERDAY, which establishes the tense for the entire story. Therefore, the English translation is written in the past tense.

2. CLASSIFIERS

The precise meaning of a classifier depends upon the context of the sentence in which it is used. How this is accomplished is shown in the following discussion of the classifiers used in the dialogue.

a. *cl-1:WALK-past-me*

The cl-1:WALK-past-me classifier tells us nothing about what walked past. You move an upright index finger past your face but does the finger represent a woman, child, teacher, friend, or some kind of animal? We don't know unless we add context to the situation in which the classifier is used. In the story, context is added:

MAN cl-1:WALK-past-me.

Now we know that it was a man who walked past. When did he walk past?

YESTERDAY, MAN cl-1:WALK-past-me.

At this point, a translation is possible.

A man walked past me yesterday.

A classifier is a powerful linguistic tool in ASL. Using the classifier cl-1:WALK-past-me, you can indicate many different kinds of movements and show the relative distance between the subject and object. For example, to show that the man ran past quickly you move the hand fast. To show that the man walked past close by, you keep the hand close to the face as it is moved past. To show that the man walked past at a distance, you keep the hand away from the body as it is moved past.

b. *cl-1:he-TURN-TOWARD-me.*

The subject and tense of this sentence have already been established in the story. Therefore, a translation of this classifier could be "He turned toward me" or "The man turned toward me" or some other close approximation.

c. *cl-1:CAME-UP-to-me.*

Two possible translations are "He came up to me" and "He walked up to me."

d. *cl-1:he-TURN-AWAY.*

An appropriate translation is "He turned away from me."

e. *cl-1:he-MOVE-AWAY.*

A couple of possible translations are "He walked away from me" and "He moved away from me."

3. GAZE-SHIFTING

Gaze-shifting is the movement of the eye and is an important part of ASL (see Chapter 9 "Body- and Gaze-Shifting"). In the story, eye gazing is used to emphasize the relationship between you, the signer, and the man you are talking about. In the first sentence,

YESTERDAY, MAN cl-1:WALK-past-me.

you sign YESTERDAY, MAN and then turn your head slightly to watch the upright finger as it moves past the face. If you are a right-handed person, the sign cl-1:WALK-past-me will start at the right side of the signing space and at this point you should be looking directly at it. As the finger moves across the face you follow it by keeping your eyes on it.

The head also will move slightly to follow the movement of the finger. In the practice activity, the eye-gazing is described for each of the classifiers used in the story.

In the sentence,

ME WATCH-go-past.

you repeat the eye gaze of the previous sentence, but this time you watch the hand signing WATCH-go-past. At the start, the fingertips of this sign (for a right-handed signer) will be pointing to the right side of the signing space. The sign will then move across the face just as the classifier cl:WALK-past-me did.

4. INDICATING THAT YOU HAVE MADE A MISTAKE

The phrase

MISTAKE ME

is a common one used to indicate that a person has made a mistake and is usually translated as "I have made a mistake" or "I was wrong." In the story, the meaning is "I had made a mistake" to account for the fact that the signer is telling a story in the past tense. More generally, English translations of ASL should always attempt to capture the sense of what the signer is trying to say. In the phrase

MISTAKE ME. ME DON'T-KNOW HIM.

a good translation might be "Whoops, I didn't know him" or "Oh no, I didn't know him" and facial expressions will help determine which one it might be. Recall that signs are glossed in English because of the necessity of facilitating discussions of ASL grammar and vocabulary. These English glosses are shown in uppercase print and are sometimes only a suitable approximation of what a sign means.

5. INDICATING A VERBATIM REMARK OR QUESTION

In the sentence,

ME SAY, ME MISTAKE SORRY.

a correct translation is

I said, "I am sorry, I have made a mistake."

The signed phrase ME SAY is translated to "I said" because the time frame was established by the signing of YESTERDAY at the beginning of the story. What the signer said, however, is translated in the present tense because the signer is telling us exactly what she or he had said a day earlier.

WHAT'S IN A SIGN (NOTES ABOUT VOCABULARY)

1. KNOW

The sign KNOW is made with the fingertips touching the forehead once. In some instances, when a signer wants to emphasize that he or she "really knows something" then the forehead can be tapped more than once.

2. LOOK

There are many signs to describe the different ways of looking at something. The hand-shape is typically the V handshape with the two fingers representing the eyes. In the story, you use the sign for LOOK in the sense of trying to recognize someone. An appropriate facial expression for this would be for you to (1) *bend your head forward slightly* and (2) *raise your eyebrows.*

3. MAN

Signs for MALE are made by the forehead. Compare this with signs for females which are made by the chin.

4. WATCH-GO-BY

The WATCH-go-by sign is a variation of the sign WATCH. The difference between the two is that in the sign WATCH the fingertips move forward, whereas in WATCH-go-by the fingertips move from one side to the other side to indicate that the eyes moved as something went by. In both cases, your eye gaze should follow the direction indicated by the sign.

5. ASL SYNONYMS

Some signs can be used to mean other things.

Sign	Also used for
CALL-OUT	YELL
HIM	HE, SHE, HER, IT
MAN	GENTLEMAN
MISTAKE	ERROR, WRONG
SAY	HEARING, PRONOUNCE, SPEAK, SPEECH

PRACTICE ACTIVITIES

1. MODEL FOR GAZE-SHIFTING, CLASSIFIERS CL-1:, AND RULES #3. SIMPLE YES/NO QUESTIONS AND #8. ORDERING OF SIMPLE SENTENCES

Signer: cl-1:WALK-past-me

1. Place the time adverb sign at the beginning of the sentence to establish the tense of the story;
2. sign the subject of the story;
3. sign the classifier *using eye gazing* to emphasize the sign's movement. Mentally note where you stopped the sign in the signing space.

Time:	YESTERDAY
Subject:	MAN
Gaze:	cl-1:WALK-past-me (eyes follow the sign as it moves across the signing space)

Signer: WATCH-go-past

1. Use gaze-shifting to emphasize what the signer did (the sign should stop moving at the same point where the sign cl-1: WALK-past-me ended);
2. ask a yes/no question *raising the eyebrows* and *tilting the head forward*.

Gaze:	ME WATCH-go-past (eyes follow the sign WATCH-go-past)
Question:	ME KNOW HIM?

Practice

Signer: [eyes follow the sign]
          YESTERDAY MAN cl-1:WALK-past-me
          [eyes follow the sign]
          ME WATCH-go-past,   ME KNOW HIM?

2. MODEL FOR CLASSIFIERS CL-1:, GAZE-SHIFTING, AND RULE #8. ORDERING OF SIMPLE SENTENCES

Signer:

1. Describe an action (The sign CALL-OUT will move in the direction of where the sign WATCH-go-past ended in the previous sentence. The eyes should be looking in the same direction);
2. fingerspell the name of the person called.

Action:	ME CALL-OUT,
Name:	P-E-T-E!

Signer: cl-1:he-TURN-TOWARD-me.

1. Make sign where sign WATCH-go-past ended.

Signer: cl-1:CAME-UP-to-me.

1. Use this sign to follow through from the previous sign. There should be a slight pause after the sign cl-1:he-TURN-TOWARD-me, and then the sign cl-1:CAME-UP-to-me is made. The eyes watch the movement of both classifiers.

Signer: me-LOOK-at-him.

1. Describe an action (the eyes look in the direction of the man).

Practice

Signer: ME CALL-OUT, P-E-T-E!
[eyes watch the hand movement]
cl-1:he-TURN-TOWARD-me.
[eyes watch the hand moving toward the signer]
cl-1:CAME-UP-to-me.
[eyes look in the direction where the man is placed in the signing space]
me-LOOK-at-him.

3.   MODEL FOR INDICATING THAT YOU HAVE MADE A MISTAKE

Signer:	1. Describe the topic;	
	2. make a comment about the mistake.	

	Topic:	MISTAKE ME.
	Comment:	ME DON'T-KNOW HIM.

Signer:	1. Describe an action;	
	2. apologize for making the mistake.	

	Action:	ME SAY,
	Apology:	ME MISTAKE SORRY.

Signer:	1. Describe an action that the man did;	
	2. describe another action that the man did.	

	Action 1:	cl-1:he-TURN-AWAY,
	Action 2:	cl-1:he-MOVE-AWAY.

Practice

Signer: MISTAKE ME.
ME DON'T-KNOW HIM.
ME SAY, ME MISTAKE SORRY.
cl-1:he-TURN-AWAY,
cl-1:he-MOVE-AWAY.

4.   MASTERY LEARNING

When you feel comfortable signing these phrases, practice signing the entire master story shown at the beginning of the lesson. Practice the story until you can sign the classifiers and use the appropriate eye gazes comfortably.

5.   FURTHER PRACTICE

Rewrite and practice the story making the following substitutions:

a. Substitute	MAN WOMAN	for	MAN
	cl-2	for	cl-1
b. Substitute	C-A-R	for	MAN
	cl-3	for	cl-1
	S-T-O-P	for	P-E-T-E

LESSON 22   EXPLORING WITH CLASSIFIERS

LANGUAGE GOALS

The student will
1. further explore how movement affects the meaning of classifiers.
2. recognize and use the classifier cl-2: to represent two people.

PRACTICE WITH CLASSIFIERS

A classifier can take on a variety of meanings depending upon how it is moved. When two classifiers are used, the number of meanings multiplies. Assigning a single word or a combination of words to represent these meanings in print is difficult. Furthermore, small changes in the movement of a classifier can drastically change the meaning of a sign. Therefore, even though it is important that you learn the handshape associated with a classifer, it is impractical for you to memorize the many meanings that a classifier can have.

What should you do? You need to *explore* the uses of classifiers using *images* of situations and practice how to sign these images. In this way you will be able to develop a *sense* of how a classifier is used. This would then prepare you for using the classifier when the situation arises.

THE MASTER CLASSIFIERS

1. cl-1: (upright 1 handshape to represent a person or animal)
2. cl-2: (upright 2 handshape to represent two persons or two animals)

PRACTICE ACTIVITIES

For each exploration sentence, do the following:

1. Close your eyes and
   - imagine the scene that each sentence describes.
   - replace the image of one of the persons (or animals) with a classifier.
   - use the classifier to make the movement described in the sentence.
   - imagine looking at the scene being described to practice eye-gazing and head movements.
   - sign the sentence. Recall that the pronoun is incorporated into each classifier.

2. Open your eyes and
   - sign the sentence using appropriate eye-gazing and head movements.

Hint #1. In some cases, it can be more convenient to switch hands rather than make a one-handed sign with the same hand all the time. For a right-handed person, signs that move off to the right side of the body are easily made with the right hand. Similarly, signs that move to the left side of the body can be made with the left hand.

Hint #2. Placement of a classifier in the signing space can show the relative size of a person or animal when compared to the signer. When the classifier cl:1 is used to represent the movement of a dog, the hand is often positioned lower than it would be when representing a person. In the former case, the hand would move at about chest height and in the latter it would move at about the same height as the head.

Hint #3. When twisting the hand to indicate that someone or something turned away, twist counterclockwise for signs made with the right hand, and clockwise for signs made with the left hand.

EXPLORATION SENTENCES
a. Use one hand with the classifier cl-1.
  1. She came straight to me.
  2. I went off to the right.
  3. She went off to the left.
  4. She walked up to me and then turned away.
  5. He came to me from my left side.
  6. She came to me from my right side.
  7. I walked straight ahead and then came straight back.
  8. I walked straight ahead and then turned to the right.
  9. I walked ahead, stopped, and then continued walking ahead.
  10. The dog ran past me quickly.
  11. The cat came up to me.
  12. The dog came straight up to me and then turned and walked away to the left.
b. Use two hands with the classifier cl-1.
  1. I went to the right and she went to the left. (**Hint:** Use two hands with your right hand representing you and your left hand representing the other person.)
  2. He came up to me from the right side, and she came up to me from the left side.
  3. They walked right past each other.
  4. I followed her. (**Hint:** Place one hand behind the other; then move both of them forward.)
  5. I walked around her. (**Hint:** Hold the left hand stationary; then move the other hand in a semicircle around it.)

6. I walked up to her and then turned and moved off to the right.
7. The dog followed the cat to the right and then the left.
8. I went up to her, and then the two of us went to the right.
9. We walked right past one another.
10. I walked in circles.

c. Use the classifier cl-2.

1. Two people came up to me on my right side.
2. I approached the two of them. (**Hint:** You must use two classifiers in this sentence, cl-1: and cl-2:. The phrase "the two of them" is made with cl-2, while the pronoun "I" is represented by cl-1.)
3. I walked right past the two of them.
4. Two people came up to me and then turned around and walked away.
5. Two people turned away from me, walked in a big circle, and then came back to me.
6. I walked up to them. ("Them" is two people.)
7. The two of them were walking past me; they stopped and then continued walking.
8. The two of them turned away quickly.
9. The two of them hopped past me. (**Hint:** Keep the fingertips pointing up.)
10. Two people followed me. (**Hint:** "Two people" will be represented by cl-2 and "me" will be represented by cl-1.)

LESSON 23   USING CLASSIFIERS IN A DIALOGUE

LANGUAGE GOALS

The student will

1. use Rules   **#3.** simple yes/no questions,

                 #5. information-seeking questions,

                 #7. rhetorical questions,

                 #8. ordering of simple sentences, and

               #10. negation.

2. review the use of the classifiers cl-1: and cl-2: in a dialogue.
3. use negation in a sentence with the sign **DON'T-WANT.**
4. use the signing space for locating pronouns.
5. use the directional verb **ASK.**
6. use five new signs in a master dialogue.

THE MASTER DIALOGUE

1.   Kaye: MAN THERE, WHO HE?
                 Who is that man?

       Fran: ME DON'T-KNOW. you-MEET-him WANT YOU?
                 I don't know. Do you want to meet him?

2.   Kaye: YES. ME WANT me-MEET-him.
                 Yes, I do want to meet him.

       Fran: YOU cl-1:you-GO-to-him, you-ASK-him NAME.
                 Go up to him and ask for his name.

3.   Kaye: cl-1:me-GO-to-him, me-ASK-him NAME? ME DON'T-WANT.
                 I don't want to go and ask him for his name.

       Fran: YOU DON'T-WANT, WHY-NOT?
                 Why don't you want to?

4.   Kaye: ME SHY.
                 I'm shy.

       Fran: YOU SHY? ME DOUBT-IT.
                 I doubt that you are shy.

5.   Kaye: TWO-of-us, cl-2:we-GO-to-him ASK-him, WHY-NOT?
                 Why don't the two of us go up and ask him for his name?

       Fran: SURE. cl-2:we-GO-to-him, NAME ASK-him.
                 Sure. The two of us can go and ask him for his name.

THE MASTER CLASSIFIERS

cl-1:me-GO-to-him

cl-1:you-GO-to-him

cl-2:we-GO-to-him

THE MASTER SIGNS

ASK

ASK-him

DON'T WANT

WANT

WHY-NOT

WHAT'S IN THE SIGNS (NOTES ABOUT THE GRAMMAR)

1. RULE #5. INFORMATION-SEEKING QUESTIONS

The signer describes the topic and then signs the wh-question.

Topic	Wh-question
MAN THERE,	WHO HE?
YOU DON'T-WANT,	WHY-NOT?
TWO-of-us, cl-2:we-GO-to-him ASK-him,	WHY-NOT?

The meaning for the sign WHY-NOT is along the line of "why don't you?" or "why don't we?" depending upon the subject of the sentence.

2. RULE #3. SIMPLE YES/NO QUESTIONS

As with many ASL yes/no questions, the question follows the topic.

topic:	YOU-MEET-him
question:	WANT YOU?

3. USING THE SIGN WANT

The sign WANT can come before or after the person or thing that is desired:

ME WANT me-MEET-him.
me-MEET-him, WANT ME.

4. DIRECTIONAL VERB

The directional verb GO is incorporated into the movement of the classifiers cl-1 and cl-2. In the story there are also two other directional verbs, ASK-him and MEET-him. The object of both sentences is "him" or the man in the story. The subject depends on the context of the sentence. The translations for just the directional verb phrases are shown here. They differ slightly from the translations in the story because the story has more information added to the sentences.

	Translation
you-MEET-him WANT YOU?	Do you want to meet him?
ME WANT me-MEET-him.	I want to meet him.
you-ASK-him NAME.	You ask him for his name.
me-ASK-him NAME?	I ask him for his name?

In the dialogue, the classifier cl:1 is used to identify subject and object associated with two of the foregoing phrases as follows:

YOU cl-1:you-GO-to-him, you-ASK-him NAME.
cl-1:me-GO-to-him, me-ASK-him NAME? ME DON'T-WANT.

5. RULE #10. NEGATION
To negate a thought, you describe a topic and then add a negative sign.

topic:	cl-1:me-GO-to-him, me-ASK-him NAME?
negative:	ME DON'T-WANT.

6. RULE #8. ORDERING OF SIMPLE SENTENCES
Sentences that use descriptive terms to describe the subject can follow a simple subject-adjective order as seen in the following sentence:

ME SHY.

7. RULE #7. RHETORICAL QUESTIONS
In the following sentences, a rhetorical question is asked and then answered:

YOU SHY? ME DOUBT-IT.
cl-1:me-GO-to-him, me-ASK-him NAME? ME DON'T-WANT.

WHAT'S IN A SIGN (NOTES ABOUT VOCABULARY)

1. ASK

The sign ASK is a directional verb. The direction of its movements indicates the subject and object of a sentence. For the sign ASK-him, the hand moves toward a place in the signing space where the person represented by HIM is placed. The subject of the phrase could be "me" as in me-ASK-him or "you" as in you-ASK-him, depending upon the context of the sentence. The subject can vary to take on other pronouns, too.

2. DON'T-WANT

The sign for DON'T WANT is another example of negative incorporation. The sign WANT is made, and then the hands are turned away to show that something is not wanted.

3. SHY

Signs for feelings can be accompanied by facial expressions that clue in on the feelings. While signing SHY a person could (1) *raise the right shoulder* and (2) *tilt the head slightly toward the same shoulder* to emphasize the withdrawal characteristic of a person being shy.

4. WHY-NOT

The sign WHY-NOT is a combination of the sign WHY and NOT. It is similar to the sign WHY except the thumb starts by the chin or in the same starting position for the sign NOT.

5. ASL SYNONYMS

Some signs can be used to mean other things.

Sign	Also used for
ASK	QUERY, QUESTION
WANT	DESIRE

PRACTICE ACTIVITIES

1. MODEL FOR DIRECTIONAL VERB ASK AND RULE #5. INFORMATION-SEEKING QUESTIONS

Signer A:	1. Describe the topic;
	2. ask a wh-question about the topic.

Topic:	MAN THERE,
Question:	WHO HE?

Signer B:	1. Respond to the question;
	2. use the directional verb MEET to describe a topic;
	3. use the sign WANT to ask a yes/no question.

Response:	ME DON'T-KNOW.
Topic:	you-MEET-him
Question:	WANT YOU?

Signer A:	1. Respond to the question affirmatively;
	2. describe what the signer wants to do.

Response:	YES.
Describe action:	ME WANT me-MEET-him.

Practice

Signer A:	MAN THERE, WHO HE?
Signer B:	ME DON'T-KNOW. you-MEET-him WANT YOU?
Signer A:	YES. ME WANT me-MEET-him.

2. MODEL FOR CLASSIFIER CL-1, DIRECTIONAL VERB ASK, AND RULES #7. RHETORICAL QUESTIONS AND #10. NEGATION

Signer A:	1. Use the classifier cl-1: to describe an action with a subject (YOU) and object (HIM);
	2. use the sign ASK to indicate a second action.

Action 1:	YOU cl-1:you-GO-to-him,
Action 2:	you-ASK-him NAME.

Signer B:
1. Use the classifier cl-1: to describe an action with a subject (ME) and object (HIM);
2. repeat the question with the sign ASK moved in a direction that identifies the subject (ME) and object (HIM) of the sentence;
3. answer the question with the negative sign DON'T-WANT.

Action:	cl-1:me-GO-to-him,
Question:	me-ASK-him NAME?
Response:	ME DON'T-WANT.

Practice

Signer A: YOU cl-1:you-GO-to-him, you-ASK-him NAME.

Signer B.   cl-1:me-GO-to-him, me-ASK-him NAME? ME DON'T-WANT.

3. MODEL FOR RULES #5. INFORMATION-SEEKING QUESTIONS, #7. RHETORICAL QUESTIONS, AND #8. ORDERING OF SIMPLE SENTENCES

Signer A:
1. Describe the topic;
2. ask a wh-question using the sign WHY-NOT.

Topic:	YOU DON'T-WANT,
Question:	WHY-NOT?

Signer B:
1. Respond to the question with a simple sentence.

Response:	ME SHY.

Signer A:
1. Ask a rhetorical question;
2. answer the question.

Rhetorical question:	YOU SHY?
Answer:	ME DOUBT-IT.

Practice

Signer A: YOU DON'T-WANT, WHY-NOT?

Signer B: ME SHY.

Signer A: YOU SHY? ME DOUBT-IT.

4. MODEL FOR CLASSIFIER CL-2, DIRECTIONAL VERB ASK, AND RULE #5. INFORMATION-SEEKING QUESTIONS

Signer A: 1. Use the classifier cl-2: to describe the first action of the subject (TWO-of-us) and the relationship of this action to the object of the sentence (HIM);

2. use the directional verb ASK to describe the second action of the subject and to indicate the object (HIM) in a sentence;

3. ask a wh-question using the sign WHY-NOT.

Action 1:	TWO-of-us, cl-2:we-GO-to-him
Action 2:	ASK-him,
Question:	WHY-NOT?

Signer B: 1. Respond to the question;

2. use the classifier cl-2: to describe an action with a subject (TWO-of-us) and object (HIM);

3. describe the topic.

Response:	SURE.
Action:	cl-2:we-GO-to-him,
Topic:	NAME ASK-him.

Practice

Signer A: TWO-of-us, cl-2:we-GO-to-him ASK-him, WHY-NOT?
Signer B: SURE. cl-2:we-GO-to-him, NAME ASK-him.

5. MASTERY LEARNING

When you feel comfortable signing these phrases, practice signing the entire dialogue shown at the beginning of the lesson. Practice the master dialogue until you can sign the part of each character smoothly.

6. FURTHER PRACTICE

Create ten ASL sentences that use a classifier. Write the English gloss for these sentences and then sign each sentence to a partner who will translate them back to English.

LESSON 24 GOING TO THE WORLD GAMES FOR THE DEAF

LANGUAGE GOALS

The student will
1. use Rules   **#1.** topic/comment,
   #5. information-seeking questions,
   #7. rhetorical questions,
   #8. ordering of simple sentences, and
   #9. conditional sentences.
2. use the directional verb FLY-to.
3. use the preposition EXCEPT.
4. use fourteen new signs in a master dialogue.

THE MASTER DIALOGUE

1. Dale: HELLO P-A-T, YOU EXCITED WHY?
   Hello Pat, why are you excited?

   Pat: ME EXCITED WHY? NEXT-WEEK JAPAN me-FLY-to-there.
   I am excited because I am flying to Japan next week.

2. Dale: JAPAN you-FLY-to-there, FOR-FOR?
   Why are you flying to Japan?

   Pat: JAPAN HOST WORLD GAMES DEAF, W-G-D.
   Japan is hosting the World Games for the Deaf.

3. Dale: W-G-D MEAN?
   What does WGD mean?

   Pat: W-G-D SIMILAR OLYMPICS EXCEPT ATHLETE ALL DEAF.
   The WGD is similar to the Olympics except all of the athletes are deaf.

4. Dale: ATHLETE ALL DEAF, INTERESTING.
   That's interesting that all of the athletes are deaf.

   Pat: SUPPOSE YOU HEARING, YOU W-G-D COMPETE, CAN'T.
   If you are a hearing person, then you can't compete in the WGD.

THE MASTER SIGNS

ALL

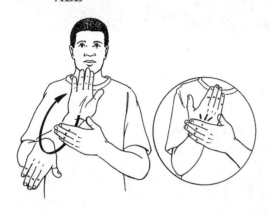

CAN'T

ATHLETE

  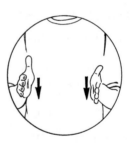

COMPETE

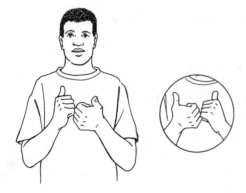

EXCEPT

THE MASTER SIGNS

FLY-to

me-FLY-to

you-FLY-to

FOR-FOR

GAMES

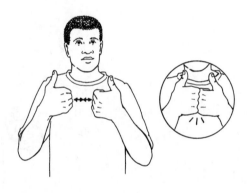

HOST

INTERESTING

THE MASTER SIGNS

JAPAN

SIMILAR

OLYMPICS

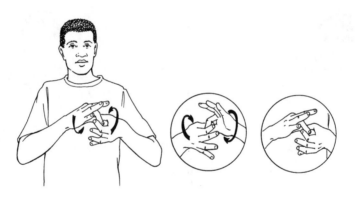

WORLD

WHAT'S IN THE SIGNS (NOTES ABOUT THE GRAMMAR)

1. RULE #5. INFORMATION-SEEKING QUESTIONS

In the dialogue, Dale begins the conversation with a wh-question:

YOU EXCITED WHY?

In this type of question, the wh-question sign comes at or near the end of the sentence.
In the following sentence:

JAPAN you-FLY-to-there, FOR-FOR?

Dale uses the sign FOR-FOR to ask a why question. The sign FOR-FOR always translates
to "why" or "why did you do that" in English. The dialogue contains another information-
seeking question:

W-G-D MEAN?

The nonmanual signals for information-seeking questions provide the clue that the sentence W-G-D MEAN? is a question.

2. RULE #8. ORDERING OF SIMPLE SENTENCES

The following is an example of a subject-verb-object (SVO) ordering of a sentence:

JAPAN HOST WORLD GAMES DEAF, W-G-D.

You fingerspell W-G-D at the end of the sentence to indicate how you will be referring to
the World Games for the Deaf.

3. RULE #7. RHETORICAL QUESTIONS

In the dialogue, Pat uses a rhetorical question to explain why she is excited.

ME EXCITED WHY? NEXT-WEEK JAPAN me-FLY-to-there.

In the second part of this sentence, the time adverb (see Rule #2) is placed at the beginning
of the response to the rhetorical question.

4. DIRECTIONAL VERB FLY-TO

> a. JAPAN me-FLY-to-there.
> b. JAPAN you-FLY-to-there.

The starting and ending positions of the directional verb FLY-to indicate the subject and object of the sentence. In both sentences a and b, the ending position of the sign FLY-to shows the location of the object of the sentence (JAPAN) in the signing space for each signer.

5. PREPOSITION: EXCEPT

The following sentence consists of two phrases joined by the preposition EXCEPT:

W-G-D SIMILAR OLYMPICS EXCEPT ATHLETE ALL DEAF.

6. RULE #1. TOPIC/COMMENT

In the sentence

ATHLETE ALL DEAF, INTERESTING.

a topic is first described followed by a comment.

7. RULE #9. CONDITIONAL SENTENCES

In the following sentence, the condition is first signed followed by the outcome of this condition:

SUPPOSE YOU HEARING, YOU W-G-D COMPETE, CAN'T.

As with all conditional sentences, you (1) *raise your eyebrows* and (2) *tilt the head forward* while stating the condition. The second part of the sentence

YOU W-G-D COMPETE, CAN'T

is an example of Rule #10. negation, which states that the negative sign typically comes at or near the end of the sentence. For the second part of the sentence, the signer may wish to shake the head while signing CAN'T.

WHAT'S IN A SIGN (NOTES ABOUT VOCABULARY)

1. ATHLETES

Some verbs can be made into a noun by adding the AGENT-sign at the end of the verb sign. The sign ATHLETE is made by adding the AGENT-sign to the verb sign COMPETE to get, COMPETE + AGENT-sign = ATHLETE. This sign is also used for COMPETITOR.

2. FLY-TO

FLY-to is a directional verb sign. The locations of the starting and ending position of this sign show the subject and object of the sentence.

3. ME-FLY-TO-THERE

The sign for me-FLY-to-there begins in front of the signer's chest to show that the signer (ME) is the subject. The hand then moves out to a position off to the right or left side of the signing space, which will then represent the place referred to as "there."

4. FOR-FOR

The meaning of the FOR-FOR sign is the same as for the sign WHY. There is no rule for determining when to use FOR-FOR or WHY because both are interchangeable. As you improve in your signing, you will use FOR-FOR in certain situations and WHY in others.

5. GAMES

There is no difference in the way GAME and GAMES are signed because the singular form (GAME) is signed with a repeated motion. Repeated motion can be used to show the plural form of a noun only if the singular form of the noun is not already made with a repeated motion. The reason for using GAMES in the phrase WORLD GAMES DEAF is because that is the appropriate English gloss for the sign given the meaning of the phrase.

6. NEXT-WEEK

The NEXT-WEEK sign is an example of how the signing space is used to indicate time. The body represents the present time, movement of the hand to the front of the body can be used to indicate the future, and movement to the back shows that something has happened in the past. In the sign NEXT-WEEK, the hand moves to the front of the body.

7. WORLD GAMES DEAF (W-G-D)

When introducing an abbreviation, you give the name or phrase first, followed by the initials or letters of the abbreviation.

8. ASL SYNONYMS

Some signs can be used to mean other things.

Sign	Also used for
ALL	WHOLE
ATHLETE	COMPETITOR, RACER
COMPETE	COMPETITION, RACE
EXCEPT	CERTAIN, EXCEPTIONAL, ESPECIALLY, PARTICULAR, SPECIAL
HOST	TAKE-UP
INTERESTING	INTEREST
OLYMPICS	CHAIN
SIMILAR	ALIKE, LIKE

MASTERY LEARNING

1. MODEL FOR RULES #5. INFORMATION-SEEKING QUESTIONS AND #7. RHETORICAL QUESTIONS

Signer A: 1. Describe the topic;
                   2. ask a question about the topic.

Topic: YOU EXCITED
Question: WHY?

Signer B: 1. Repeat the question to form a rhetorical wh-question;
                   2. answer the question.

Rhetorical question: ME EXCITED WHY?
Answer: NEXT-WEEK JAPAN me-FLY-to-there.

Practice

Signer A: YOU EXCITED WHY?
Signer B: ME EXCITED WHY? NEXT-WEEK JAPAN me-FLY-to-there.

2. MODEL FOR RULES #5. INFORMATION-SEEKING QUESTIONS, AND #8. ORDERING OF SIMPLE SENTENCES AND FOR ABBREVIATIONS

Signer A: 1. Describe the topic;

      2. ask a question about the topic using the sign FOR-FOR.

      Topic: JAPAN you-FLY-to-there,

      Question: FOR-FOR?

Signer B: 1. Sign the subject;

      2. sign the verb;

      3. sign the object;

      4. give the abbreviations for the object named in the sentence.

      Subject: JAPAN

      Verb: HOST

      Object: WORLD GAMES DEAF,

      Abbreviation: W-G-D.

Practice

Signer A: JAPAN you-FLY-to-there, FOR-FOR?

Signer B: JAPAN HOST WORLD GAMES DEAF, W-G-D.

3. MODEL FOR RULE #5. INFORMATION-SEEKING QUESTIONS AND FOR PREPOSITION EXCEPT

Signer A: 1. Describe the topic;

      2. ask a question about the topic.

      Topic: W-G-D

      Question: MEAN?

Signer B: 1. Sign the first phrase that is joined by a preposition;

      2. sign the preposition EXCEPT;

      3. sign the phrase following the preposition.

      First phrase: W-G-D SIMILAR OLYMPICS

      Preposition: EXCEPT

      Second phrase: ATHLETE ALL DEAF.

Practice

Signer A: W-G-D MEAN?

Signer B: W-G-D SIMILAR OLYMPICS EXCEPT ATHLETE ALL DEAF.

4. MODEL FOR RULES #1. TOPIC/COMMENT AND #9. CONDITIONAL SENTENCES

| Signer A: | 1. Describe the topic; |
| | 2. make a comment about the topic. |

| Topic: | ATHLETE ALL DEAF, |
| Comment: | INTERESTING. |

| Signer B: | 1. Describe the condition; |
| | 2. describe the outcome of this condition. |

| Condition: | SUPPOSE YOU HEARING, |
| Outcome: | YOU COMPETE W-G-D, CAN'T. |

Practice

Signer A: ATHLETE ALL DEAF, INTERESTING.
Signer B: SUPPOSE YOU HEARING, YOU COMPETE W-G-D, CAN'T.

5. MASTERY LEARNING

When you feel comfortable signing these phrases, practice signing the entire dialogue shown at the beginning of the lesson. Practice the master dialogue until you can sign it comfortably.

6. FURTHER PRACTICE

Practice your fingerspelling skills by fingerspelling an abbreviation and having a partner fingerspell the entire name for it. Use abbreviations for organizations, states, provinces, or anything else. For example,

| Signer A: | O-R |
| Signer B: | O-R-E-G-O-N |

| Signer A: | U-S |
| Signer B: | U-N-I-T-E-D S-T-A-T-E-S |

In the following dialogue, (1) replace the sign EXCITED with other descriptive terms from Lesson 4 or other lessons, and (2) replace the sign NEXT-WEEK with other time adverbs found in Lessons 18–20.

| Signer A: | HELLO, YOU EXCITED WHY? |
| Signer B: | ME EXCITED WHY? NEXT-WEEK JAPAN me-FLY-to-there. |

LESSON 25   SOCIALIZING AND THE WORLD GAMES FOR THE DEAF

LANGUAGE GOALS

The student will
1. use Rules
   - #1. topic/comment,
   - #5. information-seeking questions,
   - #7. rhetorical questions,
   - #8. ordering of simple sentences,
   - #9. conditional sentences, and
   - #10. negation.
2. use the classifier cl:55 to convey the thought of many people going to a particular place.
3. use the directional verbs ARRIVE and GO-to.
4. use nine new signs in a master dialogue.

THE MASTER DIALOGUE

1.   Dale: YOU W-G-D ARRIVE-there, YOU DO-what?
What do you do when you arrive at the World Games for the Deaf?

Pat: ME WATCH COMPETITION.
I watch the competition.

ME ENJOY WATCH MOST WHAT? SWIMMING.
I enjoy watching swimming the most.

2.   Dale: SUPPOSE GAMES BORING, DO-what YOU?
What do you do if the Games are boring?

Pat: GAMES BORING, NEVER!
The Games are never boring!

DEAF PEOPLE COUNTRIES VARIOUS cl-55:FLOCK-to-Games.
Deaf people from many countries come to the Games.

3.   Dale: NEAT!
Hey, that's cool!

Pat: YOU W-G-D GO-to SHOULD.
You should go to the Games.

4.   Dale: YES, ME SHOULD.
Yes, I should.

THE MASTER SIGNS

ARRIVE-there

COUNTRIES

cl-55:FLOCK-to

MOST

NEVER

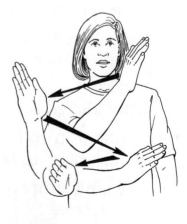

THE MASTER SIGNS

PEOPLE

SHOULD

SWIMMING

VARIOUS

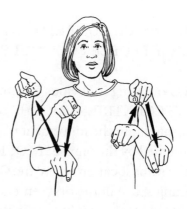

WHAT'S IN THE SIGNS (NOTES ABOUT THE GRAMMAR)

1. RULE #5. INFORMATION-SEEKING QUESTIONS AND THE DIRECTIONAL VERB ARRIVE

The opening sentence of the dialogue is the wh-question

YOU W-G-D ARRIVE-there, YOU DO-what?

The topic is described first followed by the wh-question. The sentence makes use of the directional verb ARRIVE to place the noun W-G-D in the signing space. You can either move the sign ARRIVE toward the left side of your signing space or the right side. After you have done this, you can refer to the World Games for the Deaf by merely pointing to that location.

2. RULE #8. ORDERING OF SIMPLE SENTENCES AND CLASSIFIER: CL-55

The following sentences use the subject-verb-object (SVO) ordering:

a. ME WATCH COMPETITION.
b. DEAF PEOPLE COUNTRIES VARIOUS cl-55:FLOCK-to-Games.

The SVO ordering is obvious in sentence a. In sentence b the subject is clearly signed (DEAF PEOPLE COUNTRIES VARIOUS or Deaf people from various countries), but the object is incorporated into the movement of the classifier cl:55:FLOCK-to-Games. This incorporation is represented by the phrase "FLOCK-to-Games," which is telling you to move the classifier cl-55: to the same location where the Games (i.e., the World Games for the Deaf) were located in the signing space in the first sentence of the dialogue. That is, if Pat signed ARRIVE-there to the right side of the signing space then the classifier cl-55: will also move to the right side.

3. RULE #7. RHETORICAL QUESTIONS

The following rhetorical question was used in the dialogue:

ME ENJOY WATCH MOST WHAT? SWIMMING.

4. RULE #9. CONDITIONAL SENTENCES

The conditional sentence

SUPPOSE GAMES BORING, DO-what YOU?

was translated as "What do you do if the Games are boring?" This is not the only possible translation. Other acceptable translations are "If the Games are boring, what do you do?" and "Suppose the Games are boring, what do you do?" How a sentence gets translated depends upon your command of language and your customary use of words and signs.

5. RULE #10. NEGATION

In the sentence

GAMES BORING, NEVER!

the emphasis is placed on NEVER. The emphasis can be reinforced (1) *by shaking your head* and (2) *by raising your eyebrows* as you sign NEVER!

6. RULE #1. TOPIC/COMMENT AND DIRECTIONAL VERB GO-TO

In the following sentence, Pat is urging Dale to go to the Games:

YOU W-G-D GO-to SHOULD.

Because Pat wishes to emphasize that Dale *should* go to the Games, she signs SHOULD at the end of the sentence. This sentence could also be signed YOU SHOULD GO-to-GAMES. The movement of the directional verb GO-to is to the same location in which the GAMES were placed in the signing space in the first sentence of the dialogue.

WHAT'S IN A SIGN (NOTES ABOUT VOCABULARY)

1. ARRIVE-THERE

The "there" in this sign is telling you to move the sign ARRIVE to a particular place in the signing space. Where this particular place is has to be decided by you. To what is "there" referring? The sign ARRIVE-there comes after the noun W-G-D; therefore, the concept "there" represents is the World Games for the Deaf. Because this is the first sentence of the dialogue, you must decide where in the signing space you are going to place the W-G-D.

2. NEAT

This sign is used to express a feeling about something and is typically translated as "Hey, that's cool," "Cool," "That's neat," and "Neat." It is *not* to be used to mean orderly as in "The room looked neat and tidy."

3. ASL SYNONYMS

Some signs can be used to mean other things.

Sign	Also used for
NEAT	COOL
SHOULD	NECESSARY, NEED
SWIMMING	SWIM
VARIOUS	DIVERSE, DIVERSITY, ETCETERA (ETC.), VARY

PRACTICE ACTIVITIES

1. MODEL FOR RULES #5. INFORMATION-SEEKING QUESTIONS, #7. RHETORICAL QUESTIONS, AND #8. ORDERING OF SIMPLE SENTENCES

Signer A: 1. Describe the topic and sign ARRIVE-there to either the right or left side of the signing space;
2. ask a question about the topic.

Topic: YOU W-G-D ARRIVE-there,
Question: YOU DO-what?

Signer B:
1. Sign the subject;
2. sign the verb;
3. sign the object.

Subject:	ME
Verb:	WATCH
Object:	COMPETITION.

1. Ask a rhetorical question;
2. answer the question.

| Rhetorical question: | ME ENJOY WATCH MOST WHAT? |
| Answer: | SWIMMING. |

Practice

Signer A: YOU W-G-D ARRIVE-there, YOU DO-what?
Signer B: ME WATCH COMPETITION.
ME ENJOY WATCH MOST WHAT? SWIMMING.

2. MODEL FOR RULES #8. ORDERING OF SIMPLE SENTENCES, #9. CONDITIONAL SENTENCES, AND #10. NEGATION

Signer A:
1. Describe the condition;
2. ask a wh-question about the condition.

| Condition: | SUPPOSE GAMES BORING, |
| Question: | DO-what YOU? |

Signer B:
1. Describe the topic;
2. sign the negative sign NEVER.

| Topic: | GAMES BORING, |
| Negation: | NEVER! |

1. Sign the subject;
2. sign the classifier that includes the verb and object of the sentence (sign cl-55 to the same location where the hands moved for the sign ARRIVE-there).

| Subject: | DEAF PEOPLE COUNTRIES VARIOUS |
| Verb & object: | cl-55:FLOCK-to-Games. |

Practice

Signer A: SUPPOSE GAMES BORING, DO-what YOU?

Signer B: GAMES BORING, NEVER!

DEAF PEOPLE COUNTRIES VARIOUS cl-55:FLOCK-to-Games.

3. MODEL FOR RULE #1. TOPIC/COMMENT

Signer A: 1. Describe the topic;

2. make a comment about the topic.

Topic: YOU W-G-D GO-to

Comment: SHOULD.

Signer B: 1. Respond affirmatively to the comment just made;

2. repeat the comment.

Response: YES,

Comment: ME SHOULD.

Practice

Signer A: YOU W-G-D GO-to SHOULD.

Signer B: YES, ME SHOULD.

4. MASTERY LEARNING

When you feel comfortable signing these phrases, practice signing the entire dialogue shown at the beginning of the lesson. Practice the master dialogue until you can sign it comfortably.

5. FURTHER PRACTICE

Join the master dialogue with the one in Lesson 24 and practice signing both of them until you are comfortable signing them. Note that you must select a location for the World Games for the Deaf in the signing space and maintain it through both master dialogues.

LESSON 26   SIGNING AND THE WORLD GAMES FOR THE DEAF

LANGUAGE GOALS

The student will
1.   use Rules   #3. simple yes/no questions,
   #4. long yes/no questions,
   #5. information-seeking questions, and
   #7. rhetorical questions.
2.   use the classifier cl-55.
3.   use nine new signs in a master dialogue.

THE MASTER DIALOGUE

1.   Dale: DEAF PEOPLE W-G-D cl-55:FLOCK-to-Games, YOU SOCIALIZE?
   Do you socialize with the Deaf people who go to the World Games for the Deaf?

   Pat: YES WHY? DEAF PEOPLE FROM DIFFERENT+ COUNTRIES SIGN DIFFERENT.
   Yes I do, because Deaf people from various countries sign differently.

2.   Dale: ASL NOT UNIVERSAL?
   You mean that ASL is not universal?

   Pat: RIGHT. ASL USE WHERE? UNITED-STATES CANADA.
   That's right. ASL is used in the United States and Canada.

3.   Dale: OH-I-see. W-G-D COUNTRIES INVOLVED, HOW-MANY?
   I see. How many countries are involved in the WGD?

   Pat: COUNTRIES 57.
   Fifty-seven countries.

THE MASTER SIGNS

CANADA

DIFFERENT

DIFFERENT+

FROM

HOW-MANY

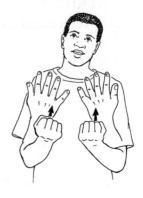

THE MASTER SIGNS

INVOLVED

SOCIALIZE

UNITED-STATES

UNIVERSAL

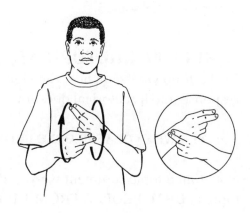

USE

WHAT'S IN THE SIGNS (NOTES ABOUT THE GRAMMAR)

1. RULE #4. LONG YES/NO QUESTIONS AND CLASSIFIER CL-55

In the following sentence, the topic is first described followed by a yes/no question about the topic.

topic:	DEAF PEOPLE W-G-D cl-55:FLOCK-to-Games
question:	YOU SOCIALIZE?

Because of the length of the sentence, the nonmanual signals would be used only when the question is signed.

The classifier cl-55:FLOCK-to-Games will be moved to the right or left of the signing space. Because this dialogue is a continuation of the two previous dialogues, you should practice moving the classifier to the location where the Games were initially placed in the signing space in Lesson 24. Also, although the noun W-G-D is inserted in this sentence, it would not have been necessary to do so if this dialogue was signed as a continuation of the dialogue in Lesson 25.

2. RULE #7. RHETORICAL QUESTIONS

In the following sentence, the signer is responding to a question and then turning the response into a rhetorical question:

YES WHY? DEAF PEOPLE FROM DIFFERENT+ COUNTRIES SIGN DIFFERENT.

Note that a topic/comment word ordering is used to respond to the WHY? question—the topic is DEAF PEOPLE FROM DIFFERENT+ COUNTRIES, and the comment is SIGN DIFFERENT.

Another rhetorical question in the dialogue was

ASL USE WHERE? UNITED-STATES CANADA.

This sentence is an example of how the sign WHERE is commonly used.

3. RULE #3. SIMPLE YES/NO QUESTIONS

The question

ASL NOT UNIVERSAL?

is distinguished from the declarative sentence "ASL is not universal" by the nonmanual signals that accompany the sentence. For yes/no questions, the nonmanual signals are (1) *the raised eyebrows* and (2) *the head tilting forward*.

4. RULE #5. INFORMATION-SEEKING QUESTIONS

The following question is asked about the number of countries involved in the WGD.

W-G-D COUNTRIES INVOLVED, HOW-MANY?

This was translated to "How many countries are involved in the WGD?" The sign INVOLVED could also be translated as "How many countries take part in the WGD?" The response to this question was COUNTRIES 57, which is an example of a noun-adjective word ordering commonly used in ASL.

WHAT'S IN A SIGN (NOTES ABOUT VOCABULARY)

1. UNITED-STATES

The sign UNITED-STATES is the same one used for America or American. That is, this sign would be used to sign AMERICA as in NORTH AMERICA and American as in AMERICAN SIGN LANGUAGE. If you wanted to ensure that the addressee understood that the meaning of the sign is United States and not America, then you could fingerspell U-S or U-S-A.

2. SOCIALIZE

The movement of the SOCIALIZE sign represents people interacting with one another. It is *not* used to mean social or society.

3. DIFFERENT+

Recall that the plus symbol (+) means to repeat a sign. When the sign DIFFERENT is repeated, its meaning is similar to the sign VARIOUS. When you sign DIFFERENT the second time, you should move both hands over to the side slightly.

4. ASL SYNONYMS
Some signs can be used to mean other things.

Sign	Also used for
DIFFERENT	BUT
DIFFERENT+	VARIOUS
SOCIALIZE	ACQUAINT, ASSOCIATE, BROTHERHOOD, EACH-OTHER, FELLOWSHIP, FRATERNITY, INTERACT, INTERACTION, INTERACTIVE, MINGLE, ONE-ANOTHER
UNITED-STATES	AMERICA, AMERICAN
INVOLVED	INCLUDE, TAKE-PART
HOW-MANY	HOW-MUCH

PRACTICE ACTIVITIES

1. MODEL FOR RULES #4. LONG YES/NO QUESTIONS AND #7. RHETORICAL QUESTIONS

Signer A: 1. Describe the topic;
2. ask a yes/no question about the topic.

Topic: DEAF PEOPLE W-G-D cl-55:FLOCK-to-Games,
Question: YOU SOCIALIZE?

Signer B: 1. Respond affirmatively;
2. ask a rhetorical question using WHY;
3. describe the topic;
4. make a comment about the topic.

Response: YES
Rhetorical question: WHY?
Topic: DEAF PEOPLE FROM DIFFERENT+ COUNTRIES
Comment: SIGN DIFFERENT.

Practice

Signer A: DEAF PEOPLE W-G-D cl-55:FLOCK-to-Games, YOU SOCIALIZE?

Signer B: YES WHY? DEAF PEOPLE FROM DIFFERENT+ COUNTRIES SIGN DIFFERENT.

2. MODEL FOR RULES #3. SIMPLE YES/NO QUESTIONS, #5. INFORMATION-SEEKING QUESTIONS, AND #7. RHETORICAL QUESTIONS

Signer A: 1. Describe the topic;
            2. ask a yes/no question about the topic.

Topic:	ASL
Question:	NOT UNIVERSAL?

Signer B: 1. Respond affirmatively to the yes/no question;
            2. ask a rhetorical question;
            3. answer the question.

Response:	RIGHT.
Rhetorical question:	ASL USE WHERE?
Answer:	UNITED-STATES CANADA.

Signer A: 1. Acknowledge that you understand what was just said;
            2. describe a topic;
            3. ask a question about the topic.

Acknowledgment:	OH-I-see.
Topic:	W-G-D. COUNTRIES INVOLVED,
Question:	HOW-MANY?

Signer B: 1. Respond to the question using a noun-adjective phrase.

Response:	COUNTRIES 57.

Practice

Signer A: ASL NOT UNIVERSAL?

Signer B: RIGHT. ASL USE WHERE? UNITED-STATES CANADA.

Signer A: OH-I-see. W-G-D COUNTRIES INVOLVED, HOW-MANY?

Signer B: COUNTRIES 57.

3. MASTERY LEARNING

When you feel comfortable signing these phrases, practice signing the entire dialogue shown at the beginning of the lesson. Practice the master dialogue until you can sign the part of each character smoothly.

4. FURTHER PRACTICE

Sign all the dialogues in Lessons 24–26 together. Remember that after you have established a place in the signing space for the World Games for the Deaf, you should refer to this location when using the classifier cl-55:FLOCK-to-Games and the directional verbs ARRIVE-there and GO-to-Games.

REVIEW OF LESSONS 21–26

Write an English translation for each of the following ASL sentences.

1. W-G-D, you-GO-to-there FOR-FOR?

2. W-G-D PEOPLE cl-55:FLOCK-to-Games, WHEN?

3. W-G-D DEAF PEOPLE COMPETE HOW-MANY?

4. YOU COMPETITION INVOLVE HOW-MANY?

5. YOU DIFFERENT+ LANGUAGE UNDERSTAND, HOW-MANY?

6. NEXT-YEAR, GAMES WHERE?

7. IN-3-YEARS GAMES WHERE? CANADA.

8. EVERY DAY TIME 7:00, MAN cl-1:WALK-past-me.

9. 4-WEEKS-AGO, GAME you-CHALLENGE-him WHAT?

10. SUPPOSE YOUR CLASS me-JOIN, you-HELP-me STUDY DON'T-MIND YOU?

ANSWERS

Note that there may be other ways of translating these sentences than the ones shown here.

1. Why are you going to the WGD?

2. When are people going to the WGD?

3. How many Deaf people compete in the WGD?

4. How many competitions are you involved with?

5. How many different languages do you understand?

6. Where are the Games next year?

7. In three years, the Games will be in Canada.

8. Every day at seven o'clock, a man walks past me.

9. In what game did you challenge him four weeks ago?

10. If I join your class, would you mind helping me study?

Deaf Organizations

12

The National Association of the Deaf (NAD) is the oldest advocacy organization of, for, and by Deaf people in the United States and possibly the world. The NAD was founded in 1880, the same year as the passage of the infamous resolution against sign language by the International Congress on Education of the Deaf in Milan, Italy. Since its inception, the NAD has served as a national leader and crusader for rights of Deaf people and global Deaf awareness. Some of its accomplishments have included lobbying for basic rights and entitlements: to drive vehicles, to marry other Deaf people, to adopt children, to insurance, and to jobs and promotions.

—ROSALYN ROSEN
Politics of Deafness

HOLD THAT SIGN . . .

In the infamous resolution that Rosalyn Rosen mentions, a group of educators decreed that all Deaf children were to be educated through the use of speech and hearing alone and that signing was an unsuitable means for teaching Deaf children. The resolution came at a time when nearly all Deaf children were being taught in ASL in the United States. The Deaf population at that time had little choice but to group themselves together to fight the effects of this resolution and have ASL reinstated as a preferable language for teaching Deaf children. They did not win the battle against the Milan resolution, and the oral method of education took control of the education of Deaf children for eighty years. Nevertheless, the founding of the NAD illustrates how many Deaf organizations are formed in response to what Deaf people view as unfairness toward them by others. The NAD is still in existence today, and the preservation of ASL is still one of its prominent goals. This chapter provides a brief description of a few selected national organizations of the Deaf in the United States.

NATIONAL ASSOCIATION OF THE DEAF

814 Thayer Avenue
Silver Spring, MD 20910
Internet address: *http://www.NAD.org/*

The NAD is a national advocacy group that works with its state affiliations to improve the lives of Deaf people. The NAD was formed in reaction to nondeaf people denying the use of ASL in the education of Deaf children and even though ASL is the focus of many of its activities, the NAD also works to improve the social conditions of Deaf people and promote the integrity of the Deaf community. It sponsors biennial conventions that are attended by thousands of Deaf people from all over the country and other parts of the world. The convention serves to remind Deaf people about their heritage and accomplishments, as well as to focus their attention on the critical issues of the times. The convention includes a Miss Deaf America pageant; presentations and workshops relating to education, rehabilitation, the workplace, technology, and other matters; exhibits promoting recent technological developments, publications, videos, and information about other events of interest to Deaf people; banquets; and theatrical performances. It is the grandest show of Deaf people in America, many of whom use the occasion as an opportunity to reunite with friends and former classmates.

The convention is also a time for NAD to determine its advocacy agenda and to formulate a united stance on various issues relating to bettering the lives of Deaf people. The *NAD Broadcaster* is the premier publication of this association.

JUNIOR NATIONAL ASSOCIATION OF THE DEAF YOUTH PROGRAM

For information: *youth@nad.org*

The NAD sponsors a Junior NAD progam for school-age Deaf children. The purpose of the program is to develop leadership skills in Deaf students who will then use these skills to build stronger Deaf organizations wherever they might one day settle. Typically, schools for the Deaf are the home base for most Junior NAD programs. Each year, selected members from each state Junior NAD chapter are invited to a summer leadership program. Here they meet adult Deaf leaders and learn about key issues in the Deaf community and what they can do to preserve and promote Deaf culture in their homes and communities.

NATIONAL FRATERNAL SOCIETY OF THE DEAF

Internet address: *http://www.nfsd.com*

The National Fraternal Society of the Deaf (NFSD) was founded in 1901 in reaction to the practice of insurance companies to either deny Deaf people any coverage or to charge them excessively high premiums for life and disability insurance. The NFSD's agenda is largely a business one, but it does advocate for legislative changes that will improve the lives of Deaf people. It also has scholarships for Deaf students and awards for Deaf athletes.

GALLAUDET UNIVERSITY ALUMNI ASSOCIATION

Gallaudet University
800 Florida Avenue, NE
Washington, DC 20002
Internet address: *http://www.gallaudet.edu/~alumweb/*

Gallaudet University is the only liberal arts university for the Deaf in the world. It is world renowned and has been referred to as the mecca of the Deaf community. Given this status, it is not surprising that its alumni exert much influence on the activities of Deaf communities. The primary goals of the Gallaudet University Alumni Association (GUAA) are to increase the influence and prestige of Gallaudet University and to promote the welfare of Deaf people, particularly in the area of education. Many GUAA members are prominent in their local Deaf communities. The GUAA also awards scholarships, and one such recipient, I. K. Jordan, went on to become the first Deaf president of Gallaudet University in 1988.

NATIONAL THEATER OF THE DEAF

Internet address: *http://www.ntd.org*

The National Theater of the Deaf (NTD) was founded in 1967 and is not an organization of Deaf people in the same sense as the NAD and NFSD. It is a group of Deaf and nondeaf actors who perform across the United States and other parts of the world. Their value to the Deaf community is that their performances are in ASL, which has helped introduce many nondeaf people to sign language as well as inspire many Deaf children to take pride in their language and culture. A part of their repertoire are skits that aim to educate people about Deaf culture and to illustrate the experiences of Deaf people in their daily living. The skits are also used to attack the negative stereotypes that nondeaf people have about Deaf people and, in the language of the stage, show that Deaf and nondeaf people are not all that much different.

UNITED STATES OF AMERICA DEAF SPORTS FEDERATION

Internet address: *http://www.usadsf.org/*

Formerly known as the American Athletic Association for the Deaf, the U.S.A. Deaf Sports Federation (USADSF) was founded in 1945 to promote athletic competitions among Deaf athletes. The USADSF provides year-round training and competition that promote physical fitness, sportsmanship, and self-esteem as well as develop elite-level athletic skills in a variety of sports at the state, regional, national, and international level. While the USADSF focuses on Deaf athletes competing against one another, it also provides opportunitites for competition with nondeaf peers. This type of competition is desirable for at least three reasons. First, both groups of people are competing on equal grounds with the use of signing and the use of hearing giving no team an advantage. Second, the competition is an opportunity to increase awareness of the Deaf community among nondeaf people. Third, the competition prepares the athletes for competition at higher levels where the competitors are all Deaf.

The USADSF recognizes that not all its athletes will know how to sign when they first begin competing on a Deaf team. Indeed, USADSF actively fosters social interactions among athletes and their supporters. As a result, many athletes who do not know ASL when they first get involved in Deaf sports activities eventually come to learn it and develop a fondness for the Deaf community. The USADSF also selects and prepares athletes for competition in the Deaflympics. The Deaflympics is a quadrennial event with summer and winter Games. The Games are held all over the world and the competitions are of high caliber with some of the Deaf athletes also representing their countries in the Olympics.

There are also several national organizations for specific sports that are affiliated with the USADSF, including the U.S. Deaf Team Handball Association, U.S. Deaf Skiers and Snowboarders Association, and the U.S.A. Deaf Basketball. The USADSF publishes a magazine called *Deaf Sports Review* and a newsletter.

THE WORLD RECREATION ASSOCIATION OF THE DEAF

Internet address: *http://www.wrad.org*

The World Recreation Association of the Deaf (WRAD) was incorporated in 1985 to promote greater participation of Deaf people in recreation and leisure activities. There are activities that are suitable for all ages and include walks through city parks, camping excursions in national parks, Caribbean cruises, skiing, beach parties, paint pistol war games, and scuba diving. The goal of all activities is accessibility, and arrangements are made for sign language interpreters who ensure that the Deaf people are able to take advantage of all that an activity has to offer. The activities of the WRAD are open to nondeaf people as well, and there are WRAD organizations in other countries including Turkey, Colombia, France, and South Africa. Information about the organization is available in *The WRAD News*.

CANADIAN ASSOCIATION OF THE DEAF

Internet address: *http://www.cad.ca*

The Canadian Association of the Deaf (CAD) is a national consumer organization for Deaf Canadians. It advocates in much the same way that the NAD does for Deaf Americans. As a consumer organization, it functions as a research and information center, an advisory council on legislative matters relating to the well-being of Deaf people, a self-help society, and a community action organization.

Over the years, the association has undertaken a number of activities that have ranged from speaking against Deaf peddlers in the 1940s, establishing a Canadian Deaf Information Centre in the 1960s, sponsoring National Education Workshops to address issues relating to the use of communication in the education of Deaf students in the 1970s, hiring a full-time staff person in the 1980s, and establishing a Hall of Fame in 1991. It is actively involved in ensuring that Deaf Canadians are represented in legislative matters relating to employment, education, human rights, and technology.

CANADIAN DEAF SPORTS ASSOCIATION

Internet address: *http://www.assc-cdsa.com*

The Canadian Deaf Sports Association (CDSA) promotes the physical fitness of Deaf persons by creating opportunities for participation in a variety of amateur sports and recreation activities. Through its provincial affiliations, the CDSA promotes participation in sports through the sponsorship of national competitions in bowling, slo-pitch, and darts. The Canadian Deaf Curling Association and the Canadian Deaf Ice Hockey Federation are also affiliated with the CDSA.

A primary goal for the CDSA is to select and prepare athletes to compete in the World Games for the Deaf, a competition that the CDSA has participated in since 1965. The CDSA hosted its first and only World Winter Games for the Deaf in 1991, in Banff, Alberta. The Summer and Winter Games are quadrennial events and occur two years apart from each other.

REVIEW EXERCISE

1. Compile a list of organizations of the Deaf in your state. You may find the Internet helpful in this activity.

2. Write to one of the organizations on your list to gather information about the types of activities it is involved in.

3. Why was the founding of the National Association of the Deaf an important event?

4. Find out the date and place of the next World Games for the Deaf.

5. Imagine that you are a reporter writing a story about an organization for the Deaf. Write five questions that you would want to ask about this organization and explain the reasons why.

ANSWER EXPLANATIONS

1. Use the Internet to find Deaf organizations.

2. Send an e-mail to one of the organizations that you listed in answer to question number 1.

3. The National Association of the Deaf (NAD) has helped protect Deaf and Hard of Hearing persons against discrimination in employment, education, telecommunication, television, and other services by involving the U.S. Congress in passing legislation like the American with Disabilities Act, the Television Decoder Circuitry Act of 1990, telecommunication rules and regulations, etc. NAD has been the voice of Deaf and Hard of Hearing citizens.

4. Check *http://deafolympics.com*

5. Suggested questions:

   a. What does the organization do? (People would need to know what services they provide.)

   b. Where is the office? (Office location is needed so that people can visit or write to the organization.)

   c. What is the phone number, e-mail address, and website? (People need this information to contact individuals and departments at these organizations.)

   d. What, when, and where is the next activity? (The public will need to know how and where they can participate in the group's activities.

   e. Who can become a member? (This question is necessary because each organization has different rules.

The Deaf and Hearing World

13

LESSON 27   SPORTS AND LEISURE ACTIVITIES: PART 1

LANGUAGE GOALS

The student will
1. use Rules
   - #1. topic/comment,
   - #2. tense with time adverbs,
   - #3. simple yes/no questions,
   - #4. long yes/no questions,
   - #5. information-seeking questions,
   - #7. rhetorical questions,
   - #8. ordering of simple sentences, and
   - #10. negation.
2. use the sign FINISH to indicate that an action occurred in the past and as the command "stop."
3. use the directional verb TEASE.
4. use fifteen new signs in a master dialogue.

THE MASTER DIALOGUE

1. Alan: BASEBALL GAME TWO TICKETS, ME BUY FINISH.
YOU WANT GO YOU?
I have bought two tickets to a baseball game. Do you want to go?

 Mary: BASEBALL ME ENJOY, NOT. ME DECLINE.
I don't enjoy baseball. I will decline.

2. Alan: ME TICKETS HAVE.
I have the tickets.

 Mary: O-H W-E-L-L. TICKETS SELL, YOU CAN.
Oh, well. You can sell the tickets.

3. Alan: FINE. TONIGHT, RESTAURANT GO OKAY?
That's fine. How about going to a restaurant tonight?

 Mary: MYSELF, RESTAURANT GO?
Go to a restaurant by myself?

4. Alan: FUNNY. you-TEASE-me FINISH.
That's funny. Stop teasing me.

 Mary: RESTAURANT, EXPENSIVE CHEAP WHICH?
Is the restaurant expensive or cheap?

5. Alan: FOR YOU? CHEAP.
For you it will be cheap.

 Mary: THANK-you. ME ACCEPT.
Thank you. I accept.

THE MASTER SIGNS

ACCEPT

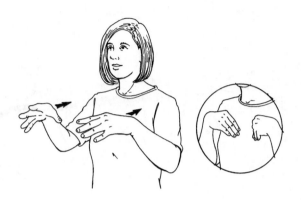

BASEBALL

BUY

THE MASTER SIGNS

CAN

CHEAP

DECLINE

EXPENSIVE

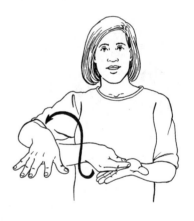

FOR

FUNNY

THE MASTER SIGNS

GO

HAVE

RESTAURANT

SELL

you-TEASE-me

TICKETS

WHAT'S IN THE SIGNS (NOTES ABOUT THE GRAMMAR)

1. RULE #1. TOPIC/COMMENT

Three sentences used the topic/comment format.

    a. BASEBALL GAME TWO TICKETS, ME BUY FINISH.
    b. TICKETS SELL, YOU CAN.
    c. you-TEASE-ME FINISH.

Note that in sentence a the sign FINISH determines the tense of the sentence but that in sentence c FINISH is used to mean stop.

2. RULE #3. SIMPLE YES/NO QUESTIONS

Two sentences asked yes/no questions.

    a. TONIGHT, RESTAURANT GO OKAY?
    b. MYSELF, RESTAURANT GO?

In sentence a Rule #2. tense with time adverbs, is also used because the tense is established directly with the use of the sign TONIGHT. Although the nonmanual signals for yes/no questions apply to both questions, the flavor of the dialogue is such that Mary asks question b with a tongue-in-cheek mannerism. You can reflect this mannerism by (1) *smiling slightly* while (2) *tilting your head* and (3) *raising your eyebrows* when signing the question.

3. RULE #4. LONG YES/NO QUESTIONS

The question YOU WANT GO YOU? can stand alone as a simple yes/no question, or it can be thought of as part of a long yes/no question because it is asking a question about the previous sentence.

BASEBALL GAME TWO TICKETS, ME BUY FINISH. YOU WANT GO YOU?

4. RULE #5. INFORMATION-SEEKING QUESTIONS

The question

RESTAURANT, EXPENSIVE CHEAP WHICH?

is an example of a question that specifies two of the possible answers. Notice that no sign for the concept "or" is in the sentence. The concept "or" is expressed in the meaning of the sign WHICH.

5. RULE #7. RHETORICAL QUESTIONS

The following sentence is another example of how the mood of the signer will influence the nonmanual signals when signing

FOR YOU? CHEAP.

The sentence does contain a rhetorical question, but there are several options for the type of nonmanual signals when signing CHEAP. It could be signed with a hint of humor, with a bland look, with a look of mock seriousness, and so forth.

6. RULE #8. ORDERING OF SIMPLE SENTENCES

   a. ME DECLINE.
   b. ME TICKETS HAVE.
   c. ME ACCEPT.

Sentences a and c use a simple subject-verb format. The objects of both sentences are implied from the dialogue. It is readily understood that in sentence a Mary is declining the invitation to go to a baseball game and in sentence c she is accepting the invitation to go to a restaurant.

7. RULE #10. NEGATION

The negation rule was applied in the following sentence:

BASEBALL ME ENJOY, NOT.

The topic is first described, followed by the negative sign NOT.

WHAT'S IN A SIGN (NOTES ABOUT VOCABULARY)

1. FUNNY

The English gloss of a sign is only the best approximation for a sign. Your facial grammar provides the clues necessary to determine the exact meaning of a sign. In the dialogue, Alan signs FUNNY, but it is clear that he does not mean that what Mary had just said is very funny or it is something to laugh at. Rather, Alan's intended meaning is more like "Yeah right, funny" or "I could almost laugh at that." Study the dialogue and decide how you might sign it. With a deadpan expression? With an exasperated look?

2. YOU-TEASE-ME

TEASE is a directional verb. The dominant hand moves toward the signer to indicate that the subject is "you" and the object is "me."

3. GO

Compare the formation of this sign with GO-to. Although the signs can sometimes be used interchangeably, there are instances when one sign feels more appropriate than the other. The sign GO-to is a directional verb and is always used when the signer wishes to indicate movement to a specific location in the signing space. The sign GO is often used when movement to a particular point in the signing space is not necessary. For example, GO is best used when the meaning of the sentence is along the lines "Let's go" and "He's gone."

4. ASL SYNONYMS

Some signs can be used to mean other things.

Sign	Also used for
ACCEPT	APPROVE
BASEBALL	BAT
BUY	PURCHASE
CHEAP	BARGAIN, INEXPENSIVE
DECLINE	REJECT, WAIVE
FUNNY	COMEDY, HUMOR, JOKE
GO	GONE

PRACTICE ACTIVITIES

1. MODEL FOR RULES #1. TOPIC/COMMENT, #4. LONG YES/NO QUESTIONS, #8. ORDERING OF SIMPLE SENTENCES, AND #10. NEGATION

Signer A:	1. Describe the topic;
	2. say something about the topic;
	3. ask a yes/no question about the topic.

Topic:	BASEBALL GAME TWO TICKETS,
Comment:	ME BUY FINISH.
Question:	YOU WANT GO YOU?

Signer B:	1. Describe the topic;
	2. negate the topic with a negative sign;
	3. describe an action with a simple sentence structure.

Topic:	BASEBALL ME ENJOY,
Negative:	NOT.
Action:	ME DECLINE.

Practice

Signer A:	BASEBALL GAME TWO TICKETS, ME BUY FINISH. YOU WANT GO YOU?
Signer B:	BASEBALL ME ENJOY, NOT. ME DECLINE.

2. MODEL FOR RULES #1. TOPIC/COMMENT AND #8. ORDERING OF SIMPLE SENTENCES

Signer A:	1. Create a simple subject-verb-object sentence.

SVO:	ME TICKETS HAVE.

Signer B:	1. Make a comment about the previous sentence;
	2. describe the topic;
	3. make a comment about the topic.

Comment:	O-H W-E-L-L.
Topic:	TICKETS SELL,
Comment:	YOU CAN.

Practice

Signer A: ME TICKETS HAVE.
Signer B: O-H W-E-L-L. TICKETS SELL, YOU CAN.

3. MODEL FOR RULES #1. TOPIC/COMMENT, #2. TENSE WITH TIME ADVERBS, AND #3. SIMPLE YES/NO QUESTIONS

Signer A: 1. Establish the tense with a time adverb;
                  2. describe the topic;
                  3. ask a yes/no question about the topic.

Tense:	TONIGHT,
Topic:	RESTAURANT GO
Question:	OKAY?

Signer B: 1. Describe the topic;
                  2. ask a question about the topic.

Topic:	MYSELF,
Question:	RESTAURANT GO?

Signer A: 1. Respond to the question with a comment;
                  2. describe an action as a topic;
                  3. indicate that the action is to stop by using FINISH to make a comment about the topic.

Comment:	FUNNY.
Topic (action)	you-TEASE-me,
Comment:	FINISH.

Practice

Signer A: TONIGHT, RESTAURANT GO OKAY?
Signer B: MYSELF, RESTAURANT GO?
Signer A: FUNNY. you-TEASE-ME, FINISH.

4. MODEL FOR RULES #5. INFORMATION-SEEKING QUESTIONS, #7. RHETORICAL QUESTIONS, AND #8. ORDERING OF SIMPLE SENTENCES

Signer A: 1. Describe the topic;
            2. ask a question about the topic.

Topic:	RESTAURANT,
Question:	EXPENSIVE CHEAP WHICH?

Signer B: 1. Ask a rhetorical question;
            2. answer the question.

Rhetorical question:	FOR YOU?
Answer:	CHEAP.

Signer A: 1. Make a courteous response;
            2. describe an action with a simple sentence structure.

Response:	THANK-you.
Action:	ME ACCEPT.

Practice

Signer A: RESTAURANT, EXPENSIVE CHEAP WHICH?
Signer B: FOR YOU? CHEAP.
Signer A: THANK-you. ME ACCEPT.

5. MASTERY LEARNING

When you feel comfortable signing these phrases, practice signing the entire dialogue shown at the beginning of the lesson. Practice the master dialogue until you can sign the part of each character smoothly while using the appropriate nonmanual signals. Try to assume the mannerism that you think each character in the dialogue is portraying.

6. FURTHER PRACTICE

Create five alternative responses for Signer B in the following dialogue:

Signer A: BASEBALL GAME, YOU WANT GO YOU?
Signer B: BASEBALL ME ENJOY, NOT. ME DECLINE.

Practice signing the dialogue and the alternative responses with a partner.

LESSON 28   SPORTS AND LEISURE ACTIVITIES: PART 2

LANGUAGE GOALS

The student will
1.   use Rules   #1. topic/comment,
                     #3. simple yes/no questions,
                     #5. information-seeking questions,
                     #8. ordering of simple sentences, and
                #10. negation.
2.   use thirty new signs to describe sports and leisure activities.

THE MASTER DIALOGUE

1.   Mary: YOU PLAY SPORT?
             Do you play sports?

     Alan: YES. MANY SPORTS, ME INVOLVE.
             Yes. I'm involved in many sports.

2.   Mary: YOUR FAVORITE SPORT, WHAT?
             What's your favorite sport?

     Alan: VOLLEYBALL, TENNIS.
             Volleyball and tennis.

THE MASTER SIGNS

FAVORITE

MANY

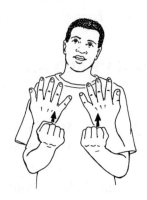

THE MASTER SIGNS

PLAY

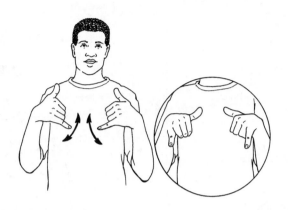

SPORTS

BASKETBALL

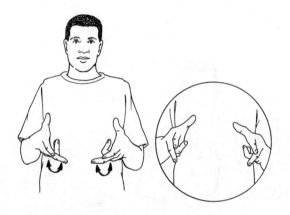

CYCLING

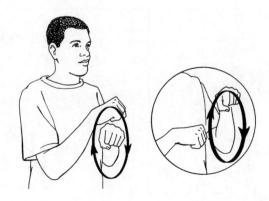

THE MASTER SIGNS

SPORTS

BOWLING

FOOTBALL

GOLF

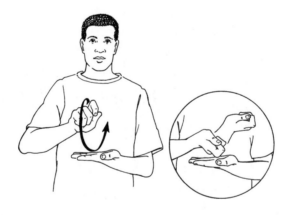

HOCKEY

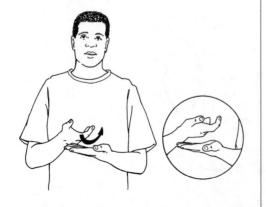

SOCCER

THE MASTER SIGNS

SPORTS

SKIING

SPORT

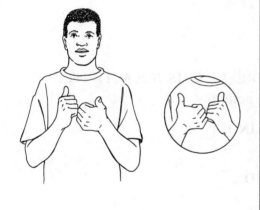

VOLLEYBALL

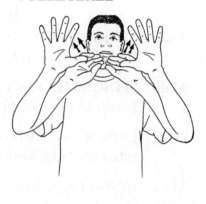

TENNIS

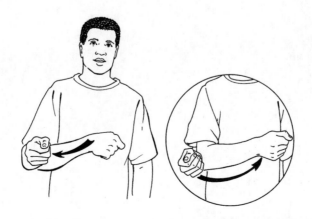

THE MASTER SIGNS

SPORTS

WRESTLING

THE MASTER DIALOGUE

1.　　Alan:　SPORTS, YOU LIKE?
　　　　　　Do you like sports?

　　　Mary:　SPORTS ME DON'T-LIKE. ME PREFER LEISURE ACTIVITIES.
　　　　　　I don't like sports. I prefer leisure activities.

2.　　Alan:　LEISURE ACTIVITIES, WHAT KIND?
　　　　　　What kind of leisure activities?

　　　Mary:　HORSEBACK RIDING, BILLIARDS.
　　　　　　Horseback riding and billiards.

THE MASTER SIGNS

ACTIVITIES

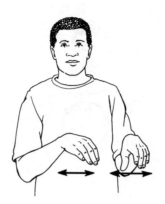

DON'T LIKE

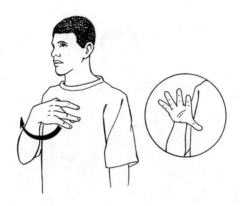

KIND

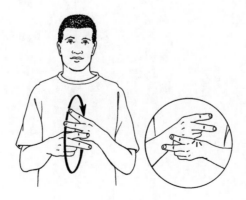

THE MASTER SIGNS

LEISURE

PREFER

THE MASTER SIGNS

LEISURE

BILLIARDS

EXERCISE

CAMPING

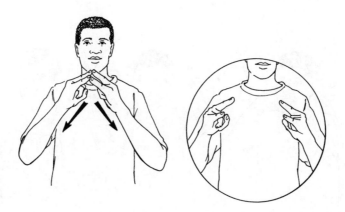

CANOEING

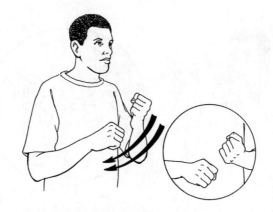

THE MASTER SIGNS

LEISURE

CARDS

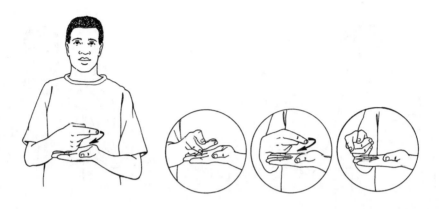

HORSEBACK RIDING

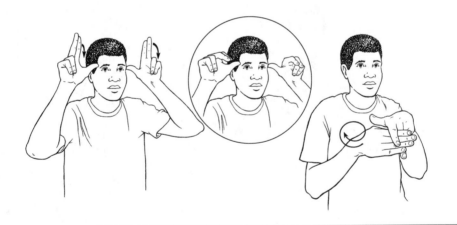

HUNTING

THE MASTER SIGNS

LEISURE

ICE-SKATING

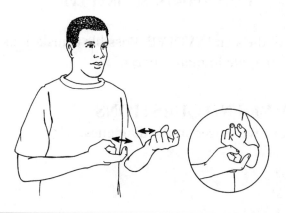

RUNNING

ROLLER-SKATING

WHAT'S IN THE SIGNS (NOTES ABOUT THE GRAMMAR)

1. RULE #1. TOPIC/COMMENT

The sentence

MANY SPORTS, ME INVOLVE.

illustrates a common use of the sign INVOLVE. Possible translations include "I'm involved in many sports" and "I participate in many sports."

2. RULE #3. SIMPLE YES/NO QUESTIONS

Two simple yes/no questions were used in the dialogues:

a. YOU PLAY SPORTS?
b. SPORTS, YOU LIKE?

Simple questions can have variable ordering of the signs. Question a uses a subject-verb-object (SVO) sentence structure, and question b uses an object-subject-verb (OSV) order.

3. RULE #5. INFORMATION-SEEKING QUESTIONS

a. YOUR FAVORITE SPORT, WHAT?
b. LEISURE ACTIVITIES, WHAT KIND?

In both questions the wh-sign comes after the topic is described. Question b could have been signed without KIND in it.

4. RULE #8. ORDERING OF SIMPLE SENTENCES

An SVO sentence order is used in the following sentence:

ME PREFER LEISURE ACTIVITIES.

11. RULE #10. NEGATION

The negative sign follows the topic in this example of how the negation rule is applied:

SPORTS ME DON'T-LIKE.

WHAT'S IN A SIGN (NOTES ABOUT VOCABULARY)

1. LIKE/DON'T-LIKE

The sign DON'T-LIKE is an example of negative incorporation. It is similar to the sign LIKE except that the hand is opened up and turned away from the body. Thus, there is no sign DON'T in the sign DON'T-LIKE.

2. LEISURE

It is also common practice to fingerspell the word "leisure" and then sign it to ensure that the intended meaning of the sign is understood clearly.

3. KIND

The meaning of the sign KIND is type. Avoid using this sign for the other meaning of kind which is generous.

4. ASL SYNONYMS

Some signs can be used to mean other things.

Sign	Also used for
ACTIVITIES	ACTIVE, DO
KIND	TYPE
SPORT	COMPETE, COMPETITION, RACE
MANY	MANIFOLD, MULTIPLE, PLURAL
INVOLVE	INCLUDE, PARTICIPATE
FAVORITE	PREFER

PRACTICE ACTIVITIES

1. MODEL FOR RULES #1. TOPIC/COMMENT, #3. YES/NO QUESTIONS, AND #5. INFORMATION-SEEKING QUESTIONS

Signer A: 1. Use the SVO sentence structure to ask a simple yes/no question.

SVO: YOU PLAY SPORT?

Signer B: 1. Respond affirmatively to the question;
2. describe a topic;
3. make a comment about the topic.

Response:	YES.
Topic:	MANY SPORTS,
Comment:	ME INVOLVE.

Signer A: 1. Describe a topic;
2. ask a wh-question about the topic.

Topic:	YOUR FAVORITE SPORT,
Question:	WHAT?

Signer B: 1. Respond to the question with the names of sports.

Response:	VOLLEYBALL, TENNIS.

Practice

Signer A: YOU PLAY SPORT?
Signer B: YES. MANY SPORTS, ME INVOLVE.
Signer A: YOUR FAVORITE SPORT, WHAT?
Signer B: VOLLEYBALL, TENNIS.

2. MODEL FOR RULES #3. SIMPLE YES/NO QUESTIONS, #5. INFORMATION-SEEKING QUESTIONS, #8. ORDERING OF SIMPLE SENTENCES, AND #10. NEGATION

Signer A: 1. Describe a topic;
2. ask a yes/no question about the topic.

Topic:	SPORTS,
Question:	YOU LIKE?

Signer B: 1. Describe a topic:
                   2. negate the topic with the negative sign DON'T-LIKE;
                   3. describe a preference for something by using an SVO sentence
                      structure.

Topic:	SPORTS
Negative:	ME DON'T-LIKE.
SVO:	ME PREFER LEISURE ACTIVITIES.

Signer A: 1. Describe a topic;
                   2. ask a wh-question about the topic.

Topic:	LEISURE ACTIVITIES,
Question:	WHAT KIND?

Signer B: 1. Respond to the question with the names of leisure activities.

Response:	HORSEBACK RIDING, BILLIARDS.

Practice

Signer A: SPORTS, YOU LIKE?
Signer B: SPORTS ME DON'T-LIKE. ME PREFER LEISURE ACTIVITIES.
Signer A: LEISURE ACTIVITIES, WHAT KIND?
Signer B: HORSEBACK RIDING, BILLIARDS.

3. MASTERY LEARNING
Practice the two dialogues until you feel comfortable with them.

4. FURTHER PRACTICE
Substitute signs in the dialogues with other signs for sports and leisure activities that are shown in the list of master signs.

LESSON 29   THE DENTIST AND YOU

LANGUAGE GOALS

The student will
1.   use Rules   #1. topic/comment,
                     #3. simple yes/no questions,
                     #4. long yes/no questions, and
                     #5. information-seeking questions.
2.   use BUT as a preposition.
3.   use the verb OPEN to indicate the location of an action on the body.
4.   use the directional verbs SHOW and PULL-OUT.
5.   use the sign PAIN to indicate the location of pain on the body.
6.   use fourteen new signs in a master dialogue.

THE MASTER DIALOGUE

1.   Dentist: HELLO D-E-N-I-S-E, FEEL+YOU?
                Hello Denise, how are you feeling?

     Denise: TODAY ME FINE BUT M-O-L-A-R PAIN-in-mouth.
                I am fine today but my molar hurts.

2.   Dentist: YOUR M-O-L-A-R PAIN? you-SHOW-me, OPEN-mouth-wide.
                Your molar is sore? Open your mouth wide and show me.

     Denise: YOU SEE WHAT?
                What do you see?

3.   Dentist: YOU TOOTH ROTTEN HAVE YOU. ME PULL-OUT HAVE-TO.
                You have a rotten tooth. I will have to pull it out.

     Denise: YOU DENTIST EXPERIENCE MANY YEAR FINISH YOU?
                Do you have many years of experience as a dentist?

4.   Dentist: RELAX, ME GOOD.
                Relax, I'm good.

     Denise: YOU SURE?
                Are you sure about that?

THE MASTER SIGNS

BUT

DENTIST

EXPERIENCE

HAVE-TO

PULL-OUT

THE MASTER SIGNS

OPEN-mouth-wide

PAIN

PAIN-in-mouth

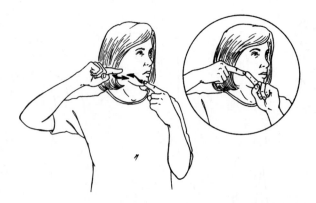

THE MASTER SIGNS

RELAX

ROTTEN

SEE

you-SHOW-me

TOOTH

WHAT'S IN THE SIGNS (NOTES ABOUT THE GRAMMAR)

1. GREETING
The dentist begins the dialogue with the greeting

HELLO D-E-N-I-S-E, FEEL+YOU?

The ASL phrase "FEEL+YOU?" translates to "How are you feeling?" in English. There is no verb to-be in ASL. Recall that a hyphenated word means to fingerspell that word.

2. PREPOSITION BUT
In the following sentence, the sign BUT is used as a preposition to express the thought "with the exception that":

TODAY ME FINE BUT M-O-L-A-R PAIN-in-mouth.

You could also substitute the sign EXCEPT for BUT in this sentence and still retain the same meaning.

3. RULE #3. SIMPLE YES/NO QUESTIONS
In the question

YOUR M-O-L-A-R PAIN?

the sign PAIN is placed at the end of the sentence because it asks a question about the molar. In the dialogue, the dentist doesn't wait for an answer, which is not an uncommon procedure used in many conversations. A person will simply ask a question to establish what is going to be said next.

4. VERB THAT SHOWS THE LOCATION OF ACTION OPEN AND DIRECTIONAL VERB SHOW
In the sentence

you-SHOW-me, OPEN-mouth-wide.

two signs make use of the signing space. First, the sign OPEN is made by the mouth to show the location of the action open or what is to be opened. Second, the sign SHOW is made from the addressee toward the signer. In the dialogue the dentist makes the sign from Denise toward herself or himself.

5. RULE #5. INFORMATION-SEEKING QUESTIONS

In the dialogue, Denise asks the following wh-question:

YOU SEE WHAT?

This is a short sentence and the ordering of the signs can vary. For example, you could also sign WHAT YOU SEE? and SEE WHAT YOU?

6. RULE #1. TOPIC/COMMENT

The dialogue contains two consecutive sentences that follow the topic comment rule.

Topic	Comment
YOU TOOTH ROTTEN	HAVE YOU.
ME PULL-OUT	HAVE-TO.

Note that HAVE and HAVE-TO are two different signs. The phrase HAVE YOU refers to the possession or ownership of something, whereas the phrase HAVE-TO refers to a requirement to do something.

7. RULE #4. LONG YES/NO QUESTIONS

The question

YOU DENTIST EXPERIENCE MANY YEAR FINISH YOU?

can be thought of as consisting of two parts. The first part describes the topic of the question, whereas the second part asks a yes/no question about the topic.

topic:	YOU DENTIST EXPERIENCE
yes/no question:	MANY YEAR FINISH YOU?

WHAT'S IN A SIGN (NOTES ABOUT VOCABULARY)

1. DENTIST
The sign DENTIST is a combination of the sign TOOTH + AGENT-sign. It is not uncommon to simply sign TOOTH alone to mean DENTIST.

2. OPEN-MOUTH-WIDE
There are several ways to sign OPEN and each one of them depends upon what object is being opened. In this sign, the hands mimic the action of the mouth opening wide. This sign is an example of a verb that shows the location of an action because of where it is made in the signing space.

3. PAIN-IN-MOUTH
The sign PAIN is made by the mouth to show the location of the pain.

4. PULL-OUT
The dentist in the dialogue signed PULL-OUT by the cheeks to show that one of the back teeth (a molar) will be pulled out. If this sign is made by the throat, it becomes TONSILITIS. If it is made by the right side of the stomach, it becomes APPENDECTOMY.

5. ASL SYNONYMS
Some signs can be used to mean other things.

Sign	Also used for
HAVE	POSSESS
HAVE-TO	MUST
PAIN	HURT, SORE
RELAX	REST
ROTTEN	ROT, RUIN, RUINED, SPOIL, SPOILED
TOOTH	DENTIST, TEETH

PRACTICE ACTIVITIES

1. MODEL FOR GREETINGS AND PREPOSITION BUT

Signer A:	1. Greet the person;
	2. ask how she is.

Greeting:	HELLO D-E-N-I-S-E,
Question:	FEEL+YOU?

Signer B:	1. Respond to greeting;
	2. sign the preposition BUT;
	3. describe the exception relating to the use of BUT.

Response:	TODAY ME FINE
Preposition:	BUT
Exception:	M-O-L-A-R PAIN-in-mouth.

Practice

Signer A:	HELLO D-E-N-I-S-E, FEEL+YOU?
Denise:	TODAY ME FINE BUT M-O-L-A-R PAIN-in-mouth.

2. MODEL FOR RULE #3. SIMPLE YES/NO QUESTIONS, USING OPEN TO SHOW THE LOCATION OF THIS ACTION, AND DIRECTIONAL VERB SHOW

Signer:	1. Describe the topic;
	2. ask a question about the topic using the sign PAIN.

Topic:	YOUR M-O-L-A-R
Question:	PAIN?

Signer:	1. Sign SHOW moving the hands from the addressee to yourself;
	2. indicate the location of the action by signing OPEN in front of the mouth.

Directional verb:	you-SHOW-me,
Location:	OPEN-mouth-wide.

Practice

Signer:	YOUR M-O-L-A-R PAIN? you-SHOW-me, OPEN-mouth-wide.

3. MODEL FOR RULES #1. SIMPLE YES/NO QUESTIONS AND #5. INFORMATION-SEEKING QUESTIONS

Signer A: 1. Describe the topic;
                2. ask a question about the topic.

Topic:	YOU SEE
Question:	WHAT?

Signer B: 1. Describe the topic;
                2. make a comment about the topic;
                3. repeat steps 1 and 2.

Topic:	YOU TOOTH ROTTEN
Comment:	HAVE YOU.
Topic:	ME PULL-OUT
Comment:	HAVE-TO.

Practice

Signer A: YOU SEE WHAT?
Signer B: YOU TOOTH ROTTEN HAVE YOU. ME PULL-OUT HAVE-TO.

4. MODEL FOR RULE #4. LONG YES/NO QUESTIONS

Signer A: 1. Describe the topic;
                2. ask a yes/no question about the topic.

Topic:	YOU DENTIST EXPERIENCE
Question:	MANY YEAR FINISH YOU?

Signer B: 1. Respond to the question.

Response:	RELAX, ME GOOD.

Practice

Signer A: YOU DENTIST EXPERIENCE MANY YEAR FINISH YOU?
Signer B: RELAX, ME GOOD.

5. MASTERY LEARNING

When you feel comfortable signing these phrases, practice signing the entire dialogue shown at the beginning of the lesson. Practice the master dialogue until you can sign it comfortably.

6. FURTHER PRACTICE

Create five simple dialogues where one person tells another person about a pain in the shoulder, stomach, knee, nose, and forehead. Practice signing each of the dialogues with a partner. Make the sign PAIN in the area mentioned. Note that when PAIN is signed by the stomach, you have produced the sign STOMACHACHE; when PAIN is signed by the forehead, you have the sign HEADACHE.

LESSON 30 THE TOOTH COMES OUT

LANGUAGE GOALS

The student will
1. use Rules   #1. topic/comment,
                    #3. simple yes/no questions,
                    #5. information-seeking questions,
                    #8. ordering of simple sentences, and
                    #10. negation.
2. use the conjunction LIKE.
3. use the directional verb PULL-OUT.
4. use the verb OPEN to indicate the location of an action on the body.
5. use nine new signs in a master dialogue.

THE MASTER DIALOGUE

1.   Dentist: FEEL YOU? CHEEK NUMB?
                        How do you feel? Is your cheek numb?

         Denise: YES, ME FEEL NOTHING.
                        Yes, I feel nothing.

2.   Dentist: GOOD. OPEN-mouth-wide YOUR TOOTH ME PULL-OUT.
                        Good, open your mouth wide and I will pull your tooth out.

         Denise: PULL-OUT-by-cheek, FINISH YOU?
                        Have you finished pulling out my tooth?

3.   Dentist: YES. YOUR M-O-L-A-R HUGE.
                        Yes. Your molar is huge.

         Denise: ME FEEL STRANGE LIKE SOMETHING MISSING.
                        I feel strange as if something is missing.

4.   Dentist: YOUR TOOTH MISSING. RELAX, YOU FEEL BETTER SOON.
                        Your tooth is missing. Relax and you will feel better soon.

         Denise: O-K.
                        Okay.

THE MASTER SIGNS

BETTER

CHEEK

HUGE

MISSING

LIKE

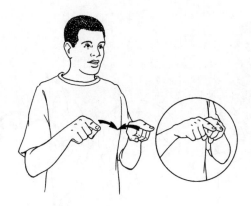

THE MASTER SIGNS

NOTHING

SOON

NUMB

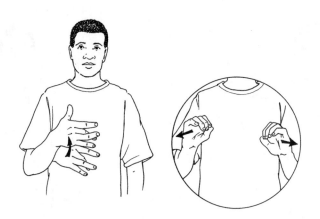

SOMETHING

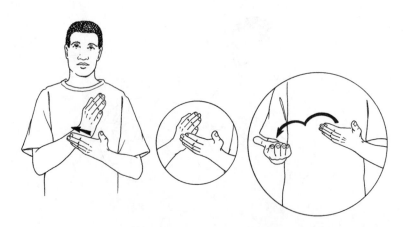

WHAT'S IN THE SIGNS (NOTES ABOUT THE GRAMMAR)

1. RULE #5. INFORMATION-SEEKING QUESTIONS AND #3. SIMPLE YES/NO QUESTIONS

The dialogue begins with two different types of questions:

FEEL YOU? CHEEK NUMB?

The first question seeks information about how a person (Denise) is feeling. The second question asks for a yes or no response. Both types of questions require a different set of nonmanual signals. Review Chapter 1 for a reminder of which nonmanual signals goes with which question.

2. RULE #10. NEGATION

The sentence

ME FEEL NOTHING

is an example of using the negation rule. The negative sign NOTHING is placed at the end of the sentence to represent what it was that Denise felt.

3. RULE #1. TOPIC/COMMENT AND DIRECTIONAL VERB PULL-OUT

The following sentence makes use of the signing space in two ways:

OPEN-mouth-wide YOUR TOOTH ME PULL-OUT.

First, the sign OPEN is made by the mouth to get OPEN-mouth-wide to show the location of an action. Second, the sign PULL-OUT can be made in a neutral position in the signing space. Alternatively, it can start with the hand held in the direction of Denise's tooth and then pulled back to show whose tooth is being pulled out.

There are two more examples of a topic/comment sentence in the dialogue.

Topic	Comment
YOUR M-O-L-A-R	HUGE.
YOUR TOOTH	MISSING.

4. RULE #3. SIMPLE YES/NO QUESTIONS AND DIRECTIONAL VERB PULL-OUT

In the sentence

PULL-OUT-by-cheek, FINISH YOU?

the starting position of the sign PULL-OUT-by-cheek is by the cheek on the side from which the tooth is pulled. The subject of the sentence is implied in the context of the dialogue, and the object of the sentence, tooth, is incorporated into the movement of the sign. The phrase FINISH YOU? asks a yes/no question about PULL-OUT-by-cheek.

5. CONJUNCTION LIKE

In the sentence

ME FEEL STRANGE LIKE SOMETHING MISSING.

the sign LIKE is used to mean as if, and it joins the phrases "ME FEEL STRANGE" and "SOMETHING MISSING."

6. RULE #8. ORDERING OF SIMPLE SENTENCES

Ordering of some sentences can be highly variable. The sentence

RELAX, YOU FEEL BETTER SOON.

could also be signed RELAX, SOON YOU FEEL BETTER or SOON YOU FEEL BETTER, RELAX.

WHAT'S IN A SIGN (NOTES ABOUT VOCABULARY)

1. CHEEK

Some parts of the anatomy are signed by pointing to them.

2. HUGE

The size and intensity of this sign indicates the relative degree of largeness. To emphasize that something is very large, you should (1) *squeeze the eyebrows together* and (2) *purse your lips together tightly*.

3. NUMB

The sign for NUMB is a compound sign made up of the signs FEEL and NONE.

4. SOMETHING

This compound sign is made up of the signs SOME and THING.

5. ASL SYNONYMS

Some signs can be used to mean other things.

Sign	Also used for
HUGE	ENORMOUS, GIGANTIC, LARGE
LIKE	AS-IF, ALIKE, SIMILAR
MISSING	ABSENCE, ABSENT
SOON	BRIEF, SHORTLY, TEMPORARY

PRACTICE ACTIVITIES

1. MODEL FOR RULES #3. SIMPLE YES/NO QUESTIONS, #5. INFORMATION-SEEKING QUESTIONS, AND #10. NEGATION

Signer A: 1. Ask a simple information-seeking question;
             2. ask a yes/no question.

             Information-seeking question: FEEL YOU?
             Yes/no question: CHEEK NUMB?

Signer B: 1. Respond to the yes/no question;
             2. use the negation rule to state how you feel.

             Response: YES,
             Negative: ME FEEL NOTHING.

Practice

Signer A: FEEL YOU? CHEEK NUMB?
Signer B: YES, ME FEEL NOTHING.

2. MODEL FOR VERBS THAT SHOW THE LOCATION OF AN ACTION OPEN, RULE #1. TOPIC/COMMENT, DIRECTIONAL VERB PULL-OUT, AND RULE #3. SIMPLE YES/NO QUESTIONS

Signer A: 1. Describe the location of an action with the verb OPEN;

     2. describe the topic;

     3. make a comment about the topic using the directional verb PULL-OUT.

Location:	OPEN-mouth-wide
Topic:	YOUR TOOTH
Comment:	ME PULL-OUT.

Signer B: 1. Describe the topic;

     2. ask a yes/no question about the topic.

Topic:	PULL-OUT-by-cheek
Question:	FINISH YOU?

Signer A: 1. Respond to the yes/no question;

     2. describe the topic;

     3. make a comment about the topic.

Response:	YES.
Topic:	YOUR M-O-L-A-R
Comment:	HUGE.

Practice

Signer A: OPEN-mouth-wide YOUR TOOTH ME PULL-OUT.

Signer B: PULL-OUT-by-cheek, FINISH YOU?

Signer A: YES. YOUR M-O-L-A-R HUGE.

3. MODEL FOR CONJUNCTION LIKE AND RULES #1. TOPIC/COMMENT AND #8. ORDERING OF SIMPLE SENTENCES

Signer A: 1. Sign a simple SVO phrase;
                 2. sign the conjunction LIKE;
                 3. sign another simple phrase.

Phrase:	ME FEEL STRANGE.
Conjunction:	LIKE
Phrase:	SOMETHING MISSING.

Signer B: 1. Describe a topic;
                 2. make a comment about the topic.

| Topic: | YOUR TOOTH |
| Comment: | MISSING. |

1. Create a simple sentence.

| Sentence: | RELAX, YOU FEEL BETTER SOON. |

Practice

Signer A: ME FEEL STRANGE LIKE SOMETHING MISSING.
Signer B: YOUR TOOTH MISSING. RELAX, YOU FEEL BETTER SOON.

4. MASTERY LEARNING

When you feel comfortable signing these phrases, practice signing the entire dialogue shown at the beginning of the lesson. Practice the master dialogue until you can sign it comfortably.

5. FURTHER PRACTICE

Join the master dialogue with the one in Lesson 29 and practice signing both of them until you are comfortable signing them.

LESSON 31   A VISIT TO THE DOCTOR

LANGUAGE GOALS

The student will
1.   use Rules   #1.   topic/comment,
                   #3.   simple yes/no questions,
                   #5.   information-seeking questions,
                   #8.   ordering of simple sentences, and
                   #10. negation.
2.   use the directional verb ACCOMPANY.
3.   use eight new signs in a master dialogue.

THE MASTER DIALOGUE

1.   Denise: EXCUSE-me, ME APPOINTMENT WITH DOCTOR.
               Excuse me, I have an appointment with the doctor.

     Nurse: YOUR APPOINTMENT TIME?
               What time is your appointment?

2.   Denise: MY APPOINTMENT TIME 11:30.
               My appointment is at 11:30.

     Nurse: RIGHT. ME NURSE ACCOMPANY-me PLEASE.
               That's right. I'm the nurse, and could you please come with me?

3.   Denise: O-K, me-ACCOMPANY-you.
               Okay, I will come with you.

     Nurse: SIT PLEASE. YOU ALLERGY MEDICATION?
               Please have a seat. Do you have an allergy to medication?

4.   Denise: NO, ME ALLERGY NONE.
               No, I have no allergy.

     Nurse: YOU SMOKE?
               Do you smoke?

5.   Denise: NO, ME SMOKE NEVER.
               No, I never smoke.

     Nurse: GOOD. DOCTOR COME SOON. WAIT PLEASE.
               Good for you. The doctor will come soon. Please wait.

THE MASTER SIGNS

ACCOMPANY-me
me-ACCOMPANY-YOU

ALLERGY

APPOINTMENT

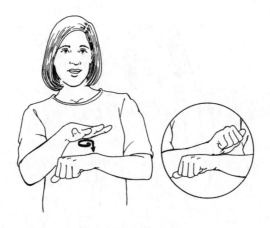

MEDICATION

NONE

THE MASTER SIGNS

PLEASE

SIT

SMOKE

WHAT'S IN THE SIGNS (NOTES ABOUT THE GRAMMAR)

1. RULE #8. ORDERING OF SIMPLE SENTENCES

The dialogue begins with a simple sentence structure:

EXCUSE-me, ME APPOINTMENT WITH DOCTOR.

The WITH in this sentence is not necessary. The sentence ME APPOINTMENT DOCTOR is acceptable because the meaning can be implied from the situation. This sentence would be readily understood if it came from a person walking up to a reception desk in a doctor's office.

Four more simple sentences in the dialogue are

a. ME NURSE ACCOMPANY-me PLEASE.
b. SIT PLEASE.
c. DOCTOR COME SOON.
d. WAIT PLEASE.

Sentence a is organized by the nurse introducing herself or himself followed by a command and the sign PLEASE. In English, you could have said, "Please come with me, I am the nurse." In ASL, it is common to set up the situation first and in the case of this sentence to introduce oneself before giving a command. Hence, in sentences c and d the nurse first informs Denise that the doctor is coming soon and then tells her to please wait. Sentence b could be translated as "Please have a seat" or "Sit down please" or some other variation. A key factor in translating is to ensure that the conventions of one language, such as those with regard to politeness, are accounted for. In English, we would not normally say "Sit please" to a patient in a doctor's office because it is too curt and may be seen as impolite.

One further example of a simple sentence is

O-K, me-ACCOMPANY-you.

The subject and object of the sentence are incorporated into the directional verb ACCOMPANY.

2. RULE #1. TOPIC/COMMENT

Telling the time for something can be done by following the topic/comment rule. You first describe what sort of time you are about to tell and then tell the time. An example of this is found in one sentence in the dialogue:

MY APPOINTMENT TIME 11:30.

3. RULE #5. INFORMATION-SEEKING QUESTIONS

To ask a time-related question, you follow the rule for information-seeking questions. This occurred in the following sentence:

YOUR APPOINTMENT TIME?

As with all questions, nonmanual signals are necessary to show that the sentence is a question and not a statement. In the response to this question

MY APPOINTMENT TIME 11:30.

the sign TIME is not translated as such. It is used because it shows that the numbers following it tell the time.

4. RULE #3. SIMPLE YES/NO QUESTIONS

The dialogue contained the following two simple yes/no questions:

a. YOU ALLERGY MEDICATION?
b. YOU SMOKE?

Both questions are dependent upon the nonmanual signals to indicate that they are asking a question. Without these signals you would get "You are allergic to medication" and "You do smoke."

5. RULE #10. NEGATION

The dialogue contained one example of a sentence using the rule for negation.

Answers a previous question	Topic	Negation
NO,	ME ALLERGY	NONE.
NO,	ME SMOKE	NEVER.

In both sentences, the signer uses two negative signs; one to answer a question and the other to negate a topic.

WHAT'S IN A SIGN (NOTES ABOUT VOCABULARY)

1. ACCOMPANY-ME AND ME-ACCOMPANY-YOU

The sign for ACCOMPANY-me starts in a neutral position and then moves to the side to indicate that the person being addressed should accompany the person signing. A proper translation is dependent upon the context of the dialogue, but it is usually just as appropriate to say "come with me" as it is to say "accompany me." The dialogue also has the sign me-ACCOMPANY-you. This sign directly incorporates the subject (me) and the object (you) because of its starting location (by the body of the signer) and its ending position (toward the body of the addressee).

2. ALLERGY

The sign for ALLERGY consists of the two signs NOSE + OPPOSITE.

3. NONE

The sign for NONE is also used to mean "no" as in "no more games for you" or "there are no rules for being lazy." Beginning signers often substitute this sign for the other sign NO, which is only to be used to express a negation as in "No, you may not go."

4. 11:30

Time is indicated by first signing TIME and then adding the correct numbers, which in this case are the signs for 11 and 30.

5. ASL SYNONYMS

Some signs can be used to mean other things.

Sign	Also used for
APPOINTMENT	ASSIGNMENT, BOOK, RESERVATION
MEDICATION	MEDICINE
NONE	NO
PLEASE	APPRECIATE
SMOKE	SMOKING
SIT	SIT-DOWN

PRACTICE ACTIVITIES

1. MODEL FOR RULES #1. TOPIC/COMMENT, #3. SIMPLE YES/NO QUESTIONS, AND #8. ORDERING OF SIMPLE SENTENCES

Signer A:
1. Initiate the conversation;
2. describe something about yourself.

Initiate: EXCUSE-me,
Description: ME APPOINTMENT WITH DOCTOR.

Signer B:
1. Describe the topic;
2. ask a question about the topic using the sign TIME.

Topic: YOUR APPOINTMENT
Question: TIME?

Signer A:
1. Describe the topic;
2. make a comment about the topic.

Topic: MY APPOINTMENT
Comment: TIME 11:30.

Practice

Signer A: EXCUSE-me, ME APPOINTMENT WITH DOCTOR.
Signer B: YOUR APPOINTMENT TIME?
Signer A: MY APPOINTMENT TIME 11:30.

2. MODEL FOR RULE #8. ORDERING OF SIMPLE SENTENCES

Signer A:
1. Introduce self;
2. give a command.

Introduction: ME NURSE
Command: ACCOMPANY-me PLEASE.

Signer B:
1. Acknowledge command;
2. describe the action that you will do.

Acknowledgment: O-K
Action: me-ACCOMPANY-you.

Signer A:
1. Give a command.

Command: SIT PLEASE.

Practice

Signer A: ME NURSE ACCOMPANY-me PLEASE.

Signer B: O-K, me-ACCOMPANY-you.

Signer A: SIT PLEASE.

3. MODEL FOR RULES #3. SIMPLE YES/NO QUESTIONS AND #10. NEGATION

Signer A:

1. Describe the topic;
2. ask a question about the topic.

| Topic: | YOU ALLERGY |
| Question: | MEDICATION? |

Signer B:

1. Respond to the question;
2. describe the topic;
3. use a negative sign to negate the topic.

Response:	NO,
Topic:	ME ALLERGY
Negation:	NONE.

Signer A:

1. Ask a simple yes/no question.

| Question: | YOU SMOKE? |

Signer B:

1. Respond to the question;
2. describe the topic;
3. use a negative sign to negate the topic.

Response:	NO,
Topic:	ME SMOKE
Negation:	NEVER.

Practice

Signer A: YOU ALLERGY MEDICATION?

Signer B: NO, ME ALLERGY NONE.

Signer A: YOU SMOKE?

Signer B: NO, ME SMOKE NEVER.

4. MODEL FOR RULE #8. ORDERING OF SIMPLE SENTENCES

Signer: 1. Describe an action;
                          2. give a command.

                          Action: DOCTOR COME SOON.
                          Command: WAIT PLEASE.

Practice

Signer: DOCTOR COME SOON. WAIT PLEASE.

5. MASTERY LEARNING

When you feel comfortable signing these phrases, practice signing the entire dialogue shown at the beginning of the lesson. Practice the master dialogue until you can sign the part of each character smoothly.

6. FURTHER PRACTICE

Create five to ten simple dialogues using various signs for time adverbs to discuss the time of an appointment. For example,

Signer A: YOU DOCTOR APPOINTMENT TIME?
                   What time is your doctor appointment?

Signer B: ME DOCTOR APPOINTMENT TOMORROW AFTERNOON TIME
                   4:30.
                   My doctor appointment is tomorrow afternoon at 4:30.

Signer A: YOU ARRIVE-there EARLY, YOU SHOULD.
                   You should arrive there early.

Signer B: ME EARLY ALWAYS.
                   I'm always early.

LESSON 32 WHAT THE DOCTOR SAID

LANGUAGE GOALS

The student will
1. use Rules   #1. topic/comment,
                             #2. tense with time adverbs,
                             #3. simple yes/no questions, and
                             #8. ordering of simple sentences.
2. use the preposition BUT.
3. use the directional sign GIVE.
4. use ten new signs in a master dialogue.

THE MASTER DIALOGUE

1.   Doctor: HELLO D-E-N-I-S-E, YOU SICK YOU?
                        Hello Denise, are you sick?

         Denise: YES, SINCE THREE-DAYS ME STOMACH-ACHE.
                        Yes, I have had a stomachache for three days.

2.   Doctor: SINCE THREE-DAYS VOMIT YOU?
                        Have you been vomiting for three days?

         Denise: YES, ME VOMIT OCCASIONALLY.
                        Yes, I have been vomiting occasionally.

3.   Doctor: YOU FEEL HOT, COLD?
                        Do you feel hot and cold?

         Denise: (nods) BUT MOST FEEL HOT.
                        Yes, but mostly I feel hot.

4.   Doctor: OH-I-see. YOU F-E-V-E-R HAVE.
                        I see. You have a fever.

         Denise: YOU THINK?
                        Do you think so?

5.   Doctor: YES. YOU REST MUST. MEDICATION me-GIVE-you.
                        Yes. You must rest. I will give you medication.

         Denise: THANK-YOU.
                        Thank you.

THE MASTER SIGNS

me-GIVE-you

MOST

OCCASIONALLY

REST

SICK

SINCE

THE MASTER SIGNS

STOMACH-ACHE

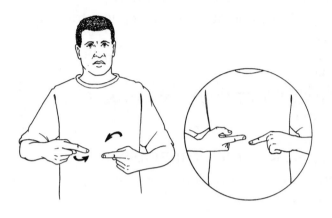

THINK

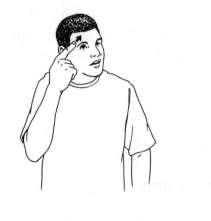

THREE-DAYS

VOMIT

WHAT'S IN THE SIGNS (NOTES ABOUT THE GRAMMAR)

1. RULE #3. SIMPLE YES/NO QUESTIONS

As with doctors in general, the doctor in the dialogue relied on yes/no questions to get information from Denise.

    a. YOU SICK YOU?
    b. SINCE THREE-DAYS VOMIT YOU?
    c. YOU FEEL HOT, COLD?

Sentence b includes the phrase "SINCE THREE-DAYS," which translates to "for the past three days," "since three days ago," or "from three days ago until now."
    Denise also used a yes/no question:

    d. YOU THINK?

This question can also be signed THINK YOU? Note that the nonmanual signals are critical with question d. The signals for a yes/no question are (1) *a raised eyebrow* and (2) *the head tilted forward*. If you signed this question with a squeezed eyebrow then you are asking for information and the meaning of the question changes from "Do you think so?" to "What do you think about that?"

2. RULE #2. TENSE WITH TIME ADVERBS

The phrase "SINCE THREE-DAYS" is used in the sentence

SINCE THREE-DAYS ME STOMACH-ACHE.

It can be translated in several ways such as "I have had a stomachache for three days," "I have had a stomachache for the past three days," or "For three days now I have had a stomachache." All the translations indicate that something took place in the past and continues to the present time.

3. RULE #1. TOPIC/COMMENT

It is common in ASL to place signs for time (or time adverbs) at the beginning of the sentence. When the time adverb is not used to establish the tense of a sentence but rather to comment on the occurrences of a particular event, then it usually follows the action sign. This is seen in the following sentence:

YES, ME VOMIT OCCASIONALLY.

The sign MUST often comes at the end of a sentence when it is the emphasis of the sentence as in the following:

YOU REST MUST.

This sentence can be signed YOU MUST REST without any change in the meaning. However, placing MUST at the end of the sentence in this dialogue fits well with what a doctor would sign when admonishing a patient.

4. CONJUNCTION BUT

A head nod can take the place of the sign YES. Thus, in the following sentence the sign BUT is used to join an affirmative thought (indicated by the head nod) and an exception.

(nods) BUT MOST FEEL HOT.

5. RULE #8. ORDERING OF SIMPLE SENTENCES

The simple sentence

MEDICATION me-GIVE-you.

has the subject (me) and object (you) incorporated into the movement of the directional sign GIVE. The movement begins in front of your body and moves toward the addressee. Another simple sentence in the dialogue was

YOU F-E-V-E-R HAVE.

WHAT'S IN A SIGN (NOTES ABOUT VOCABULARY)

1. ME-GIVE-YOU

This is a directional sign whereby the subject and object are incorporated into the movement of the sign.

2. STOMACH-ACHE

The sign for PAIN is made by the stomach to show the location of the pain.

3. THREE-DAYS

The 3 sign is used to make the sign DAY. This is an example of number incorporation, which is common in ASL.

4. ASL SYNONYMS

Some signs can be used to mean other things.

Sign	Also used for
MEDICATION	MEDICINE
OCCASIONALLY	ONCE-IN-A-WHILE, PERIODICALLY, SOMETIMES
REST	RELAX
SICK	ILL
SINCE	ALL-ALONG, BEEN, EVER-SINCE, SO-FAR, UP-TO-NOW
VOMIT	THROW-UP

PRACTICE ACTIVITIES

1. MODEL FOR RULES #1. TOPIC/COMMENT, #2. TENSE WITH TIME ADVERBS, AND #3. SIMPLE YES/NO QUESTIONS AND FOR CONJUNCTION BUT

Signer A:
1. Initiate the conversation with a greeting;
2. describe the topic;
3. ask a yes/no question about the topic.

Initiate:	HELLO D-E-N-I-S-E.
Topic:	YOU SICK
Question:	YOU?

Signer B:
1. Respond to the question;
2. describe the time that something took place;
3. describe what took place.

Response:	YES,
Time:	SINCE THREE-DAYS
Describe:	ME STOMACH-ACHE.

Signer A:
1. Describe the time that something took place;
2. describe the action;
3. ask a yes/no question.

Time:	SINCE THREE-DAYS
Action:	VOMIT
Question:	YOU?

Signer B: 1. Respond affirmatively to the question;
                 2. describe the action;
                 3. describe the time of the action.

Response:	YES,
Action:	ME VOMIT
Time:	OCCASIONALLY.

Signer A: 1. Describe the topic;
                 2. ask a question about the topic.

Topic:	YOU FEEL
Question:	HOT, COLD?

Signer B: 1. Respond affirmatively to the question with a head nod;
                 2. sign the conjunction BUT;
                 3. describe the exception.

Response:	(nods)
Conjunction:	BUT
Exception:	MOST FEEL HOT.

Practice

Signer A: HELLO D-E-N-I-S-E, YOU SICK YOU?
Signer B: YES, SINCE THREE-DAYS ME STOMACH-ACHE.
Signer A: SINCE THREE-DAYS VOMIT YOU?
Signer B: YES, ME VOMIT OCCASIONALLY.
Signer A: YOU FEEL HOT, COLD?
Signer B: (nods) BUT MOST FEEL HOT.

2. MODEL FOR RULES #1. TOPIC/COMMENT, #3. SIMPLE YES/NO QUESTIONS, AND #8. ORDERING OF SIMPLE SENTENCES

Signer A: 1. Demonstrate you understood something;
                 2. sign the subject;
                 3. sign the object;
                 4. sign the verb.

Understanding:	OH-I-see.
Subject:	YOU
Object:	F-E-V-E-R
Verb:	HAVE.

Signer B: 1. Ask a yes/no question relating to Signer A's statement.

                 Question: YOU THINK?

Signer A: 1. Respond affirmatively to the question;
                 2. describe a topic;
                 3. make a comment about the topic.

                 Response: YES.
                 Topic: YOU REST
                 Comment: MUST.

                 1. Name the object that is given;
                 2. sign the verb.

                 Object: MEDICATION
                 Verb: me-GIVE-you.

Signer B: 1. Respond by expressing your gratitude.

                 Response: THANK-YOU.

Practice

Signer A: OH-I-see. YOU F-E-V-E-R HAVE YOU.
Signer B: YOU THINK?
Signer A: YES. YOU REST MUST. MEDICATION me-GIVE-you.
Signer B: THANK-YOU.

5. MASTERY LEARNING

When you feel comfortable signing these phrases, practice signing the entire dialogue shown at the beginning of the lesson. Practice the master dialogue until you can sign the part of each character smoothly.

6. FURTHER PRACTICE

Join this dialogue with the one in Lesson 31 and sign them together.

LESSON 33   VOCABULARY BUILDING: HEALTH AND BODY RELATED

LANGUAGE GOALS

The student will
1.   use Rule   #1. topic/comment,
    #3. simple yes/no questions,
    #8. ordering of simple sentences, and
    #10. negation.
2.   use sixteen new signs in the master dialogue and in a self-created dialogue.

THE MASTER DIALOGUE

1.   Rebecca: YOU SICK?
    Are you sick?

    Jenny: ME MEASLES HAVE.
    I have the measles.

2.   Rebecca: SIGN MEASLES, ME DON'T UNDERSTAND. FINGERSPELL PLEASE.
    I don't understand the sign MEASLES. Please fingerspell it.

    Jenny: M-E-A-S-L-E-S.
    Measles.

3.   Rebecca: OH-I-see. SORRY. YOU GET-WELL QUICK, ME HOPE.
    I see. I'm sorry. I hope you get well quickly.

    Jenny: THANK-you.
    Thank you.

THE MASTER SIGNS

HOPE

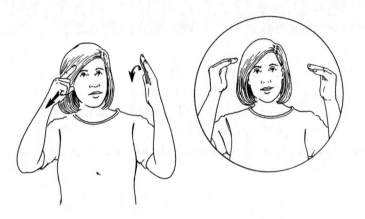

GET WELL

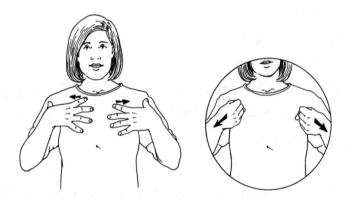

MEASLES

THE MASTER SIGNS

QUICK

WHAT'S IN THE SIGNS (NOTES ABOUT THE GRAMMAR)

1. RULE #1. TOPIC/COMMENT

A topic/comment sentence structure used in the dialogue was

YOU GET-WELL QUICK, ME HOPE.

2. RULE #3. SIMPLE YES/NO QUESTIONS

A simple structure can be used to inquire about a person's condition:

YOU SICK?

Although this is a simple question, in the absence of appropriate nonmanual signals it would mean "You are sick."

3. RULE #8. ORDERING OF SIMPLE SENTENCES

The following two simple sentence strutures were illustrated in the dialogue:

a. ME MEASLES HAVE.
b. FINGERSPELL PLEASE.

Sentence a is an example of a subject-object-verb (SOV) sentence order. Sentence b is an example of what you can say when you do not understand the meaning of a sign.

4. RULE #10. NEGATION

In the sentence

SIGN MEASLES, ME DON'T UNDERSTAND.

the phrase ME DON'T UNDERSTAND is in reference to the phrase SIGN MEASLES. When expressing a negative thought, it is always important to first describe the topic that is not understood.

WHAT'S IN A SIGN (NOTES ABOUT VOCABULARY)

1. GET-WELL

You must avoid falling into the trap of trying to find a sign for each English word. The sign GET-WELL is a single sign and not a compound sign made of the signs GET and WELL.

2. ASL SYNONYMS

Some signs can be used to mean other things.

Sign	Also used for
GET-WELL	HEALTHY, ROBUST
HOPE	EXPECT

PRACTICE ACTIVITIES

1. MODEL FOR RULES #1. TOPIC/COMMENT, #3. SIMPLE YES/NO QUESTIONS, #8. ORDERING OF SIMPLE SENTENCES, AND #10. NEGATION

Signer A:	1. Ask a simple yes/no question.
	Question: YOU SICK?
Signer B:	1. Respond to the question with an SOV sentence.
	SOV: ME MEASLES HAVE.

| Signer A: | 1. Describe a topic; | |
| | 2. sign a negative phrase about the topic. | |

| | Topic: | SIGN MEASLES, |
| | Negative: | ME DON'T UNDERSTAND. |

1. Use a simple sentence to make a request.

| | Request: | FINGERSPELL PLEASE. |

| Signer B: | 1. Fingerspell the name of the sign that Signer A did not understand. | |

| | Fingerspell: | M-E-A-S-L-E-S. |

Signer A:	1. Indicate that you understand;	
	2. sign a sympathetic remark;	
	3. describe a topic;	
	4. make a comment about the topic.	

	Indication:	OH-I-see.
	Remark:	SORRY
	Topic:	YOU GET-WELL QUICK,
	Comment:	ME HOPE.

| Signer B: | 1. Express your appreciation. | |

| | Appreciation: | THANK-you. |

Practice

Signer A:	YOU SICK?
Signer B:	ME MEASLES HAVE.
Signer A:	SIGN MEASLES, ME DON'T UNDERSTAND. FINGERSPELL PLEASE.
Signer B:	M-E-A-S-L-E-S.
Signer A:	OH-I-see. SORRY. YOU GET-WELL QUICK, ME HOPE.
Signer B:	THANK-you.

2. MASTERY LEARNING

Practice the above dialogue until you feel comfortable signing it.

3. FURTHER PRACTICE

Create dialogues using the health-related signs shown below. Write the English gloss and translation for your dialogue and practice signing it with a partner.

ADDITIONAL HEALTH-RELATED SIGNS

Also used for

DIZZY   LIGHT-HEADED

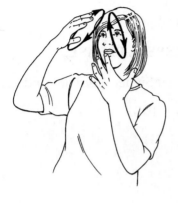

UPSET

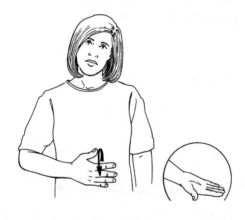

PALE

ADDITIONAL HEALTH-RELATED SIGNS

Also used for

HEART-ATTACK

COUGH   SNEEZE

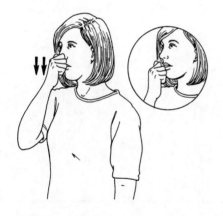

BREATH   BREATHE

ADDITIONAL HEALTH-RELATED SIGNS

Also used for

MUMPS

PREGNANT

BLOOD   BLEED

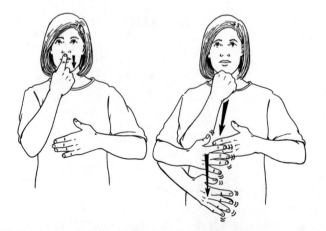

ADDITIONAL HEALTH-RELATED SIGNS

Also used for

TEMPERATURE   DEGREE

THERMOMETER

OPERATION   CUT, DISSECTION, SURGERY

REVIEW OF LESSONS 27–33

Write an English translation for each of the following ASL sentences.

1. FOOTBALL GAME ME WATCH FINISH.

2. TOMORROW NIGHT RESTAURANT TWO-of-us GO-to, TIME?

3. YOU PREFER SPORTS, LEISURE ACTIVITIES WHICH?

4. ME LIKE WHAT? HOCKEY, GOLF, CYCLING.

5. SUPPOSE YOU PAIN-in-mouth, YOU APPOINTMENT DOCTOR DENTIST WHICH?

6. ME FEEL AWFUL WHY? MY TOOTH ROTTEN.

7. YOU HURT WHERE? you-SHOW-me.

8. ME ALLERGY WHAT? P-E-N-I-C-I-L-L-I-N.

9. ME SICK, ME FEEL HOT.

10. MORNING YOU HOCKEY PLAY, AFTERNOON YOU FOOTBALL WATCH, NOW SICK YOU?

ANSWERS

Note that there may be other ways of translating these sentences than the ones shown here.

1. I watched the football game.

2. What time are we going to the restaurant tomorrow night?

3. Do you prefer sports or leisure activities? or Which do you prefer, sports or leisure activities?

4. I like hockey, golf, and cycling.

5. If you have a pain in your mouth, do you make an appointment to see the dentist or the doctor?

6. I feel awful because I have a rotten tooth.

7. Show me where you are hurt.

8. I have an allergy to penicillin.

9. I am sick and I feel hot.

10. You played hockey in the morning, watched football in the afternoon, and now you are sick?

Poems and Humor

14

When word got out of NBC's plans to show "Experiment in Television," which was the first major production using sign language on national television, the network received a telegram from the Alexander Graham Bell Association [for the Deaf] objecting to such plans and arguing that the exposure of sign language on television would undermine the efforts of "thousands of parents of deaf children and teachers of the deaf who are trying to teach deaf children to speak." . . . NTD [National Theater of the Deaf] Director David Hays . . . responded to the Bell objections and pointed out that such programs would "bring enormous cultural benefit to the deaf who are deprived of theatre" and "show highly gifted deaf people working in a developed art form of great beauty."

—JACK R. GANNON
Deaf Heritage

HOLD THAT SIGN . . .

The objections of the A.G. Bell Association to the showing of sign language on national television in the 1960s might seem a bit odd given that sign language on television is no longer a novelty. But objections to signing have long been a part of the history of Deaf people. Even after a generation of children have graduated from watching Linda Bove use ASL on *Sesame Street,* to watching Marlee Matlin charm and chastise her fellow attorneys on *Reasonable Doubts,* the Deaf community still must contend with people who are against the use of sign language to teach Deaf children. This is why so many of their poems and humor appear to be centered around showing nondeaf people the natural side of Deaf—a world shaped by what one sees. This chapter presents five poems written by Deaf people that illustrate this world. A number of jokes popular in the Deaf community are also presented.

POEMS

How We Are by Kathleen B. Schreiber

You hear the sound of laughter,
I see a smiling face,
You hear the rapid footsteps,
I see the stride and grace,
You hear a joyous greeting,
I see a friendly hand:
Yours is a word that's spoken,
Mine is an act as planned.

You hear a shrieking siren,
I see a flashing light,
You hear the blare of traffic,
I see the glare at night,
You hear the lilting music,
I feel the catchy beat:
Yours is the sound of motion,
Mine is the mute repeat.

You hear a tree that rustles,
I see the swaying leaves,
You hear a wind that whistles,
I feel a steady breeze,
You hear a songbird calling,
I see its graceful flight:
Yours is the sound of nature,
Mine is the gift of sight.

You hear the preacher praying,
I see the way he stands,
You hear the people singing,
I see it signed by hands,
You hear the final Amen,
I see the bow above:
Yours is a vocal worship,
Mine is an act of love.

On His Deafness by Robert F. Panara

My ears are deaf, and yet I seem to hear
Sweet nature's music and the songs of man,
For I have learned from Fancy's artisan
How written words can thrill the inner ear
Just as they move the heart, and so for me
They also seem to ring out loud and free.
In silent study, I have learned to tell
Each secret shade of meaning, and to hear
A magic harmony, at once sincere,
That somehow notes the tinkle of a bell,
The cooing of a dove, the swish of leaves,
The raindrop's pitter-patter on the eaves,
The lover's sigh, the strumming of guitar—
And if I choose, the rustle of a star!

Language for the Eye by Dorothy Miles

Hold a tree in the palm of your hand,
or topple it with a crash.
Sail a boat on finger waves,
or sink it with a splash.
From your finger tips see a frog
leap at a passing butterfly.
The word becomes the picture
in this language for the eye.

Follow the sun from rise to set,
or bounce it like a ball.
Catch a fish in a fishing net,
or swallow it, bones and all.
Make traffic scurry, or airplanes fly,
and people meet and part.
The word becomes the action
in this language of the heart.

Words from a Deaf Child by Mervin D. Garretson

I need to perceive life through native eyes,
not yours, which after all are yours.
you're sailing on a vastly foreign sea
it's my country—you're the stranger
listen to me.

we sign a language all our own
our hands are yours to share
the word, I think, is communication
we speak through sign and both together
whatever and by all the means to the end.

millions of stars do not make me a star
millions of dreams may not be my dream
the pilgrims were a handful on a newfound shore
that was their own.

let me choose if I will
to be different from the mass
learn that there is beauty in a single star
peace and grace in being what you are.

like an almighty wave this flash of scorn
for you who do not try to understand
that every sunset, every sunrise born
is different as each single grain of sand.

this life is yours to know but mine to command
teach me, love me, like you'd love a work of art
or a mountain pine
don't try to lead me, own me, force me
into a mold that's not my own.

water, feed, nourish the growing tree
don't hold it, fold it, circumscribe
let it flower, let it grow
if you love me, let me go.

My Clipped Wings by Ken Glickman

Unbeknownest to me, my wings got clipped
A long time ago by somebody
Who found me not responsive
To chirping . . .
And who believed the bill speaks louder—
Louder than the wing.
Thus I was grounded—
Holed up in a nest—
And was taught to chirp . . .
And to chirp . . .
And to chirp . . .
Until I was big enough
To go forth on my own . . .
Only to soon find out
My wings are for freedom
Of expression, also.
Thus did I try to grow back
A couple of feathers in my wings
Just so that I can soar.

HUMOR

The Motel

A newly married Deaf couple are spending their first night in a motel. The wife wakes up in the middle of the night and says that she has a headache and wants some medication. Her new husband eagerly bounces out of bed, kisses his wife, turns off the light, and drives off to an all-night drugstore to buy some aspirin. Upon returning he realizes that he has forgotten the room number and his motel key is unmarked. Thinking about how to find his room he latches on to an idea. He goes back to his car and begins honking the horn. Almost immediately, the lights are turned on in every room in the motel except one. With a smile he heads to this room.

The Deaf Bank Robber

A Deaf bank robber is caught and the sheriff uses a sign language interpreter to find out where the money was hidden.

While the Deaf man signs, the interpreter translates: "He does not know what you are talking about."

This goes on for an hour. The sheriff finally takes out his gun and points it at the robber's head and says, "If you don't tell me where the money is, I am going to kill you!"

The interpreter signs what the sheriff has said to which the Deaf man signs, "I give up. I hid the money under the stairs at the back of the house."

It is obvious to the sheriff that the Deaf man has changed his tune and so he asks the interpreter, "What did he say?"

The interpreter quickly replies, "He says he is not afraid to die!"

The Tree

A lumberjack is chopping trees one day when he encounters one that will not fall. Even after yelling "Timber!" several times, the tree still will not fall. He calls a tree doctor who comes out and examines the tree. The doctor determines that the tree is Deaf, so he fingerspells "T-I-M-B-E-R" and the tree falls.

There Is Plenty More Back Home

Three Deaf men, a Russian, a Cuban, and an American, were traveling together on a train in Europe.

The Deaf Russian was enjoying an expensive dish of caviar when he suddenly opened the window and tossed it out. The American asked why he threw away the expensive caviar. The Russian responded, "Oh, I don't need it. There is plenty more back home."

The Deaf Cuban was enjoying a cigar when he suddenly opened the window and tossed a whole box of cigars out. The American asked why he threw away the cigars. The Cuban responded, "Oh, I don't need them. There are plenty more back home."

Feeling hungry, the Deaf American ordered a sandwich from the waiter. When the waiter brought the sandwich, the American suddenly opened the window and tossed the waiter out. Both the Russian and the Cuban were shocked, and they asked the American why he threw the waiter away. The American responded, "Oh, I don't need him. There are plenty more hearing people back home."

REVIEW OF CHAPTER 14

1. With a partner or a group of people, discuss the meaning of each poem in this chapter.

2. For a research project, find three more poems written by Deaf authors.

Traveling with ASL

15

LESSON 34   TRAVEL PLANS

LANGUAGE GOALS

The student will
1.   use Rules
- #1. topic/comment,
- #2. tense with time adverbs,
- #3. simple yes/no questions,
- #5. information-seeking questions,
- #8. ordering of simple sentences, and
- #9. conditional sentences.
2.   use the directional verbs **HELP** and **JOIN**.
3.   use nine new signs in a master dialogue.

THE MASTER DIALOGUE

1.   Paul: HELLO, DO-what YOU?
        Hello, what are you doing?

    Jenny: ME NEED VACATION. GO-to ENGLAND ME WANT.
        I need a vacation. I want to go to England.
        NOW W-E-B S-I-T-E ME CHECK.
        I am checking websites now.

2. Paul: W-E-B S-I-T-E CHECK FOR-FOR?
    Why are you checking out websites?

    Jenny: PAST, SUPPOSE ME WANT TRAVEL, TRAVEL A-G-E-N-T HELP-me ALWAYS.
    In the past if I wanted to travel, a travel agent always helped me.
    TODAY, ME TRAVEL MYSELF PLAN, COMPUTER HELP-me.
    Today, I do my own travel planning and a computer helps me.

3. Paul: COOL! TECHNOLOGY TODAY, AWESOME.
    Hey, that's cool! Today's technology is really awesome.
    YOU VACATION HOW LONG?
    How long will your vacation be?

    Jenny: FOUR-WEEKS.
    Four weeks.

4. Paul: me-JOIN-you, DON'T-MIND YOU?
    Do you mind if I join you?

    Jenny: FINE.
    That's fine.

THE MASTER SIGNS

AWESOME

CHECK

ENGLAND

THE MASTER SIGNS

me-JOIN-you

MYSELF

PLAN

TRAVEL

TECHNOLOGY

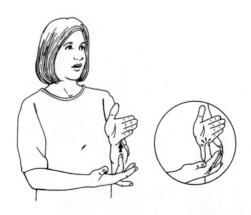

THE MASTER SIGNS

VACATION

WHAT'S IN THE SIGNS (NOTES ABOUT THE GRAMMAR)

1. GREETING

The dialogue begins with the following greeting:

HELLO, DO-what YOU?

The phrase DO-what YOU? is commonly used to initiate a conversation.

2. RULE #1. TOPIC/COMMENT

The following phrases follow the topic/comment rule:

Topic	Comment
GO-to ENGLAND	ME WANT.
W-E-B S-I-T-E	ME CHECK.
TECHNOLOGY TODAY,	AWESOME.
ME TRAVEL	MYSELF PLAN,
COMPUTER	HELP-me.

3. RULE #2. TENSE WITH TIME ADVERBS

Each of the following sentences relies on a time adverb to establish the tense of the sentence. The time adverb is placed at the beginning of the sentence.

    a. NOW W-E-B S-I-T-E ME CHECK.
    b. PAST, SUPPOSE ME WANT TRAVEL, TRAVEL A-G-E-N-T HELP-me ALWAYS.
    c. TODAY, ME TRAVEL MYSELF PLAN, COMPUTER HELP-me.

In the dialogue, sentences b and c follow one another and demonstrate how a signer uses time adverbs to change the tense of a conversation. If the sign TODAY was left out of sentence c, then the sentence "TRAVEL PLAN MYSELF COMPUTER HELP-me" would be in the past tense in the dialogue because the sentence before it contained the time adverb, PAST.

4. RULE #3. SIMPLE YES/NO QUESTIONS

In the question

me-JOIN-you, DON'T-MIND YOU?

the topic is described (me-JOIN-you) followed by a yes/no question about the topic (DON'T-MIND YOU?).

5. RULE #5. INFORMATION-SEEKING QUESTIONS

In the sentences

W-E-B S-I-T-E CHECK FOR-FOR?
YOU VACATION HOW LONG?

the questions FOR-FOR? and HOW LONG? follow the description of the topic. Recall that FOR-FOR means why and is interchangeable with the sign WHY.

6. RULE #8. ORDERING OF SIMPLE SENTENCES

The sentence

ME NEED VACATION.

follows a subject-verb-object (SVO) word ordering.

7. RULE #9. CONDITIONAL SENTENCES

In the following conditional sentence

PAST, SUPPOSE ME WANT TRAVEL, TRAVEL A-G-E-N-T HELP-me ALWAYS.

the time adverb is placed at the beginning of the sentence and before the sign SUPPOSE. The comment relating to the comment is modeled on a topic/comment format.

8. DIRECTIONAL VERBS JOIN AND HELP

The dialogue contained the following two examples of directional verbs or verbs that change the meaning of a sentence in the signing space:

me-JOIN-you
HELP-me

In the dialogue, HELP-me is used twice. The first time it is used the subject is the travel agent, and the second time the subject is the computer. In both instances the subject of the sentence is implied in the signing. That is, the sign HELP-me begins in a neutral position and then moves toward the signer. It would also be proper to sign he- or she-HELP-me and it-HELP-me, which would more clearly indicate the subject of the sentence. But before you can sign either of these, you must first place the travel agent and the computer in your signing space and then begin the sign he- or she-HELP-me and it-HELP-me from that location.

WHAT'S IN A SIGN (NOTES ABOUT VOCABULARY)

1. FOUR-WEEKS

The sign for 4 is incorporated into the sign for WEEK.

2. JOIN

This sign is not to be used to mean to join things together as in "join the two ropes together." It is to be used only when referring to the concept of becoming a member of something or to participate in something. In the dialogue, Paul wants to join Jenny on her trip to England.

3. MYSELF

The pronoun MYSELF and all other pronouns containing -*self*, are made with the A handshape replacing the pointing finger, which is used to make the pronouns ME, YOU, SHE, IT, THEM, and so forth. The sign is also used to mean *self-* as in *self-esteem* and *self-concept*.

4. ASL SYNONYMS

Some signs can be used to mean other things.

Sign	Also used for
AWESOME	EXCELLENT, FABULOUS, FANTASTIC, SUPERB, WONDERFUL
CHECK	EXPLORE, INVESTIGATE
ENGLAND	BRITAIN, BRITISH, ENGLISH
MYSELF	SELF-
PLAN	ARRANGE, PREPARE
TECHNOLOGY	TECHNICAL
TRAVEL	TOUR, TRIP
VACATION	HOLIDAY

PRACTICE ACTIVITIES

1. MODEL FOR GREETINGS AND RULES #1. TOPIC/COMMENT, #2: TIME ADVERBS, AND #8. ORDERING OF SIMPLE SENTENCES

Signer A: 1. Greet the person;
2. ask what the person is doing.

Greeting: HELLO,
Question: DO-what YOU?

Signer B: 1. Respond to the question with an SOV sentence.

Response: ME NEED VACATION.

1. Describe a topic;
2. make a comment about the topic.

Topic: GO-to ENGLAND
Comment: ME WANT.

1. Use a time adverb to establish the time frame of a sentence;
2. describe a topic;
3. make a comment about the topic.

Tense: NOW
Topic: W-E-B S-I-T-E
Comment: ME CHECK.

Practice

Signer A: HELLO, DO-what YOU?

Signer B: ME NEED VACATION. GO-to ENGLAND ME WANT.
NOW W-E-B S-I-T-E ME CHECK.

2. MODEL FOR RULES #2. TENSE WITH TIME ADVERBS, #5. INFORMATION-SEEKING QUESTIONS, AND #9. CONDITIONAL SENTENCES

Signer A: 1. Describe a topic;
2. ask a question about the topic using the sign FOR-FOR.

Topic:	W-E-B S-I-T-E CHECK
Wh- Question:	FOR-FOR?

Signer B: 1. Indicate the tense with a time adverb;
2. describe the condition;
3. describe an outcome of the condition using the directional verb HELP.

Tense:	PAST,
Condition:	SUPPOSE ME WANT TRAVEL,
Outcome:	TRAVEL A-G-E-N-T HELP-me ALWAYS.

1. Change the tense by placing the time adverb TODAY at the beginning of a sentence;
2. describe a topic;
3. make a comment about the topic;
4. describe another topic;
5. make a comment about the topic.

Tense:	TODAY,
Topic:	ME TRAVEL
Comment:	MYSELF PLAN,
Topic:	COMPUTER
Comment:	HELP-me.

Practice

Signer A: W-E-B S-I-T-E CHECK FOR-FOR?

Signer B: PAST, SUPPOSE ME WANT TRAVEL, TRAVEL A-G-E-N-T HELP-me ALWAYS.
TODAY, ME TRAVEL MYSELF PLAN, COMPUTER HELP-me.

3. MODEL FOR RULES #1. TOPIC/COMMENT AND #5. INFORMATION-SEEKING QUESTIONS

Signer A: 1. Use the sign COOL to make a comment relating to the use of computers to help a person make travel plans;
2. describe the topic;
3. ask a question about the topic.

Comment:	COOL!
Topic:	TECHNOLOGY TODAY,
Question:	AWESOME.

1. Describe a topic;
2. ask a question about the topic.

Topic:	YOU VACATION
Comment:	HOW LONG?

Signer B: 1. Respond to the question.

Response:	FOUR-WEEKS.

Practice

Signer A: COOL! TECHNOLOGY TODAY, AWESOME.
YOU VACATION HOW LONG?
Signer B: FOUR-WEEKS.

4. MODEL FOR RULE #3. SIMPLE YES/NO QUESTIONS

Signer A: 1. Describe the topic;
2. ask a yes/no question about the topic.

Topic:	me-JOIN-you,
Question:	DON'T-MIND YOU?

Signer B: 1. Respond to the question.

Response:	FINE.

Practice

Signer A: me-JOIN-you, DON'T-MIND YOU?
Signer B: FINE.

5. MASTERY LEARNING

When you feel comfortable signing these phrases, practice signing the entire dialogue shown at the beginning of the lesson. Practice the master dialogue until you can sign it comfortably.

6. FURTHER PRACTICE

Create five to ten ASL sentences about traveling that use time adverbs and descriptive terms for feelings. Write the English gloss for these sentences; then practice signing them to a partner. The partner should write the English translation of your ASL sentences.

LESSON 35   TRAVEL SCHEDULES

LANGUAGE GOALS

The student will
1.   use Rules   #1. topic/comment,
                            #3. simple yes/no questions,
                            #5. information-seeking questions,
                            #6. pronominalization,
                            #8. ordering of simple sentences, and
                      #10. negation.
2.   use the directional verb FLY.
3.   use the question WHAT'S-WRONG?
4.   use seventeen new signs in a master dialogue.

THE MASTER DIALOGUE

1.   Paul: ENGLAND point-right TWO-of-us FLY-to-right WHEN?
               When do the two of us fly to England?

       Jenny: J-U-L-Y 21.
               July 21st.

2.   Paul: right-FLY-back WHEN?
               When do we fly back?

       Jenny: A-U-G-U-S-T 18.
               August 18th.

3.   Paul: TWO-of-us ARRIVE-there DO-what?
               What do we do when we get there?

       Jenny: FIRST, LONDON VISIT. THEN TRAIN GET-on COUNTRY TRAVEL-
               AROUND.
               First we visit London. Then we get on a train and travel around the country.

4.   Paul: TRAIN RIDE-on WILL?
               We will ride on a train?

       Jenny: YES. WHAT'S-WRONG?
               Yes. What's wrong?

5.   Paul: BEFORE ME TRAIN RIDE-on, NEVER. ME NERVOUS.
            I have never been on a train before. I'm nervous.

     Jenny: REALLY? TRAIN RIDE-on NOTHING-to-it. YOU ENJOY, WILL.
            Really? Riding on a train is nothing to worry about. You will enjoy it.

6.   Paul: YOU THINK?
            You think so?

     Jenny: YES. TRUST ME.
            Yes. Trust me.

THE MASTER SIGNS

FIRST

FLY-back (right-FLY-back)

FLY-to

GET-on

THE MASTER SIGNS

LONDON

NERVOUS

NOTHING-to-it

RIDE-on

THE MASTER SIGNS

THEN

TRAIN

TRAVEL-around

WHAT'S-WRONG

THE MASTER SIGNS

TRUST

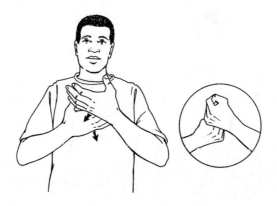

VISIT

WILL

WHAT'S IN THE SIGNS (NOTES ABOUT THE GRAMMAR)

1. RULE #5. INFORMATION-SEEKING QUESTIONS AND #6. PRONOMINALIZATION

In the first sentence of the dialogue, England is placed to the right side of the signing space:

ENGLAND point-right TWO-of-us FLY-to-right WHEN?

The sign FLY-to-right moves from a neutral point in the signing space to the right side where England was placed. The sign FLY-to-right starts in a neutral position because it is referring to both people in the dialogue.

The sentence is also an example of a wh-question in which the first part of the sentence describes the topic and the sign WHEN asks a question about the topic. Another example of a wh-question that includes pronominalization is

TWO-of-us ARRIVE-there DO-what?

The sign ARRIVE-there moves from a position in front of the body to the right side of the signing space, which is where England was placed.

In the following sentence:

right-FLY-back WHEN?

the sign right-FLY-back starts in the same location in the signing space where England was placed, which was in the right side of the signing space. The topic of this question is right-FLY-back and the wh-question sign is WHEN?

2. RULE #8. ORDERING OF SIMPLE SENTENCES

The sentence

FIRST, LONDON VISIT.

is translated to "First, we will visit London." This ASL sentence does not contain a sign for a pronoun because it is readily implied from the context of the dialogue. The second sentence provides an example of how sentences can be organized by laying out events in the way that they occurred:

THEN TRAIN GET-on COUNTRY TRAVEL-AROUND.

Two more examples of simple sentences found in the dialogue are

ME NERVOUS.

TRUST ME.

3. RULE #3. SIMPLE YES/NO QUESTIONS

In the sentence

TRAIN RIDE-on WILL?

the topic is first described followed by a yes/no question about it. Signing WILL at the end of the sentence highlights the sentence as a question. Another yes/no question in the dialogue is

YOU THINK?

4. RULE #10. NEGATION

There are two points to consider in the following sentence:

BEFORE ME TRAIN RIDE-on, NEVER.

First, it is an example of the negation rule: a topic is described and then negated by a negative sign (NEVER). The second point is the use of the sign BEFORE. This sign is made in the same manner as PAST because its meaning is related to what a person has done in the past.

5. RULE #1. TOPIC/COMMENT

The sign NOTHING-to-it is either signed alone or placed at the end of a sentence as in the following:

TRAIN RIDE-on NOTHING-to-it.

It is always used to make a comment about something. Another topic/comment sentence in the dialogue was

YOU ENJOY, WILL.

The sign WILL is often used to emphasize that a person is going to do something and that is why it fulfills the role of a comment in the foregoing sentence.

WHAT'S IN A SIGN (NOTES ABOUT VOCABULARY)

1. FLY-TO/FLY-BACK

FLY is a directional verb because its movement tells about the subject and object of a sentence. The sign FLY-to moves toward the outside of the signing space, and the sign FLY-back moves from the outside of the signing space toward the inside. The exact starting and ending positions of both signs is dependent upon who is flying: the signer, or someone whom the signer is talking about.

2. GET-ON/RIDE-ON

The difference between the signs for GET-on and RIDE-on is that the hand does not move forward in the sign GET-on, whereas in the sign RIDE-on the hand moves forward to represent going someplace.

3. WRONG-WRONG, WRONG-WHAT

The common English gloss for this sign is "What's wrong?" or "What's the matter?" It is often signed by itself as a means of inquiring about something.

4. WILL

Although the sign WILL is used to indicate the future time, it is also commonly used to emphasize that a person will do something.

3. ASL SYNONYMS

Some signs can be used to mean other things.

Sign	Also used for
NOTHING-TO-IT	INSIGNIFICANT, PUNY, TRIVIAL
TRUST	CONFIDENT

PRACTICE ACTIVITIES

1. MODEL FOR RULES #5. INFORMATION-SEEKING QUESTIONS AND #6. PRONOMINALIZATION

Signer A: 1. Sign the object of the sentence, ENGLAND;
                 2. place England in the signing space by pointing to the right (note that you could also point to the left);
                 3. describe the topic;
                 4. ask a question about the topic.

Object:	ENGLAND
Placement of object:	point right
Topic:	TWO-of-us FLY-to-right
Question:	WHEN?

Signer B: 1. Respond to the question.

Response:	J-U-L-Y 21.

Signer A: 1. Describe the topic;
                 2. ask a question about the topic.

Topic:	right-FLY-back
Question:	WHEN?

Signer B: 1. Respond to the wh-question.

Response:	A-U-G-U-S-T 18.

Practice

Signer A: ENGLAND-point-right TWO-of-us FLY-to-right WHEN?
Signer B: J-U-L-Y 21
Signer A: right-FLY-back WHEN?
Signer B: A-U-G-U-S-T 18.

2. MODEL FOR RULES #5. INFORMATION-SEEKING QUESTIONS AND #8. ORDERING OF SIMPLE SENTENCES

Signer A:	1. Describe the topic;	
	2. ask a question about the topic.	
	Topic:	TWO-of-us ARRIVE-there
	Question:	DO-what?
Signer B:	1. Establish the initial sequence of events by signing FIRST;	
	2. describe an action;	
	3. establish the next sequence of events by signing THEN;	
	4. describe an action.	
	Initial sequence:	FIRST,
	Action:	LONDON VISIT.
	Next sequence:	THEN
	Action:	TRAIN GET-on COUNTRY TRAVEL-AROUND.

Practice

Signer A: TWO-of-us ARRIVE-there DO-what?

Signer B: FIRST, LONDON VISIT. THEN TRAIN GET-on COUNTRY TRAVEL-AROUND.

3. MODEL FOR RULES #3. SIMPLE YES/NO QUESTIONS, #5. INFORMATION-SEEKING QUESTIONS, #8. ORDERING OF SIMPLE SENTENCES, AND #10. NEGATION

Signer A:	1. Describe the topic;	
	2. ask a yes/no question using the sign WILL.	
	Topic:	TRAIN RIDE-on
	Question:	WILL?
Signer B:	1. Answer the question affirmatively with the sign YES;	
	2. ask a question using the sign WHAT'S-WRONG?	
	Response:	YES.
	Question:	WHAT'S-WRONG?

Signer A: 1. Describe the topic;

2. use a negative sign to negate the topic;

3. use a simple sentence structure to describe how you feel.

Topic:	BEFORE ME TRAIN RIDE-on,
Negation:	NEVER.
Simple sentence:	ME NERVOUS.

Practice

Signer A: TRAIN RIDE-on WILL?

Signer B: YES. WHAT'S-WRONG?

Signer A: BEFORE ME TRAIN RIDE-on, NEVER. ME NERVOUS.

4. MODEL FOR RULES #1. TOPIC/COMMENT AND RULE #3. SIMPLE YES/NO QUESTIONS AND USING WILL IN ITS EMPHATIC SENSE

Signer A: 1. Describe the topic;

2. make a comment about the topic;

3. describe an action;

4. emphasize the action with the sign WILL.

Topic:	TRAIN RIDE-on
Comment:	NOTHING-to-it.
Action:	YOU ENJOY,
Emphasis:	WILL.

Signer B: 1. Ask a simple yes/no question.

Question:	YOU THINK?

Signer A: 1. Respond affirmatively to the yes/no question;

2. use a simple sentence to make a command.

Response:	YES.
Simple sentence:	TRUST ME.

Practice

Signer A: TRAIN RIDE-on NOTHING-to-it. YOU ENJOY, WILL.

Signer B: YOU THINK?

Signer A: YES. TRUST ME.

5. MASTERY LEARNING

When you feel comfortable signing these phrases, practice signing the entire dialogue shown at the beginning of the lesson. Practice the master dialogue until you can sign it comfortably.

6. FURTHER PRACTICE

Join the master dialogue with the one in Lesson 34 and practice signing both until you are comfortable signing them.

LESSON 36   MORE PLACES TO VISIT

LANGUAGE GOALS

The student will
1. use twenty-two new signs to describe countries to visit.
2. use the signs TRAIN, CAR, MOTORCYCLE, and BUS as vehicles in which to travel around.
3. practice fingerspelling the months of the year, numbers for the days of the months, and the names of cities in various countries.

PRACTICE ACTIVITIES

For practice in expanding your sign vocabulary you will substitute the signs learned in this lesson for various signs learned in the previous lessons. Therefore, the master dialogue for this lesson is taken from Lessons 34 and 35. Do not attempt to learn all the new signs in this lesson in one day. Divide up the signs and learn them over a period of a few days. Because you will not use some of these signs in your everyday conversations, you may find it more difficult to remember them when you do need to use them. Refer back to this lesson from time to time to refresh your memory of these signs. Do keep in mind that at anytime during a signed conversation you can always fingerspell the proper nouns. This lesson will also provide practice in fingerspelling the months of the year, numbers for the days of the month, and the names of cities in various countries.

In each of the following dialogues, substitute the word in bold with a sign or fingerspelled word from the appropriate list.

NOTE: Each country has its own signs which may be local, regional, or national. The signs we are showing are the ones most commonly recognized in the United States and Canada for that country. When the name of a country is in doubt, it should be fingerspelled.

COUNTRIES

Paul: HELLO, DO-what YOU?
Jenny: ME NEED VACATION. GO-to **ENGLAND** ME WANT.

THE MASTER SIGNS

Countries	Major Cities (fingerspelled)
Countries	**Major Cities (fingerspelled)**

Countries

ITALY

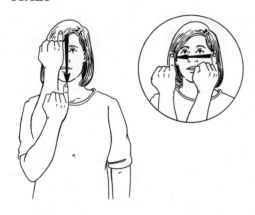

Major Cities (fingerspelled)

ROME

FRANCE

PARIS

BRAZIL

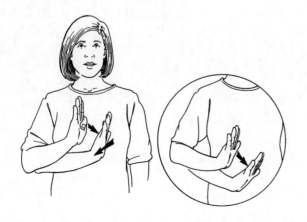

SAO PAULO
RIO DE JANEIRO

THE MASTER SIGNS

Countries

Major Cities (fingerspelled)

AUSTRALIA

CANBERRA
SYDNEY

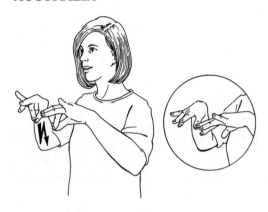

NETHERLANDS

AMSTERDAM

CHINA

BEIJING
SHANGHAI

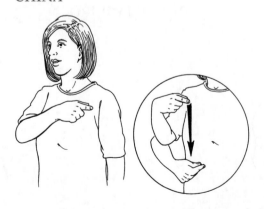

THE MASTER SIGNS

Countries	**Major Cities (fingerspelled)**

ISRAEL

TEL AVIV
JERUSALEM

EGYPT

CAIRO

GREECE

ATHENS

THE MASTER SIGNS

Countries	**Major Cities (fingerspelled)**
SWEDEN	STOCKHOLM

FINLAND	HELSINKI

NORWAY	OSLO

THE MASTER SIGNS

Countries	**Major Cities (fingerspelled)**
KOREA	SEOUL

POLAND	WARSAW

SWITZERLAND	ZURICH

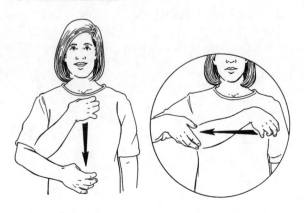

THE MASTER SIGNS

Countries	Major Cities (fingerspelled)

MEXICO

MEXICO CITY

DENMARK

COPENHAGEN

GERMANY

BONN
BERLIN

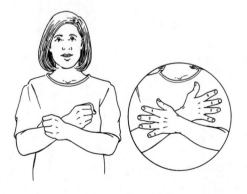

THE MASTER SIGNS

Countries   **Major Cities (fingerspelled)**

RUSSIA   MOSCOW

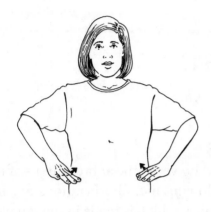

SPAIN   BARCELONA
                                                 MADRID

MONTHS, DATES, AND COUNTRIES

1. Paul: **ENGLAND** point-right TWO-of-us FLY-to-right WHEN?
    Jenny: **A-P-R-I-L 13**.

2. Paul: right-FLY-back WHEN?
    Jenny: **M-A-Y 8**.

THE MASTER SIGNS

Substitute signs from the list of countries already shown.

THE MASTER FINGERSPELLED WORDS

All months of the year can be fingerspelled completely; however, the abbreviations of many of the months can also be fingerspelled. In the following list, abbreviations are noted where they are appropriate. There is a sign for September, which is made in the same manner as the sign AUTUMN.

Months	Abbreviated fingerspelling
JANUARY	J-A-N
FEBRUARY	F-E-B
MARCH	
APRIL	
MAY	
JUNE	
JULY	
AUGUST	A-U-G
SEPTEMBER	S-E-P-T
OCTOBER	O-C-T
NOVEMBER	N-O-V
DECEMBER	D-E-C

THE MASTER NUMBERS

For the dates, substitute any numbers from 1 through 31.

CITIES AND VEHICLES

Paul: TWO-of-us ARRIVE-there-right DO-what?

Jenny: FIRST, **LONDON** VISIT. THEN **TRAIN** GET-on COUNTRY TRAVEL-AROUND.

THE MASTER CITIES

Although there are signs for the names of all the major cities listed previously, almost all of them are unknown to most Deaf people in the United States and Canada. They are typically known only by Deaf people who travel to international conferences and international Deaf sporting events. Therefore, in this lesson you will practice fingerspelling the names of some of the major cities of each of the countries listed. Fingerspelling is a complex art, and all beginning signers are advised to seek instruction from ASL instructors.

THE MASTER VEHICLES

B-U-S

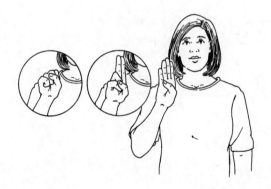

CAR

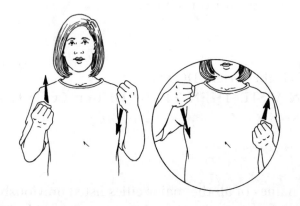

MOTORCYCLE

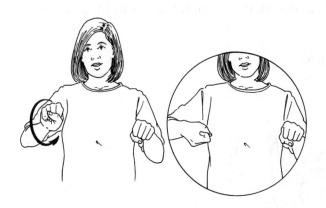

REVIEW OF LESSONS 34–36

Write an English translation for each of the following ASL sentences.

1. SUPPOSE YOU VACATION NEED, YOU TRAVEL WHERE?

2. YOU SWITZERLAND GO-to, FOR-FOR?

3. ME VACATION HOW-LONG? THREE-WEEKS.

4. LAST-YEAR YOU TRAVEL WHERE?

5. YOU VACATION PLAN, COMPUTER HELP-you HOW?

6. POLAND YOU ARRIVE-there, DO-what YOU?

7. YOU RIDE-on TRAIN, YOU NERVOUS YOU?

8. B-U-S TICKET, ME BUY FINISH.

9. you-FLY-to SPAIN WHEN?

10. IN-TWO-YEARS ME NEW-YORK VISIT WILL.

ANSWERS

Note that there may be other ways of translating these sentences than the ones shown here.

1. If you needed a vacation where would you travel? or Where would you travel if you needed a vacation?

2. Why are you going to Switzerland?

3. My vacation is three weeks long.

4. Where did you travel last year?

5. How does the computer help you plan your vacation?

6. What are you going to do when you arrive in Poland?

7. Are you nervous when you ride on a train?

8. I have bought the bus ticket.

9. When are you flying to Spain?

10. I will visit New York in two years.

Appendix

THE ASL ALPHABET

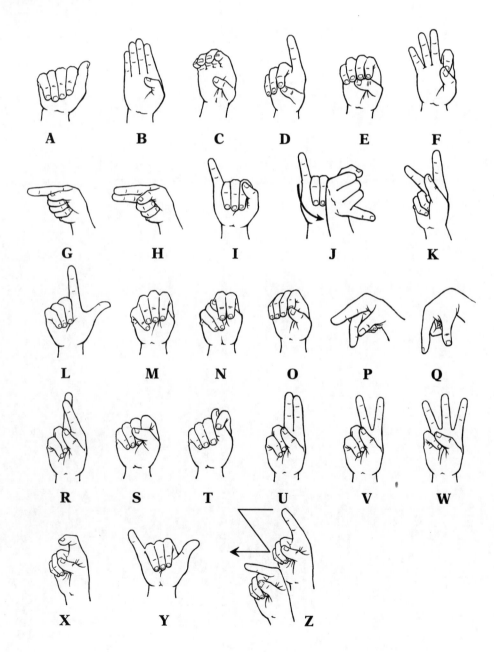

Index

Bold-faced entries are vocabulary words and/or phrases that have been illustrated in the text.